the
Color
of Love

the Color of Love

A Mother's Choice in the Jim Crow South

Gene Cheek

The Lyons Press
Guilfod, Connecticut
An imprint of the Globe Pequot Press

The Lyons Press is an imprint of The Globe Pequot Press

10 9 8 7 6 5 4 3 2 1

Printed in the United States of America

Designed by Lisa Reneson

ISBN 1-59228-626-7

Library of Congress Cataloging-in-Publication Data is available on file.

Dedication

This book is dedicated to the memory of three remarkable people: my Grandma Anderson, Mama, and Tuck. Together—from a better place—they look down on me. I hope they're proud.

Preface

This is a true story, the recollections of a little boy. Accordingly, it is his story and skewed appropriately by the events that influenced his life and the world around him. Though it would be impossible to remember word for word conversations that took place forty years ago, I have remained true to the people having those conversations. Some names were changed to protect the innocent—and the not-so-innocent as well. The story is told chronologically and the way the events unfold to me now—like a snowball rolling downhill.

The forces that affect our lives, the influences that mold and shape us, are often like whispers in a distant room, teasingly indistinct, apprehended only with great difficulty.
—Charles Dickens

Acknowledgments

I'd like to first thank my family for putting up with me all these years, God knows it wasn't easy. Thanks to Anne Siddens at the Black Mountain Library for her help and advice. Thanks to Allan Zullo, whose help was instrumental in this dream coming true. And a special thank-you to my editor Tom McCarthy and The Lyons Press for believing in this story; Mama and Tuck, thank you all as well. There are others, and you know who you are; thanks.

the Color of Love

1

Saints

On March 2, 1959, I turned eight years old. Grandma Pearl threw a birthday party for me in her tiny two-bedroom, tin-roofed mill house. The living room with its faded linoleum floor, worn and frayed upholstered furniture, overflowed with party regalia. A small banner made from butcher paper and watercolors hung from the ceiling and read HAPPY BIRTHDAY, GENE.

Fragrant aromas of chicken and dumplings, pinto beans, and corn bread wafted through the small but neat living room crammed with my relatives—the Anderson clan—and my best friend, Larry, with his mother, Becky. The Andersons were a hardworking, God-fearing, dirt-poor family who clung to each other like honeysuckle vines to a picket fence. The patriarch of the clan had been William Anderson, my grandfather. He had fallen dead on this living room floor when his heart wore out. Though he died before I was born, the legend of his kindness and charity filled up Grandma's house like the aromas from her kitchen.

Grandpa, a house painter by trade, had been famous for his sweet disposition. "Slow to anger," Grandma said, "but a whirlwind when he was riled." I knew his face and features from the many black-and-white photos of him throughout Grandma's house. He had been a tall man, rawboned and thin as a cane pole. From the years of exposure to the intense Carolina sun, his skin looked like rawhide. His face, with the exception of the wavy blond hair and the lack of a beard, could have belonged to Abe Lincoln. A smiling, lean face interrupted by a large hook-shaped nose and flanked by ears the size of catcher's mitts.

The Andersons lived by a simple creed: A man should not be judged for what he is, but for who he is. They also believed in sharing what the good Lord had given them. They believed in family and friends, and the Golden Rule, which they applied with equal vigor to everyone, even strangers.

My mother, Sallie Adillian Anderson, was the youngest of four children born to William and Pearl Anderson. Born on November 14, 1930, in Winston-Salem, North Carolina, she had been the apple of her daddy's eye. At fifteen she felt the pain of life's first arrow when her beloved father died. His death broke her heart and forced her to drop out of Gray High School after her sophomore year. She laid aside her dreams of becoming a nurse and went to work in a textile mill to help support the family.

Sitting on a straight-backed wooden chair near the kitchen door was her brother, my uncle Bill, his strong hands and muscular arms turning the crank on an ice cream maker. Grandma's delicious home-made vanilla ice cream, piled high onto Mama's mouthwatering choco-late cake, would top off this celebration. The oldest of the three sur-viving children and a long-distance truck driver, Uncle Bill had left school in the sixth grade because, as Grandma put it, "He couldn't pay attention." With a childlike heart—and to some who misjudged him, a childlike mind—he was now the head of the Anderson clan. His mis-sion in life was taking care of his sisters and mother.

Aunt Goldie, Mama's sister, was sitting on the worn-out green couch beside her husband. She had married a hardworking farm boy from Davidson County named Ed. Together they had three boys—my cousins Tim, Jerry, and Denny. Aunt Goldie spent her days cooking, cleaning, and chasing those three wild-eyed boys around their yard and the neighborhood. Uncle Ed worked two full-time jobs. He took time off once a year to drag the family to Carolina Beach for their annual vacation. There was another son born into the Anderson clan, Eugene, my namesake, but he died a few minutes after his birth.

One person was missing from this gathering—my father.

"I wonder where Jesse's at," Mama said as she walked to the win-dow and pulled back the lacy, cream-colored curtains.

4

My father was nowhere in sight. He'd promised he'd come straight to my party from his job as a meter reader for the city's water department.

"Maybe he forgot," Uncle Bill said, chewing on a Hav-A-Tampa as he cranked away on the ice cream maker.

Mama glanced at Uncle Bill in wonder. "How could he forget his son's birthday?"

"We can't wait much longer, Sallie," Aunt Goldie said, glancing at her watch. "It's close to five and Ed has to work tonight."

Uncle Bill, a big grin showing teeth that looked like they'd been thrown into his mouth from across the room, said, "Y'all don't have to leave, Goldie. I can take you and the boys home after the party."

"I hope nothing's happened to Jesse," Grandma said from her squeaky maple rocking chair. She sat facing the black-and-white TV, watching Arthur Smith singing "The Old Rugged Cross" and playing his banjo. Grandma's tiny fingers tapped in time to the music.

Tired of waiting, Mama decided that I should start opening my presents. From Larry and his mother I received a balsa wood glider. From my cousins, Uncle Ed, and Aunt Goldie, a U.S. Navy aircraft carrier that launched little metal jet planes. From Uncle Bill, a model car, a 1959 Chevy Impala, just like his new one parked on the street in front of Grandma's house.

I was about to open Grandma's present when the front door flew open and in staggered my father. Everyone knew at once that he was drunk. I wanted to melt into the floor. His chestnut-brown hair stood out like porcupine quills. His work uniform—dark green pants and a matching shirt with JESSE on the left pocket and CITY OF WINSTON-SALEM on the right—had grease and dirt smeared from top to bottom. The grease on his face couldn't hide his puffy, bloodshot eyes. The smell of liquor on his breath was strong enough, as Grandma would say, "to peel paint."

Mama took a deep breath and tried to remain calm. "Where have you been, Jesse?" she asked.

My father replied, "I was helpin' Barney fix his truck." Barney Todd was a self-employed plumber whose pink, flat-roofed house, with a yard full of pink flamingos, sat up the hill from our house on Brookline

Street. Barney was Dad's hunting, fishing, and drinking buddy—and it was the drinking that took up most of their time together.

Mama was unconvinced. "On your son's birthday?"

"I forgot, damn it," he said, his voice so loud it removed all doubt that he was drunk. Had his brain not been swimming in alcohol he wouldn't dare cuss or raise his voice in Grandma's house—not with her sitting right there across the room. Uncle Bill glared at him and muttered "Jesus Christ!" before he squashed his cigar in an ashtray and jumped up from his chair. "Who the hell do you think you are bargin' in here and—"

Grandma cleared her throat, and Uncle Bill stopped in midsentence as if he'd been struck by lightning. When Grandma cleared her throat in that special way, everyone stopped and listened. All eyes focused on the short woman with the round face and cotton-colored hair pulled back into a tight bun.

Grandma, who was fifty-six, had once been a heavyset woman, but she had lost weight after Grandpa died. The folds of loose skin on the back of her arms danced and jiggled when she worked or laughed.

It was Grandma's mouth and eyes that commanded the attention of everyone in the living room now. From years of smiling, deep-cut dimples flanked both sides of her mouth. Her blue eyes—alive, bright, and intelligent—were glistening pools of love, compassion, and understanding. But not now. Her mouth took on that stern set as the withering glare of her steel-blue eyes fixed themselves like a spotlight on Uncle Bill and then on Dad. Grandma was a simple but virtuous matriarch. She insisted that her house be the house of the Lord, that her children be exemplary in their behavior, and that her guests be respectful of her and her hospitality. In Grandma's house being poor, uneducated, or even drunk was no excuse for bad manners.

"Did I just hear cussin' in my house?" Grandma said, pronouncing each word for everyone to hear.

"Sorry, Ma," Uncle Bill said in a regretful voice.

"And you," Grandma said to Dad in a voice dripping with contempt. "How dare you come into my house drunk? And how dare you cuss and raise your voice after what you've done to disappoint your own son?"

My father hung his head. In a voice more contrite than Uncle Bill's, he said, "Sorry, Pearl. I'm real sorry. I clean forgot it was Gene's birthday. But honest, I was helpin' Barney fix his pickup, and we had a couple of beers. I thought Gene's birthday was next week. Honest I did."

Grandma wasn't someone to beat a dead horse. The repentance expressed by Uncle Bill and Dad smoothed her ruffled feathers, and she pursued the subject no further. Instead she took her seat in the rocking chair, and her face regained its permanent smile.

My focus turned back to my presents. I opened Grandma's and jumped for joy to find a bright yellow dump truck. As Mama and Aunt Goldie began to set the table, my cousins and I passed around my birthday gifts, inspecting each one as though it were a rare gem.

My father, sobered by Grandma's scolding, did his best to behave. He and Uncle Ed sat in a corner and began talking about their jobs. Dad hated his. "It's demeaning for a white man to make stops in Colored Town. That's not a fit place for a respectable white man. It's just plum full of niggers livin' like savages." Grandma didn't approve of such words, or opinions, so Dad kept his voice low while he talked to Uncle Ed. But I heard him.

What he wanted was a job at R. J. Reynolds Tobacco Company, the town's biggest employer. Beer had made Milwaukee famous. Well, the sweet smell of kiln-dried tobacco had done the same for Winston-Salem. Dad's brother, Uncle Bobby, and Uncle Ed worked at RJR, as did most of the men in our blue-collar neighborhood. Dad had made his ambition known to Mama many times. Her response was always the same: "Maybe if you stopped drinking, Bobby would get you the job."

Everybody sat around the red Formica table as we passed plates and bowls of Grandma's special birthday supper. After cake and ice cream my cousins, Larry, and I trooped outside to play with the tiny wooden glider. We tossed it into the cool evening air and watched in wonder as it sailed around the yard. We chased it, laughing and shouting and challenging each other to see who could make it fly the farthest.

My cousin Tim—the oldest and biggest among us—reached back and with all his might let the glider fly. It soared upward, climbing above the tin roof of Grandma's house. When I thought it was going to end up stuck on top, it veered near the chimney and glided back toward the ground, coming to rest in the thorny holly bushes at the corner of Grandma's front porch.

I gazed at Tim, awed by his strength as he reached into the bushes to retrieve the little plane. He had just pulled it out when a commotion erupted from the house. "Someone's fighting!" yelled Tim as he clambered over the old white banisters and onto Grandma's front porch.

"Who?" I asked, running toward Tim, who now stood on his tiptoes and was peering in through the small window. The question was unnecessary; I knew if anyone was fighting, my dad was in the middle of it.

"Uncle Bill," Tim said. "But I can't see who he's fighting with."

I reached the window and stood next to Tim, craning my neck for a better look. What I saw horrified me. Dad was sprawled in the middle of the living room floor and Uncle Bill was sitting on top of him—strangling him!

"How dare you insult my sister, you drunken bum!" cried Uncle Bill, squeezing Dad's throat with his huge hands.

"Oh, my God!" cried Aunt Goldie, clutching her mouth with her hand. "Stop him, Ed, or he'll kill Jesse!"

"Easy now, Bill," said Uncle Ed in a soft voice.

"Let me go!" my father croaked.

"Let him go, Bill," ordered Mama as she and Uncle Ed tried to pull Dad out from under Uncle Bill's massive body.

"Stop it, Bill!" Grandma shouted, rising from her rocker. "I said stop it, you hear? I don't want no fightin' in my house!"

Hearing Grandma's voice, Uncle Bill let go of Dad's throat and, without a word, got up, went straight to his bedroom at the far end of the kitchen, and shut the door.

"Jesse, you better leave my house this minute," demanded Grandma. "How dare you call your own wife such horrible names? Get out! And don't ever set foot in here drunk again, you hear? Now get!"

My father, still dazed, didn't budge.

"I said get."

Still he didn't move. Instead he kept rubbing his neck and cussing under his breath. Grandma was no one to trifle with, and what happened next didn't surprise me. She grabbed a broom from behind the kitchen door and held it in front of her like it was the Excalibur. "Didn't you hear me? I said get!"

She lifted it high over her head and, without hesitation, brought the straw broom crashing down hard on his head. "I said get!" she shouted, raining more blows on his head.

"I'm sorry, Pearl," he said, backing toward the front door, hands raised to ward off the blows while stumbling over furniture and bodies. "Please stop hittin' me with that darn broom. I promise I'll stop actin' foolish."

"Yes sir, you will!" Grandma said. "Now get!" She continued driving him out the front door, across the porch, and down the sidewalk with the broom. By now Larry and my cousins were roaring with laughter at the sight of the tiny, frail woman driving my drunken father out of her house. I squirmed with shame at the sight of my dad, who, it seemed, spent most of his time drunk, or trying to get that way. His boozing and foolish actions often ended in scenes just like this one. Grandma stopped hitting him when she noticed neighbors were congregating outside to witness the spectacle. Muttering under his breath, Dad turned and walked down the sidewalk toward our house on Brookline Street.

2

Sinners

The Friday after my birthday party Mama and I were sitting on the old hooked rug in the living room floor playing Parcheesi. It was around six in the evening, and we were waiting for Dad so we could go to Grandma's for supper. The two of us played a lot of games together. We loved games. We played board games, Parcheesi, Monopoly, and Chinese checkers. We played card games like Old Maid, Go Fish, and rummy. We'd play together and laugh so hard we'd roll on the floor.

We played games that required nothing but an imagination, like Counting Cows or "Riga-ma-riga-ma-re." Counting Cows was a simple game. I'd take one side of the road, Mama the other, and we'd count cows as we rode along in the car. Whoever counted the most by the time we got where we were going, won. Riga-ma-riga-ma-re went like this: "Riga-ma-riga-ma-re, I see something you don't see and it's blue"—or red, or whatever the color might be. The object of the game was to guess what the other person was looking at.

We had just ended one game of Parcheesi and were about to start another when I asked, "Can I tell you a secret?"

"Sure, honey."

"You won't get mad at me?"

"Of course not."

"Promise?"

"I promise."

"I hate Dad," I declared.

"Why do you hate him, honey?" she asked in a gentle voice.

"Because he's a drunken bum," I replied, repeating Uncle Bill's favorite description of my father. "And he's no fun to be around anymore."

She looked at me with understanding eyes and said, "I know, honey. But you shouldn't hate him for it."

"Why not?"

"Because he's your father."

"Not when he's drunk, he ain't. I don't like him. He's mean."

There was a long, awkward pause; Mama was searching for something to say. Her golden-green eyes glistened with tears.

"Will he ever stop drinking?"

"I don't know, honey," she said with a heavy sigh. "I just don't know."

Before I could ask another question, there was a rattling noise at the door, and I jumped up and opened it. Standing there drunk and cussing, fumbling with his keys, trying to unlock an unlocked door, was Dad. I stood staring at him in silent amazement.

"What are you gawkin' at, brat?" he demanded as he stumbled through the open door. Before I could say anything, he slapped me hard across the face with his open hand. Hollering with pain, I hurried to Mama's side.

Stunned and furious, she stood up and shouted at Dad, "You drunken son of a bitch, why did you do that?"

I was stunned. This was something new—I'd never heard words like that come out of the mouth of my God-fearing mother. Dad turned livid, his growing anger made evident by the birthmark glowing red in the middle of his forehead. He started yelling and cussing, the spit flying from his mouth with each word that he screamed at her: *whore, fat bitch, white trash.*

Without warning, he grabbed the thick brass lamp on the side table next to the rocking chair and threw it. Mama ducked just in time. The lamp missed her head by inches and smashed into the white plaster wall behind her, leaving a huge dent. Terrified and crying, Mama grabbed me and started for the door. My father, his eyes full of hate and his birthmark now turning white-hot, blocked her path.

"Where the hell do you think you're goin'?" he hissed.

"To my mama's house," she answered in a trembling voice.

"No you ain't, bitch," he said.

"Leave her alone, you drunk!" I screamed at him.

"Who are you calling a drunk, you little shit," he growled, trying to grab me.

Mama pulled me behind her dress. "Leave the boy alone, you hear!" she screamed at Dad.

"He needs to be taught a lesson. Let him go!"

"No, I won't. You ain't goin' to hit him again. You'll have to go through me first." Her voice sounded steady, but I could feel the fear as she clutched my hand. Those words had barely left her mouth when my father punched her in the face. The force of the blow sent her reeling backward; she stumbled and almost fell on top of me as she struggled to regain her balance. Blood oozed from her mouth, and tears streamed down her cheeks mixing with her blood.

"I'll kill you for hurting Mama!" I yelled at him, trying to pull free from her grasp. "I'll kill you!"

"Why you—" He lunged at me. Mama ducked to one side and, still gripping my hand, rushed for the open door. Dad grabbed at the empty air and lost his balance, falling to the floor with a thud. We scrambled down the steps and disappeared into the night, heading for Grandma's. I held on to Mama's hand as we walked up the hill on Urban Street. With each step, she cried, and I squeezed her hand. I was helpless to do anything for her, but I swore to myself that it wouldn't always be this way. Moments later I saw Grandma sitting in her old gray porch swing, wrapped up in a warm colorful shawl and humming "What a Friend We Have in Jesus." She was gazing up at the star-filled night sky.

"Where's Jesse?" she asked, never taking her eyes off heaven.

"He's home," Mama said.

"Ain't he coming for supper?"

She started crying harder as she stepped up onto the porch. In the yellow glow of the porch light Grandma noticed the blood on Mama's face.

"Lord have mercy, child! What happened to your face?"

"It's Jesse," she said, fighting back tears. She walked into the house and plopped onto the faded green couch. Grandma went into the kitchen and came back with a wet washcloth. She sat down beside her daughter and handed it to her. "He's drunk again," Mama said, dabbing at her mouth. "He's lost his mind, he's so drunk. He slapped poor Gene just for looking at him. Then he punched me in the face when I tried to stop him."

Grandma's peaceful face knotted with rage—one of the few times I'd seen her mad. She turned to me, took my face in her dainty hands, and lifted it so that our eyes met. "Did your daddy slap you, honey?" she asked.

"Yes, Grandma."

She shook her head. "My goodness! What's gotten into your father?"

"I don't know," Mama said, wringing her hands. "I just don't know. His drinking has gotten worse since he started hanging around with Barney."

"Uncle Bill needs to beat him up again," I suggested.

"Hush," Grandma said. "Why don't you turn on the TV and watch cartoons? I need to talk to your ma alone for a minute. Okay, honey?"

"There ain't no cartoons at night, Grandma," I said.

"Well, then play."

"By myself?"

"Yes. We'll have supper soon. I've made fried chicken, potato salad, and fried apple pies for dessert, your favorites. Let me talk to your ma first and then we'll sit down and eat. Can you wait that long?"

"I reckon," I said. "Is Uncle Bill eating with us?"

"No, honey. He's still on the road."

I sulked. "Shoot, I wanted to race him."

"Practice for a little while and I'll race you after supper," Grandma said, and they headed to the kitchen.

Racing to Grandma was something you did on the kitchen floor—with sewing spools. She came up with the game one day during a downpour when she saw that I was bored out of my mind. Taking spools that once held her sewing thread, she sat down on the kitchen floor, which featured a cluster of floorboards that had buckled and created a series of mini hills and valleys. She patted the spot next to her, encouraging me to join her. Curious as to what she was up to, I sat on the floor. She placed the spools at the apex of one of the floor's hills and, with all the excitement she could muster, yelled out, "On your mark, get set, go!" As the spools raced off down the floor, Grandma and I yelled at the top of our lungs, urging our imaginary drivers to go faster.

But on this day, as she and Mama talked about Dad, I wasn't in the mood to play the game, so I decided to watch *Gunsmoke*. I had just settled into Grandma's rocking chair when I heard a car pull up outside. I tensed, thinking it was Dad. *If it is*, I thought, *I'm not going to let him in. If I don't let him in, he can't hit Mama again.*

I tiptoed to the window, drew aside the lacy curtains, and peeked outside. It wasn't Dad's old rusty-gray 1949 Chevy coupe, which would have disappeared in front of a junk pile. This was a new car, a clean, polished 1959 gray-blue Chevy Bel Air gleaming in the streetlight. The driver got out of the car, and I saw that he was a colored man. To my shock, the stranger headed straight toward Grandma's front door. I almost bolted, but instead stood frozen by the window and waited for the man to knock. *Maybe*, I thought, *he's drunk and he'll turn back after he realizes he's lost and in the wrong neighborhood.* Except for his dark skin, he looked normal, which surprised me. After all the "black savage" this and "crazy nigger" thats I'd heard from Uncle Bill and my dad, this man didn't seem to be wild and crazy at all.

I heard a gentle knock on the door. I had the urge to open it and say to the stranger, *Sorry, mister, you're in the wrong part of town. This is my Grandma's house, and she's white.*

But I didn't. Instead I stood at the window, captivated by the stranger's appearance. He was dressed in a dark blue pin-striped suit, red striped tie, and black fedora hat. His wing-tip shoes reflected the porch light like polished glass.

3

The Stranger

The stranger knocked again, but the noise was swallowed up by the muffled sounds of conversation from the kitchen and Frankie Avalon's "Venus" coming from Grandma's old RCA Victor, no doubt tuned to her favorite radio station, WTOB. I didn't know whether to open the door and ask him what he wanted, or go to Grandma and tell her there was a colored man at her door.

I recalled a breathless dog day last August when Dad and I had gone fishing at Winston Lake. We were following a path that wound its way along the lakefront when we passed a colored man sitting on a five-gallon bucket in the shade of a catalpa tree. He was dressed in old worn-out overalls and was shirtless. There was a scar running across his cheek and down his shoulder, a bright raised angry scar. When we were out of sight, I asked Dad, "Did you see the scar on that man's face?"

"Yeah, I saw it. It was probably from a straight razor. I ain't never known a nigger who didn't carry a straight razor, and it looks like that one ended up on the wrong end of one. They're savages, they drink and fight and cut each other just for the hell of it." Recalling this story and others like it, and having a colored man now standing at Grandma's front door, I lost what courage I had and ran to the kitchen.

"Grandma, Grandma!" I shouted. "There's a colored man at the door."

A concerned look came over their faces. "Are you sure it's a colored man, honey?" Mama asked.

"Sure I'm sure," I said.

"What does he want?" Grandma asked.

"I don't know. I was afraid to open the door."

"Go find out," Grandma said.

I ran back to the door, my heart racing. What would I say to this colored man? What would he do when I opened the door? What would I do? This was much better than watching TV; I opened it a crack and peered up at the stranger. Before I could even ask him his name, he said, "Young man, is Mrs. Anderson in?"

The gentleness in his voice surprised me as much as his ready smile. I half expected him to growl and pull out his razor—something frightful to justify the horrible images Dad had put in my head. "Yes sir," I said. Mama and Grandma had taught me to address adults as *sir* or *ma'am* and they made no distinctions based on color, so it never occurred to me that I should address this colored man any differently.

"Can you tell her that Mr. Tucker is here?"

"Yes sir."

I scampered back to the kitchen. "That man says his name is Mr. Tucker."

Instantly a smile of recognition creased Grandma's leathery face. "Oh, Mr. Tucker. Please ask him in."

With a puzzled look on her face, Mama asked Grandma, "Who is this Mr. Tucker, and what's he doing here?"

I wanted this confusion cleared up before I went back to Mr. Tucker and ushered him in, whoever he was. Grandma wiped her small hands with a dish towel she kept hanging on the handle of the refrigerator.

"There's nothin' to worry about," she said, putting the towel down. "I know Mr. Tucker. He's a handyman. He fixes things for me from time to time." Turning to me, she said, "Go on and show him in, honey. And mind your manners. Now stop gaping at me and tell Mr. Tucker to come in."

"Yes ma'am." I stumbled back to the front door, opened it, and said in a respectful tone of voice, "Mr. Tucker, my grandma says for you to come on in."

"Thank you," Mr. Tucker said, removing his hat.

I had never seen a colored man up close before, at least not this close. He didn't look like a handyman. The handymen I'd seen around the neighborhood wore greasy overalls, grimy boots, and had dirty hands. Not Mr. Tucker. I noticed that his hands were clean. Dad's hands weren't even clean when he came to the supper table. Almost every day Mama would say, "Jesse, wash your hands." His usual response, depending on his mood, was either "Leave me alone" or "Kiss my ass!"

"Please, Mr. Tucker, sit down," Grandma said from behind me. With a dumbfounded look still on my face, I shuffled over to Mama, who was sitting on the couch. I just stood there, too confused to speak.

"Thank you, Mrs. Anderson," Mr. Tucker said. His eyes glanced around the living room, looking for a place to sit. Since Mama was sitting on the couch, and the other available chair was Grandma's rocking chair, I figured that Mr. Tucker, being a colored man and all, would just stand up while he conducted his business, whatever it was. To my surprise, Mr. Tucker, without the slightest hesitation, sat down on the couch next to Mama.

"I'm on my way to church, Mrs. Anderson. I just stopped by to let you know that I've found a screen door for you. It's a dollar and fifteen cents with tax. I'll pick it up tomorrow and come by and install it this Saturday if that's okay."

"Sure, Mr. Tucker," Grandma said, sounding grateful. "That's fine by me."

"So I'll see you on Saturday, then," Mr. Tucker said.

"Can you come in the afternoon?" Grandma said. "I have a funeral to attend at church in the morning."

"Yes ma'am."

"Can I offer you something to drink before you go?"

"Come to think of it, I'd appreciate a glass of water."

Grandma turned to me and said, "Honey, please fetch Mr. Tucker a glass of water from the kitchen."

"Which glass should I use?" I just blurted it out, knowing full well before the words had even gotten to Grandma's ears that I'd messed up. Grandma gave me a look that would have melted steel.

"Use my glass," she said.

Grandma's expression told me that I'd made a big mistake asking that question, innocent though it was. I had asked it because one time Dad and I were downtown and I made the mistake of rushing to a coloreds-only water fountain to get a drink; water looked like water to me. But my father had jerked me away from it like I was about to be snakebit, and pulled me over to another water fountain. "Boy," he scolded me, "have you lost your damn mind? You don't drink from no nigger water fountain. Hell, you might catch one of them nigger diseases."

While I was in the kitchen, I heard Grandma say, "By the way, Mr. Tucker, this is my daughter, Sallie Cheek. She lives just down the road from me."

"Nice to meet you, Mrs. Cheek."

Then Mama said something that embarrassed me. She said it in a hushed tone, so I wouldn't get my feelings hurt. But I heard it anyway. "I'm sorry for what my son said, Mr. Tucker. He didn't mean any disrespect. He's just a boy. He hears things that he shouldn't hear, and then says them without knowing what they mean."

"I understand, Mrs. Cheek. Like you said, he's just a boy."

I was ashamed and red-faced when I handed Mr. Tucker Grandma's favorite crystal glass filled with cold water from the refrigerator.

"I'm sorry for saying that, sir. I didn't mean to hurt your feelings," I said, my head bowed, my face on fire. Mama smiled and Grandma nodded, which meant they were pleased with my manners.

"No problem, young man," Mr. Tucker said with a smile. "I know you didn't mean any harm. Are you in school?"

"Yes sir."

"What grade are you in?"

"Second."

"Do you like it?"

"Yes sir. I like it all right I guess."

"Good."

"He also likes to get into a little mischief every now and then," Grandma said. "But he's a good boy, ain't he, Sallie?" Mama nodded.

Mr. Tucker was about to say something when the front door burst open and in walked my father. He stared around the living room. His birthmark lighting up his forehead, Dad's livid eyes came to rest on Mr. Tucker, sitting near Mama on the couch. "What the hell is going on here?" he demanded, glaring first at Grandma and then at Mama. "And why are you sitting next to a nigger?"

I tried to fade away because I knew this was not going to be a pretty scene. But Grandma was not in a trifling mood. She stood up, narrowed her eyes, and warned, "Watch your mouth, Jesse Cheek. This is my house. And in my house, I won't allow anyone to use that word. Not even you." Grandma paused so her words could sink in. "This here is Mr. Tucker," she said, pointing with her tiny hand. "He fixes things for me. He's a good man. He respects me and I respect him."

"I don't care who he is," my father sneered, heading toward the couch. "I don't want my wife sitting next to a goddamn nigger! Get away from there, Sallie."

Mr. Tucker didn't move; didn't even flinch. He sat there calm as could be. Mama was about to get up when Grandma said, "Sit down, Sallie."

Mama hesitated.

"I said sit down." Grandma meant it. Her tone of voice left no doubt about that. "He may be your husband, but I am your mother. I raised you as a proper Christian, and I taught you to respect all people. And, by Jesus, unless your husband calls my guest by his proper name, you ain't going nowhere."

Grandma and my father glared at each other like two roosters about to go at it. I knew my grandma and I knew my dad. He was as stubborn as a mule. But Grandma's will was forged steel. When she believed she was right—and in line with what the Good Book said—not even the hounds of hell could make her back down.

"Jesse, I'm waiting," said Grandma, growing impatient. "Either you respect this man, who is my guest, or you get out right this minute. And if you walk through that door, don't come back, ever."

"I want my wife and son."

"They ain't going anywhere until you behave like a Christian."

Mr. Tucker sat on the couch unfazed; in fact, he seemed to be watching the exchange with fascination. Here stood a frail, petite, white woman, staring down a man half her age and full of liquor and hate, and insisting that he treat a colored handyman as an equal. I stood in awe of Grandma. But I doubted that she could make my proud, stubborn father do something most southern white men would never do.

After what seemed like an eternity, I heard, as if in a dream, my father mumble, "I'm sorry for disrespectin' you, Mr. Tucker." His words were not much more than a whisper, but the room had been so silent and tense that I heard them as if he had shouted them out.

To this day, I don't know how my father managed to utter those words, but hearing them gave me a new measure of respect for him: Somewhere, deep down, he knew right from wrong. Mr. Tucker stood up now for the first time, turned, and faced Dad. In a strong voice he said, "I know you didn't mean it, Mr. Cheek. We all say things in the heat of the moment that we later regret. But I'm a Christian like Mrs. Anderson, and I believe in forgiveness." Mr. Tucker turned to Grandma and said, "I guess I'll be going, Mrs. Anderson. I'll see you Saturday afternoon." Then he went out the door and drove away.

Tears came to my father's eyes. I was stunned. It was the first time I'd ever seen him cry. "I'm so sorry for hurtin' you and Gene," he said. "I don't know why I do it. Honest I don't. Can you both forgive me?"

Mama kissed his cheek and said, "Of course we'll forgive you, won't we, honey?" she said to me.

I nodded and said, "I forgive you, Dad." But they were just words. In my heart the grudge against him grew like a cancer.

"It's the liquor, that's what makes you do these stupid things," Grandma told him. "It's the devil's drink, and no good comes from it."

4

The Apple Tree

Jesse William Cheek was the youngest in a family of three sisters and a brother. At five foot seven, he was a small man with slight features, a bright toothy smile, long chestnut brown hair slicked back with Vitalis, and mischievous brown eyes. His family, by the standards of the day, was rich. Grandma Pearl, who placed pretentiousness right alongside slothfulness and thievery, would say, "They have just enough money to consider everyone else beneath them." The Cheeks owned a small farm about five miles outside of town and lived in a sprawling two-story white brick house. To most of the poor country folks who scrounged a desperate living out of the red clay hills around Forsyth County, the Cheeks' home was a mansion.

Grandpa Cheek, the patriarch of the clan, was a short man built like a fire hydrant, thick-bodied and full of muscles. He favored bib overalls, an old straw hat, and a big wad of Old Mule chewing tobacco. His hair was as dark as coal dust, and he kept it slicked back and tucked under his hat. He had a broad, brooding face and a nose chiseled out of granite. According to him, he inherited his nose from his father, who was part Cherokee Indian.

Once in the local feed store, just down the road from the Cheek farm, I'd heard Grandpa tell the old men gathered around the potbellied stove, "My old man was the finest maker of corn liquor in the foothills of Wilkes County." He then added, with a note of pride in his voice, "He could drink most of his customers under the table." The apples that fell from my great-grandpa Cheek did not fall far from the tree.

Grandpa Cheek worked at R. J. Reynolds Tobacco Company and farmed. He raised hogs, cows, chickens, a large garden, and hay for the animals. He was a boisterous and fear-inspiring man—and, like his father before him, an incurable whiskey drinker.

Grandma Cheek, on the other hand, was a deferential woman who considered herself a quiet Christian lady with a weakness for TV preachers. She was small and fragile looking with straight chestnut hair and a proclivity for Bruton peach-flavored snuff. She walked around the house with an empty Luck's pinto bean can, which she used as a spittoon. She was an almost southern belle, often seen but seldom heard.

The Cheeks were what Grandma Pearl called "Sunday Saints and Monday Ain'ts." They went to church to be admired for their possessions, not their godliness. They were none too happy when my father announced that he'd fallen in love with that strong-willed Anderson girl, the one with the long sandy-blond hair, fine porcelain complexion, piercing gold-green eyes, and a voice that was sweet enough for God's own choir. According to my mother, all they cared about was that she was from "a dirt-poor family" and therefore unfit to marry a Cheek.

My father was stubborn in wanting to marry her, but his family was just as stubborn in their resistance. In the end Dad won that battle. But try as he might, nothing he ever did was good enough to satisfy his proud and domineering father. Dad was the odd man out in the Cheek family, the black sheep. Though he was a "chip off the old block," that fact went unnoticed by the block himself. He was not the apple of his father's eye. That honor fell to his brother Bobby. Living in the shadow of his brother was a burden my father couldn't bear.

He quit school during his senior year in high school and joined the army, but was discharged when they discovered he had epilepsy. It was a condition he had suffered from since receiving a blow to the head in a childhood fistfight. My father must have seen marriage to my mother as the perfect escape from his ornery dad. Mama once told me that while he was courting her, Dad was the nicest and kindest man she'd ever known. "Your father was a charmer," she would say. He took her dancing, shopping, and to the picture show. At family gatherings he would cradle her in his arms for all to see. In turn she would beam each time he walked into a room, and tell her friends that she couldn't wait for them to get married.

They wed on August 18, 1949, at the Urban Street Baptist Church. A few weeks after they married, they moved into a small two-bedroom row house at 318 Brookline Street. It was their dream house, just four blocks from church and five blocks from Grandma Pearl's home.

According to Mama, Dad started drinking heavily after I was born, but I didn't notice until I was around five years old. I saw him as a kind man with a great sense of humor. His kindness was evident in those days, like the time he came home with a crow that had been shot in the wing. He brought it into the house in a cardboard box and said, "There ain't no excuse for anyone who shoots a defenseless animal. Hunting, and eating what you hunt, is one thing, but this is just down-right ignorance." That crow followed him around the yard like a dog until one day its wing healed up and it flew off.

Once his drinking became obvious, even to me, the kindness started to fade. I never saw that he needed a reason to drink. I saw him drunk, getting drunk, or hung over from a drunk almost every week, and I never found any connection between the act itself and a cause. There was one exception, though, and that was our visits to the Cheek farm. On most Sundays after church, the clan would gather, and on those days Dad's drinking seemed purposeful. I didn't enjoy those gatherings; more often than not they ended in name-calling and threats of an ass whoopin'. Dad never said he disliked going; he just poured in more courage and went, his disposition growing bleaker as Sunday approached.

Today was Sunday, and Dad's mood was black. He'd been sitting on the couch drinking Pabst Blue Ribbon beer while Mama and I went to church. Mama had cooked all day Saturday for the family gathering. That was her job, to cook. It seemed—at least to me—that none of the Cheek women had learned to cook. We loaded pots and containers of green beans, potato salad, fried chicken, and Mama's special yeast rolls into the car. Then we headed down Old Thomasville Road toward the farm, Dad cussing under his breath with each passing mile.

The Cheek property, several acres in all, covered one of the hills that dotted the countryside. The grand farmhouse sat at the apex of a hill and looked down on the rest of the world. Giant white cedars defined the property lines and separated the farm from the outside world. Behind the house and off to the left stood a small wooden barn, weathered in shades of gray and brown, its tin roof streaked with rust. Connected to the far end of the old barn was a chicken coop where the hens that dared to stop laying eggs became Sunday dinner. Grandpa Cheek would stride into the coop, survey the panicked chickens, and snatch up the offender by the head and swing it around, snapping its neck. A few hundred yards beyond the barn, at the edge of the woods and downwind, was the hog pen. The few cows Grandpa raised were kept in a fenced, rolling pasture that looked like a rose-colored bedspread in the deepening dusk.

Dad turned off Teague Road and onto the unpaved, oak-lined driveway of the farmhouse and followed it around to the backyard. A line of cars all parked in a neat row faced the barn. Uncle Bobby, Aunt Irene, and my cousin Susan had ridden in their new Buick Regal. It was first in line. Next were Aunt Norma and Uncle Louis's white Ford Fairlane. Their son, Eddie, who was standing at the far end of the chicken coop, turned and walked away when we pulled up.

Dad parked our old rusty Chevy next to Aunt Lucille and Uncle John's new Pontiac Bonneville. *Great*, I thought. It meant that their sneaky kids John-John and Melissa would be waiting for me inside. Waiting and sitting, their hands folded in their laps, every bit the picture of the perfect kids. Dad shut off the old car, but, as it was prone to do, it continued to run, spitting and sputtering until it died in a cloud of blue smoke.

It was around four o'clock when we stepped out. Dad glared down at me, his head cocked to accentuate the moment, and said, "Don't start no shit with your cousins or I'll drag you out behind the barn and beat your ass. You got that?"

I nodded and took Mama's hand. We turned and walked toward the back door of Grandpa's house. Grandpa scared me. When I had a nightmare, it was his snarling face I saw.

5

The Goddamn Dog

Gathered around the kitchen table with Grandma were my aunts Norma, Lucille, and Irene. My seven-year-old cousin Susan—reserved, well behaved, and the clan's future debutante—sat in shy silence on the bench next to the kitchen door. Pretty as usual, she looked at me, smiled, and said, "Hey, Gene."

"Hey, Susan," I replied with a return smile. Cousins John-John and Melissa were sitting in the den against the far wall, and just as I'd predicted their hands were folded and lying in the laps of their new clothes. They gave me their usual dirty looks as I passed from their view. Aunt Millie, Uncle Dale, and their brood of redheads hadn't showed up yet. Their new red-and-white 1959 Rambler would be the last to arrive.

Grandpa relaxed in his overstuffed armchair, his muscular arms and stumpy fingers splayed out on its sides. I looked at the breast pocket of his Sunday overalls and spotted the familiar outline of his fancy whiskey flask. Uncle Bobby sat to the right of Grandpa in a rocking chair while the rest of my uncles assembled around the two like the Knights of the Round Table. They all looked up as we entered the kitchen.

I kept close to Mama in the kitchen as she began to warm up the food. The rest of the women went about setting the table. Dad walked off to join the rest of the knights in the den. The women started talking, and the men were laughing as I sat down on the bench next to Susan. "How's your horse?" I asked.

Susan smiled and said, "Oh, he's just fine I reckon. I rode him yesterday afternoon. When are you going to come out and ride him with me?"

"Heck, I don't know, one of these days I guess when Daddy brings me out there."

Susan and I used to play together a lot when my parents and I visited her family's nice brick house. The adults would gather around the kitchen table and play rook or rummy while Susan and I would play outside or watch TV together. The last time I had visited Susan, we'd been in the basement playing doctor. Susan was the doctor and she was leaning over me listening to my heart with her plastic stethoscope. Aunt Irene came to the basement door and yelled down, "What are y'all doing down there?" Susan answered, "Playing doctor." We loaded up and left soon after that and hadn't been back since.

Susan was just about to say something to me when a gravel voice snatched me back into reality. "Gene, come in here a minute." It was Grandpa's voice, and I pretended not to hear him. My eyes searched and found Mama, my look pleading for her to do something. She shook her head as if to say *It'll be okay*, and I reluctantly went to Grandpa.

"Why don't you sit here with me and watch TV while your mama serves up the food?" The men were watching the Washington Redskins play the Baltimore Colts. He pushed me onto his lap but I squirmed my way out and sat down on the floor. I liked the Redskins, in particular their diminutive quarterback Eddie LeBaron. He was the smallest player in the NFL, but his fiery style and fearlessness made him the undisputed leader of the Redskins and an inspiration to all us little people.

Mama continued on into the kitchen. Once she was gone, Grandpa got up.

"On second thought . . . ," he said with a mischievous grin. "Gene, come outside with me. I got something to show you."

I wanted to yell for Mama but I couldn't. As I followed Grandpa outside, I was shaking. I wondered what newfangled type of torture he had in store for me now, out of sight of everyone else. Between the house and the old barn stood Grandpa's most prized possession—a large, angry, vicious bulldog. The beast lived on a circle of ground twenty-eight feet in diameter. An iron stake driven into the middle of the circle, and fourteen feet of logging chain, tethered the dog to this one spot. The dog had paced the ground around the iron stake until the circle was void of all life, except itself. An old wooden doghouse and table scraps were its lone comforts. Grandpa loved torturing this poor animal. I once heard him say, "Torturing this damn dog makes him mean. I want him to be so mean that he'll chew the leg off anyone who comes near him." The dog had no name. Grandpa called it "dog," or "damn dog," or "dumb dog," and, when he was drunk, "goddamn dog." Clutching my hand, Grandpa half dragged me toward the abused animal, who was lying beside the stake.

"Please, Grandpa, don't," I pleaded and began to cry.

Grandpa wheeled around and glared down at me. "Are you afraid?"

"Yes sir."

"Well, you shouldn't be afraid of this goddamn dog," he said. "Watch this." He let go of my hand and walked toward the dog. I backed up several steps and wondered why he would venture so close to a dog who would tear his throat out if given the chance. I thought he was too drunk to realize what he was doing, although he didn't seem any drunker than usual. The dog began to stir as Grandpa approached.

"Be careful, Grandpa," I warned, inching backward.

"Don't worry," he said, chuckling as he got closer to the dog's circle. The dog turned to face him and let out a low, deep belly growl. The hair on its back stood up like the bristles on a Fuller brush. I was terrified. I wanted to dart back inside and tell someone that Grandpa had lost his mind and was about to be eaten by the dog. It growled again, glaring at its tormentor with red, spiteful eyes. Its mouth watered, and slobber dripped from the corners, soon, I figured, to be replaced by Grandpa's blood. "Come on, you goddamn dumb dog!" he yelled. "I ain't afraid of you!" The dog growled again.

"Watch out!" I shouted as the dog lunged to its feet and charged full speed toward Grandpa, its mouth twisted into a hideous snarl. To my horror, Grandpa didn't turn and run.

"Grandpa, get away!" I yelled.

The dog left its feet and flew toward Grandpa. Then, as if by magic, it stopped in midair less than a foot from Grandpa's throat. It hung there for a second, and then as if some giant invisible hand had reached out and smacked the dog, it turned in midflight and slammed hard into the ground. The chain had reached its limit. The dog, stunned by the harsh impact, whimpered.

"Goddamn dumb dog does that every time," Grandpa said with satisfaction in his voice. He turned and walked toward me while the dog staggered back to his dilapidated doghouse. "You see, boy?" Grandpa said. "There's no need to fear something that stupid."

"Yes sir," I said. But I wondered what would happen if the chain ever broke.

6

Even in Death

The goddamn dog didn't kill Grandpa—a massive heart attack did. But even in death, it seemed he was determined to torment me. When Uncle Bobby called with the news, my father insisted that all of us attend the wake.

"Gene is too little, Jesse," Mama said.

"I don't care, he's coming with us."

She knew better than to argue with him. Grandpa's death had sent Dad spiraling into the worst alcohol-fueled depression I'd ever seen, and he was in a nasty mood as we piled into the old Chevy. As he drove toward the Cheek farm, he gripped the steering wheel like he was driving us all to the gates of hell. I was consumed with terror; no one had bothered to tell me how Grandpa had died, and I just figured that the dog had broken the chain and exacted its revenge.

When we arrived, I looked in the dog's circle. All I could see was the logging chain going into the doghouse. The goddamn dog was nowhere in sight. As we walked into the kitchen, we found my aunts, uncles, and cousins gathered in a line leading toward the den where Grandpa's coffin sat not far from his chair. It was leaning at a slight angle so that even from the kitchen I could see his ashen white face. I wanted to stay as far from the coffin as possible, so I slumped to the floor in the corner behind the kitchen door and tried to become invisible. My father joined the long line of those giving condolences to Grandma Cheek, and I heard Uncle John say, "Couldn't even show up sober at his own father's wake."

Mama found me. "Why are you hiding in the corner?" she asked, bending down so that our eyes met.

"I'm scared of the goddamn dog."

"Honey, don't call the dog that. It's not nice."

"Well, that's what Grandpa called it." I then explained what had happened during my last visit here. "Did the dog kill Grandpa?"

"No, honey. Don't you want to go in and see your grandma or say good-bye to your grandpa?"

"No, I don't want to," I said, trembling.

"I understand, honey. You won't have to if you don't want to."

"Will you tell that to Dad?"

"Yes, I'll tell him now." She walked into the den and whispered into my father's ear. His face contorted in anger and he shook his head. I could tell from the expression on her face that she was getting nowhere with him, and short of making a big scene there was nothing more she could do. Mama turned to express condolences to Grandma, who was sitting in Grandpa's chair with her Luck's can in her right hand and her bottom lip pooched out like she'd been stung by a bee.

Dad walked over to me. "Your ma tells me you don't want to say good-bye to your grandpa," he said, breathing whiskey all over me.

"No sir."

"Don't tell me you're afraid of a dead man now, boy."

I made no reply. I continued to tremble.

"Well, it's your turn to kiss him good-bye." He clutched my arm.

"No!" I screamed as he started dragging me toward the open casket. "I don't want to kiss him! I don't want to kiss him! I don't want to kiss him!"

Dad was unmoved by my pleas. Mama left Grandma and rushed to my side. She made a futile grab for my arm as my father lifted me off my feet and carried me toward the coffin. "Jesse, don't do this to your son," she begged. "Can't you see he's terrified?"

He shoved her away while I kicked and struggled to get loose. His powerful hands under my arms, he held me over the open casket. I looked down in horror at the pasty, stone-cold corpse. For a moment I thought his eyes would fly open and he would reach out and grab me and pull me into the casket with him; that it was another one of his cruel jokes just to scare me—pretend to be dead and then seize me.

"Now kiss your Grandpa good-bye," I heard my father say from a thousand miles away. He lowered me toward the dead face of a man who had scared me in life, and I shrieked in terror. Mama regained a grip on my arm and was trying to tear me from his grasp. Everyone stared as they battled over their screaming child. Grandpa's face seemed to leer at me before it morphed into the hideous face of the goddamn dog. I could feel his coldness as I was lowered ever closer to his pallid face. I was about to faint when Mama succeeded in pulling me away.

"You stupid, stupid bastard!" she yelled at Dad. "Can't you see the child is scared to death?" She cradled me in her arms, trying to soothe my whimpers. Then we went out the back door, followed by the eyes of everyone in the house. My father trailed us, shouting at Mama and accusing her of making a sissy out of me. She ignored him, and we got into the old Chevy and drove off, leaving him standing in the yard cussing.

7

Close to the Tree

One Saturday morning in November, about a month after Grandpa's funeral, I was lying on the living room floor in an old pair of red flannel pajamas watching *Huckleberry Hound*. Mama was in the kitchen shelling beans and singing her favorite song:

Que sera sera
Whatever will be, will be

Despite her singing, she was worried.

Dad hadn't come home from work Friday evening, and we didn't know why. We had walked up to Barney Todd's pink house before breakfast to see if they knew where he was. Barney's short, plump wife came to the door with her apron on and her hands covered in biscuit dough. She told Mama that Barney had gone coon hunting Friday night with my dad. Coon hunting wasn't hunting. It was a good excuse for a few good old boys to sit out in the woods, away from their wives and rug rats, and drink. The coon dogs did all the work, finding the scent and then chasing the coon through the hills and hollers until the coon was run up a tree.

The men, at least those who were still sober enough to walk, would find the dogs at the bottom of some big old tree, yapping and snapping up at the coon. Some fool would then climb the tree, trying to catch the coon and throw it in a sack, or knock it out of the tree.

Huckleberry Hound was explaining something to Boo Boo when the old man knocked on the screen door. He wasn't a stranger—not exactly. He was a black man as old as dirt who lived across the creek in Colored Town. He wore tattered overalls and a blue gingham shirt frazzled at the collar and sleeves. In his hands he held a bent and stained baseball cap with JOHN DEERE written on the front. We all knew him. Mama and Dad knew him by name; everyone called him Uncle Joe. The kids in the neighborhood called him "the Walking Man." He'd stagger up Urban Street mumbling and cussing to no one we could see. Sometimes he'd walk through the field behind the houses on our side of Brookline Street headed toward Old Thomasville Road.

The field, a strip of hardwoods, and a creek separated us civilized white folks from the colored hordes and, according to my dad, certain death or torture at the hands of the "black savages." "Boy don't you ever cross that creek, if you do I'll beat you to within an inch of your life. There ain't no telling what them worthless drunken niggers might do to you. Do you hear me!"

I nodded and said, "Yes sir." Dad had also told me to stay away from the Walking Man. "He's just another crazy drunk nigger, and there's no telling what he might do." I wasn't scared of him; none of us kids was. First off, he was no bigger than a cornstalk. He was shorter than my mama, who was five foot two inches tall. Uncle Joe was crazy, I reckoned—his brain swimming around in whatever concoction he could find—but he was always friendly to us kids.

He'd smile and wave at us. "How you children doin' on this fine day? Playin' and laughin', that's what you 'posed to be doin'." We didn't see Uncle Joe as much of a threat.

Mama came to the door. "Uncle Joe, I ain't got no work for you today. What you doing out so early anyway?"

"Well, Miss Sallie, I was a hopin' you could spare a quarter for me, I needs a drink real bad." I could see his hands shaking as he held his old cap.

"Now, Uncle Joe, you know I ain't got no money, and if I did I wouldn't give it to you for drinkin'."

"No'm, I don't reckon, but I'm in a bad way this mornin', I'm in a real bad way. Could you let me have some paregoric, you know, to just settle my nerves a bit?"

Mama looked at the old man. "If I give it to you, will you promise to go home and go to bed?"

"Yes'm, I promise that's surely what I'll do." Mama walked into the bathroom and came out holding a small brown bottle. I didn't see how it could help him much, it was so small, but she opened the screen and handed it to him. "Here; now you go home, and don't you come back wanting nothing else to drink."

"God bless you, Miss Sallie. No'm, I won't ask you no more."

Mama closed the screen door and looked at me. "He'll be back." I walked to the door and watched as the Walking Man walked off down the road. He drained the bottle and tossed it into the woods. Just then Dad rounded the corner and pulled the car in front of the house. He got out, slammed the door, turned, and stared down the road at the old man.

"What the hell did that drunken nigger want? You didn't give him no damn money, did you?"

Mama shook her head. "No, I didn't give him money."

"Well, it's a damn good thing. He's a piece of shit, that nigger. He stays drunk all the time and ain't fit for nothing." She didn't say a word, just walked off toward the kitchen.

Dad had just walked in on Saturday morning after not coming home from work on Friday. His eyes looked like they were about to bleed, his hair was a mess, and his work clothes looked like they'd been dragged behind a mule. He'd been drunk since he'd gotten off work, and still was for the most part. Frankly, I couldn't see much difference between him and Uncle Joe. Except for their color—and the fact that I wasn't scared of the Walking Man.

Dad stood watching Mama walk off. "Did you get any coons?" I was glad to see he was all right and not dead in a ditch somewhere, which is how Uncle Bill said they were going to find Dad one day.

He glared at me. "Do you see any coons?"

I started to turn my attention back to the cartoons when without warning he slapped me with the back of his hand.

"That's for starin' at me," he growled. I didn't cry. I clenched my teeth to smother the pain and watched him stumble and mutter down the narrow hallway and into the kitchen. A minute later I heard a loud

34

crash and the shattering of glass. I jumped up, ran to the kitchen door, and peeped inside to see if Mama was okay.

"Why ain't the dishes done?" my father screamed at her. An empty milk bottle lay shattered on the yellow linoleum floor. She had retreated to a far corner of the kitchen.

"I wanted to finish shelling these crowders," she said. "I was planning on making them for supper tonight."

"Beans, beans, beans!" he yelled. "What's a man got to do to get a little meat in this damn house?"

"When you start giving me your paycheck I'll buy meat. You got paid yesterday and you didn't come home. Instead, you went out drinking. Why did Barney tell his wife you were coon hunting?" Dad said nothing. "You ought to be ashamed of yourself, Jesse Cheek. Most men spend time with their families, but not you. You waste your time and money drinking. Look at you. You're nothing but an alcoholic. If you don't change, you're going to end up just like your father." The words were no sooner out of her mouth than she realized she had gone too far.

The veins on the side of his neck bulged, and his birthmark turned bright red. "Shut your ugly trap! Don't you talk about Daddy like that or I'll kick your fat face in!"

Dad hated comparisons to his father. Before Grandpa died, Dad had cussed him behind his back, calling him a demanding, heartless, drunken SOB who cared more for his farm animals than he did his own children. But now that Grandpa was dead, he had become a saint in Dad's memory.

"I'm sorry, Jesse. I shouldn't say bad things about the dead, but you know it's the truth. Your father was an alcoholic and it killed him, and if you don't stop it's going to kill you, too. Now go to bed and sleep it off and let me finish shelling these peas."

Dad snatched the colander out of her hands and smashed it against the kitchen floor. Tiny purple-hulled crowders hit the floor and rolled off in all directions like ball bearings. "Well, you're done with 'em now, ain't you? Now do them dishes."

Furious, her arms resting on her hips, Mama said, "What's wrong with you, Jesse? Have you gone mad? Look at your son." She turned to me, still cowering outside the kitchen door. "He's afraid of you. He's even started to hate you. And he's been waiting for you to come home so we could go Christmas shopping like you promised."

"I don't give a rat's ass if he hates me. And we ain't goin' Christmas shoppin'.'."

"Why not?"

He hesitated for a moment, and then said, "Because I was fired yesterday, that's why."

Mama was stunned. For a moment, she was speechless. "Fired? You're kidding, right?"

"Do I look like I'm kiddin'?"

"My God, Jesse. What are we going to do now? It's bad enough that you drink up most of your pay, but now you've gone and got yourself fired."

"I'll find another job," he mumbled.

She looked up at him and shook her head. "Doing what?"

"I'll figure something out."

"And what's your brother going to say? He got you that job, remember? It's going to make him mad."

"I don't give a shit. To hell with Bobby. I didn't like that shitty job anyway. He could have gotten me a job at R. J. Reynolds, but he didn't, did he? Instead he got me a job that has me seeing goddamn niggers all the time. Why didn't he get me a job fit for a white man? He didn't think I was good enough to work beside him, that's why. So he can kiss my ass."

Just then we heard a knock on the door. I hurried to the front door, peered out the little side window, and saw a shiny new blue Ford pickup parked at the curb. It was Uncle Bobby.

8

Brothers

I hurried back to the kitchen. "Mama," I whispered, pointing toward the front door, "Uncle Bobby is here. You want me to let him in?"

"No. Wait a minute." She swept the shards from the broken milk bottle and the remaining peas into the dustpan and dumped them into the trash can. "Okay, go let him in."

As I opened the door, I heard Dad mutter on his way into the bathroom, "Now what the hell does he want?"

Uncle Bobby took off his green-and-red flannel hunting cap and stepped into the living room. Short and stout, he was the spitting image of Grandpa and he was always well dressed—unlike Dad, whose day-to-day attire consisted of an old pair of patched bib overalls and a T-shirt that was as thin as onionskin. Uncle Bobby wore starched pants, pressed shirts, and shined work boots. A perfect smile and green eyes completed the image he cultivated with great care. An ambitious man, Uncle Bobby had followed in Grandpa's footsteps. After he got out of the army, he went to work at R. J. Reynolds. He was now a supervisor with considerable clout.

Dad always complained that Uncle Bobby, like the rest of his family, looked down on him and never liked the fact that he had married Mama. But Mama believed that Uncle Bobby was a kind man. After all, he had been best man at their wedding and had gone out of his way—and out on a limb—to get Dad a decent job with the city, despite his ever-increasing drinking problem.

Uncle Bobby stood in the living room fidgeting with his hat and mumbled a hello to Mama and me. He glanced around our small living room, filled with a hodgepodge of worn-out hand-me-downs. Our home was a far cry from his sprawling brick house in the country situated on land near the Cheek farm on Teague Road. Dad had worked long hours helping him build that house. "And what'd I get in return?" Dad once said with considerable bitterness. "A pat on the back and a kick in the ass, that's what I got."

"Is Jesse home?" asked Uncle Bobby.

"He's in the bathroom," Mama said. She picked up my Jughead and Richie Rich comic books from the frayed old couch and motioned for him to sit down. Studying Uncle Bobby's face, she asked, "Is something wrong?"

"I'm afraid so. It's about Jesse. He did it again."

"Did what?" she asked. "Is it about his job?"

"Yeah. His supervisor got a call from a customer yesterday afternoon, complaining that Jesse was lying in his yard passed out under a tree. He went over and found him drunk. You know that wasn't the first time it's happened. So he fired him on the spot."

"You're a damn liar!" Dad yelled, emerging from the bathroom. "I wasn't drunk. I had a spell."

"Jesse, he says you smelled like a still when he found you."

"You believe him over your own brother?"

"It's not the first time you've been drunk on the job. Remember that time last summer—"

Dad cut him short. "Tell me the truth, Bobby. Are you ashamed of me?" He said it in such a pitiful voice that I thought he was about to cry. "I want to know, Bobby. Are you ashamed of me, your own brother?"

There; he'd said it. For the first time, he'd asked the question that had stuck in his craw his whole life. I stood in the corner, waiting for the answer.

"Of course not," Uncle Bobby said.

"What about Sallie?"

"What about her?"

"What'd you call her, Bobby? White trash? Isn't that what you called her?"

Uncle Bobby's face flushed, and he looked down at the floor to avoid Mama's intense gaze. I didn't know if the tears in the corner of her eyes were from anger or pain. I fumed at the thought that Uncle Bobby considered Mama white trash. Grandma had told me, *White trash are people who don't try to better themselves.* Heck, Mama worked like a dog at a thankless, mind-numbing job at the mill trying to keep our family together.

"Are you afraid that associatin' with my family will tarnish your mighty fine reputation?"

"Jesse, you know that's not true. Sallie is my sister-in-law. She's not white trash. And you're my brother. And Gene is my nephew. I care about all of you."

"The hell you do. You're a smooth talker, Bobby, I'll hand you that much. Anybody who thinks you're a Christian sure don't know you like I do. You're a selfish, prideful man, that's what you are. How many times have I asked you for help when I was down? And have you helped me? No. You make excuses. Christians don't make excuses. You must be a mighty rich man by now considerin' you still got the first dollar you ever made."

"Please, Jesse," Mama pleaded. "Bobby's your brother." By speaking up, she was taking the chance that Dad would turn his wrath on her. Instead he started crying. I stared at him in disbelief. Mama, with tears in her eyes, walked over and put her arms around him. He was sitting on the edge of the couch, leaning over crying into his hands. My hate for him vanished. I put my arms around them both, and we all wept.

I believed deep down that he was a good man and that he wanted to be a good father and husband. But he had no mirror in which to judge himself. After all, his example had been Grandpa.

From the corner of my eye I saw Uncle Bobby's face twitch at the sight of us clinging to each other. "I'm sorry, Jesse, I didn't mean to hurt you," he said, fidgeting with his cap again. "Believe me. I care about you all. I want to help. That's why I came over. Is there anything you need, Sallie?"

Mama stood up straight, pulled a tissue from her apron pocket, and wiped her eyes. It was not an easy thing for her to ask anyone for help, above all Bobby. It was hard on her pride to admit we needed help, but we did, and she knew it. "Well, we're behind on rent and utilities, and the phone has been disconnected. I can pay the rent and some of the utilities, but not all of it. With Christmas around the corner, I don't know what we'll do about that. Gene's been looking forward to this Christmas in particular."

Uncle Bobby turned his gaze toward me. "What do you want Santa Claus to bring you?"

"A bike," I said. "My best friend, Larry, got a bike last Christmas. He says Santa gave it to him for looking after his mama."

"Well, Santa just might bring you a bike on Christmas, because I know you look after your mama. All you gotta do is let him know."

"Maybe I should write Santa a letter and ask for one. Do you think I could ask him to find Daddy a new job, too?"

9

Friends in Need

The next day after church I changed my clothes, grabbed a leftover biscuit off the stove, and ran down the hill to Larry's house. He hadn't been at church and I couldn't wait to tell him the good news about my bike.

Larry's house had been the first one built in the neighborhood, and it sat all by itself on a little knoll. It had a big side yard shaped like a bowl. On summer days when thunderstorms roared through the Piedmont and rain fell in buckets, the bowl filled up like a swimming pool. A big hill at the back of Lake Larry, as we called it, provided us with a ready-made sliding board. We would rip up old cardboard and slide down the hill on the pieces, screaming and laughing at the top of our lungs as we splashed into the water.

I knocked on the door and Larry's mother, who was Mama's best friend, opened it just a crack. "Larry's not home, Gene," she said. "He left about an hour ago. I don't know where he went. I'm worried."

Through the tiny opening, I could see that she had a swollen lip, black eye, and bruises on her neck. She stepped back from the door when she saw me staring at her. I knew what had happened. John, her wife-beating, alcoholic husband, had beaten her again, and Larry, who was more terrified of his violent father than I was of mine, had run off.

"I think I know where Larry is, Mrs. Brooks," I said.

"You do?"

"Yes ma'am. He's down at the creek."

She sighed. "Can you please make sure he's all right and keep him company? I have to take John to work and I'll be gone for a little while."

"Sure, Mrs. Brooks."

"Thank you, honey."

From inside the dark house I heard Larry's father bellow, "Who the hell are you calling honey?"

"It's just Gene."

"Well, get your ass back in here," he ordered. "I can't find a clean pair of socks."

Fear spreading across her otherwise pretty face, she closed the door and hurried back to her abuser.

Shaking my head, I ran to the small creek—our sanctuary. The tiny brook cut its way through a stand of maple trees that stood on the right side of Larry's house. I found him sitting on the little wooden bridge dropping maple seeds into the shallow water.

We called the maple seeds "whirlybirds" because they twirled in the wind like helicopter blades. We'd spend hours tossing them into the air and watching them spin downward until they plopped into the water and disappeared around the bend.

Larry's large brown, puppy-dog eyes brightened when he saw me coming. I could tell he'd been crying from the streaks on his chubby cheeks. "Dad beat up Mama again."

"I saw her," I said, tossing a pebble into the creek. "She looked real bad. What was it about this time?"

"The same old thing. He came home drunk and they started arguing, then he started beating her. He almost choked her to death."

It was hard to imagine Larry's father, who was a giant of a man with meaty hands, battering and choking such a fragile, elfin woman. Larry broke down again and buried his face in his palms. I put my hand on my friend's shoulder and searched for something to say, some words that would make him feel better, something to make this hurt go away.

"Guess what?" I said, trying to cheer him up.

"What?" he asked.

"Santa is bringing me a bike."

"No kiddin'?"

"Yep, all I have to do is write him. Then you and I will have a great time riding together."

We talked and then raced stick-boats down the majestic waterway. Despite being overweight and knock-kneed, Larry stayed with me step for muddy step as we chased the boats down the creek. When we got tired, we climbed onto the bridge and dangled our feet over the side. Our sanctuary again had worked its magic. The outside world and all its problems had faded away as we lay on our backs and enjoyed the warming rays of the afternoon sun.

While Larry and I sat on the bridge talking, we heard shouting and cussing coming from the two-story house down on the corner. The house belonged to Frank, a childless, hard-drinking garbage man, and his wife. Like all the other drunks in the neighborhood, Frank lived for Fridays when he would drown his troubles in cheap bathtub gin. After work he'd walk the few blocks into Colored Town and spend his paycheck on some cheap homemade liquor made from pure grain alcohol and God knows what else. Instead of being made in a still, it was mixed up in someone's bathtub. It was so potent that it was said a man could stay drunk for an entire week—or could get poisoned. Stories of men blinded and pushed to insanity from drinking this concoction were common.

Frank was smaller than my dad—about five foot five inches tall—and skinny as a fence post. He seemed so much smaller because his foreign-born wife, Rose, was a giant of a woman. In the neighborhood we knew her as Big Mama, and these weekly fights between her and Frank were known as "the Friday night fights," though they didn't always take place on Friday. Sometimes Frank's drunken escapades lasted all weekend and ended when he finally staggered home. When he did, Rose was waiting on him, and she wasn't the least bit afraid of Frank. In fact, it was the other way around. He was petrified of her.

When we reached the edge of Larry's yard, the yelling and cussing intensified. The back door to Frank and Rose's house burst open and Frank came staggering out and tumbled to the ground. Moving as fast as his drunken legs allowed, he scrambled to his feet and tried to run. His weather-beaten face twisted in pure terror, he looked like he'd seen the devil himself. The screen door flew open.

It wasn't the devil chasing Frank. It was Big Mama, and she was holding high over her head a greasy black cast-iron frying pan big enough to fry two chickens in.

"Come back here, you drunken piece of shit!" she shouted.

"Rose, darlin', goddamn it, leave me alone!" Frank yelled. The fact that Frank had just called his wife *darlin'* as she chased him around the yard with a frying pan sent Larry and me into fits of laughter. Frank stumbled and weaved his way around the backyard, scattering the couple's chickens and goats. Another beast from their menagerie, a shaggy sheepdog named Rascal, who had never experienced the feel of soap and water, bounded after Frank, barking.

Running from his wife, Frank kept stumbling and falling like it was his first day with a new pair of legs. Soon enough Big Mama Rose and the stinking, slobbering dog caught Frank. While she worked him over with the frying pan, Rascal gnawed his ankles raw. As a growing crowd of neighbors roared with laughter, Larry turned to me and said, "Boy, I sure wish I had a mother like that."

"Me, too. Just look at her swing that skillet! She's got an arm like that guy on the box of baking soda." After Rose had hammered Frank's head, legs, and arms with the frying pan, Larry and I sat by the creek discussing ways to fatten our moms to Rose's size. We figured that fat was muscle; if we fed our mamas enough, they could garner the strength they needed to beat our fathers into submission with a frying pan. After we'd talked, I suggested we go to my house and watch *Mighty Mouse* on TV before I wrote that letter to Santa.

"That letter's gotta be written on special paper," Larry said in a knowing tone. "I have some."

"You do?"

"Yeah. I use it for all my letters to Santa. Mama bought it for me year before last. I'll give you some."

We walked up to Larry's front door. No one was home, and the door was locked. Larry turned over a rock next to their cement porch, picked up a key, and unlocked the door. We went to his bedroom, where he opened the top drawer of his desk and pulled out white stationery decorated with a picture of old Saint Nick riding in a sleigh full of presents. The address read THE NORTH POLE.

"Where's the North Pole?" I asked.

"Mama says its way, way north of Winston-Salem, past Mount Airy."

"We should go there someday."

"Mama says it's real far," my best friend said.

10

Friends in Deed

The next morning at school Larry and I were sitting outside on a brick wall behind the Forest Park Elementary School cafeteria. We were both in Mrs. Brown's second-grade class. Mrs. Brown had taught at this school since it first opened and had been, in fact, Mama's first-grade teacher. She was a tall woman who reminded me of Olive Oyl, Popeye's girlfriend, all arms and legs and a tiny head covered in short black hair.

Instead of playing with the other kids on the playground, Larry and I were talking. He was still upset over the beating his mama had taken Saturday night. I was telling Larry not to worry, that his mom would be all right. As if things weren't bad enough, Mickey, the school bully—who picked on Larry without mercy—began calling him names like "fat crybaby" and "lard ass."

"Leave him alone, you retard," I shouted. "His mama is sick."

"Mama's boy, Mama's boy," Mickey chanted.

"Don't call my friend names, you hear." I stood up, my face red with fury. Mickey was bigger than I was; he was in the third grade—for the second time. I didn't care. I was tired of him hurting Larry's feelings.

"Why don't you make me," Mickey said, sticking out his chest.

I'd never been in a fight before. Mama told me that fighting was wrong, and that if provoked I should walk away because Jesus had turned the other cheek. "I don't want no trouble," I told the bully.

"You're yellow," Mickey declared and shoved me in the chest, almost knocking me down. I stumbled back against the brick wall but didn't fall.

"I ain't yellow," I said. Then I remembered what Uncle Bill once told me: *Don't back down from bullies; most of them are all bark and no bite. You stand up to them. You can't let people start pushing you around because if you do, they'll keep on pushing. If you have to fight, make sure you get in the first punch, and go for the nose. Nothing takes it out of a bully like seeing his own blood.*

"Yeah, you're yellow," Mickey said, and then he spit on my shirt.

That did it. Enraged, I lowered my head like a football player and charged him, crashing my head into his stomach and knocking him down. In an instant I was on top of him punching his face with my fists. Uncle Bill had been right; Mickey was more bark than bite. He wasn't fighting back. Instead he began hollering as blood oozed from his nose. Several students gathered around us and egged me on, all of them wanting to see the notorious bully get what was coming to him. Larry tried to pull me off but I clung to Mickey like a snapping turtle as we rolled around on the playground dirt.

A female voice shouted out, "Stop it, you two!" It was Mrs. Terrell, the principal, who was also a member of the Urban Street Baptist Church where she sang with Mama in the choir. "What's going on?"

"He spit at me and he was picking on Larry," I said, pointing to Mickey.

"He's lying," retorted Mickey, blood leaking through the fingers that covered his nose.

"Gene, go to my office right this minute and wait for me there," Mrs. Terrell said. She grabbed Mickey by the hand, led him to the long row of water fountains, and started washing his bloodied face and hands.

Alone in her office, I squirmed and waited for Mrs. Terrell, wondering what punishment I faced. I was embarrassed. Mrs. Terrell considered me one of her favorite students, a fact that made both Grandma and Mama proud—and kept me on the straight and narrow. Until now. I figured that Mrs. Terrell would tell Mama about the fight and that she would spank me. She didn't like spanking me, but when words failed or the situation called for it, she didn't hesitate to send me into the yard to find a switch. And I didn't make the mistake of coming back with some little flimsy switch, either, because that would make it worse. I figured I could handle the spanking—just as long as Grandma and Mama didn't lose their pride in me.

My eyes wandered to Mrs. Terrell's desk in front of me. Hanging from the side of her chair was a smooth black patent leather purse just like the one I'd seen weeks earlier in the window of the Mother and Daughter Department Store. Mama had stood at that window one Saturday morning admiring that purse for what seemed like forever. I walked over to Mrs. Terrell's desk and picked up the purse. My fingers rubbed against the leather. *It sure would be nice if Mama had a purse like this for Christmas. Boy, would she be surprised. Then she could throw that old worn-out thing in the trash. Heck, the zipper is even broken on hers. I wonder if Uncle Bill would help me get her one. I bet he would if I ask him.* Out of curiosity, I opened Mrs. Terrell's purse and peeked inside. I let out a low whistle. Mixed in with the lipstick, makeup mirror, hankie, and coins was a big wad of twenties. *I ain't never seen so much money in my life. Why, I bet it could buy a house and lots of Christmas presents.* For one fleeting moment I wanted to take it all and run home and give it to Mama. But I didn't move a muscle. *Don't touch it. My God, can you imagine what Mama and Grandma would think if I was stealing?* Just the thought sent chills down my back. Still, I stood holding the open purse, staring at that wad of money, like it was the face of Jesus.

"Gene, what are you doing with my purse?"

I jerked from surprise at Mrs. Terrell's entrance. "I was just looking at it, ma'am." I closed the purse and put it back over the chair.

"And why were you looking at my purse?"

I didn't want to tell her that I was admiring it because Mama's own purse was ratty and torn up, and she couldn't afford a nice one. That would have been embarrassing to Mama, and we didn't tell our business like that outside the family. I lowered my eyes and stared at my ragged PF Flyers. I was so mortified I couldn't look her in the eye. My face felt like it was about to break out in flames. "I wasn't going to take nothing, Mrs. Terrell. Honest, I swear I wasn't." I hung my head in shame that she'd even think such a thing.

"Well, it sure looked like you were going to take something."

She's right. I should have never touched her purse. I know better. What in the world will Mama and Grandma think now?

"Wait until I tell your mother about this. I'm going to believe you weren't taking anything because I know your mama and grandma. I also believe you were protecting Larry, we know all about young Mister Mickey and his ways. I'm going to let your mama handle you, but I don't want to see you back in my office. Do I make myself clear?"

"Yes ma'am."

I spent the rest of the day worrying about what I was going to say to Mama—and Grandma, too. They were both going to be ashamed of me. When the bell rang, I walked outside to wait on my fate. Larry now became the comforter, but it was no use. I was beyond comfort.

When Mama arrived at the school grounds to pick me up—it was her day off—Mrs. Terrell told her what I'd done. As we walked home, she turned to me and said, "Gene, I'm ashamed of you. Why did you do a thing like that? Didn't I teach you that stealing is wrong?"

"I wasn't going to take nothing. I swear, I'd never do anything to make you and Grandma ashamed of me."

"Well, Mrs. Terrell caught you standing there holding her purse. Can you explain that to me?"

"Yes ma'am," I said, tears in my eyes.

"I believe you when you say that you fought Mickey to protect Larry. I been expectin' that, but why in the world were you looking in Mrs. Terrell's purse?"

Crying, I said, "I wanted to buy you one like it and give it to you for Christmas. I mean, your purse is all torn up and raggedy and hers was so nice, I wanted you to have a nice one, too."

"Oh, honey," she said, hugging me tight. There were tears in her eyes. "Having nice things like Mrs. Terrell's purse is all right, but nice things are not as important as having people around you who love you, and whom you love. Of all the things you could give me for Christmas, the best thing, the nicest thing of all, you have already given me, your love."

11

Sallie's Street

As Christmas drew nearer, my father drew farther away. His drinking got worse, and arguments with Mama became as regular as beans and 'taters on the supper table.

One morning they had a vicious fight just as Mama was leaving for work. Dad demanded money and she refused. "Over my dead body will I give you money for liquor," she declared, storming out of the house.

"Don't come back, you bitch!" he shouted. Just a few minutes later, without a word to me, he left. He was supposed to drop me off at Grandma's because school was out for the holidays, and Mama couldn't depend on him to stick around and take care of me. I stayed with Grandma most of the time anyway. *Good-bye*, I thought. *I'll walk to Grandma's myself.* It was just a few blocks and I'd done it a hundred times before.

I was gathering my toys and comic books when someone knocked on the door. I peeked through the window and saw my hero Uncle Bill on the porch. I opened the door. "Hey, honey," he said, lifting me high in the air. Uncle Bill always called me honey; I'd have fainted if he ever called me anything else. He'd been on the road and we hadn't seen each other all week.

"Hi, Uncle Bill."

He put me down. "Is your dad home?"

"No. He left a while ago."

Uncle Bill muttered something under his breath. I could tell he was angry, and figured he'd heard about the fight. I knew it was just a matter of time before he'd beat the living crap out of Dad. There were many times when I wanted him to, but sometimes I hated the thought of Dad all bloodied and bruised.

"Your mama says she forgot her purse and lunch. Do you know where they are?"

"Her lunch is in the refrigerator and her purse is in my toy box."

"In your toy box?"

"Yeah, I put it there after she left without it. I didn't want Dad to find it. He'd have taken all the money and got drunk with it." I handed him the purse. "You know, Uncle Bill, Mama could use a new purse for Christmas."

He studied the ratty purse in his hands and nodded. "She sure could." He winked at me. "And I bet you know just where to get the one she wants, huh?"

"Yep."

"Good job," he said. "You sure do look out for your mama, don't you, honey."

"I try," I said, beaming with pride that I was doing something that Uncle Bill had done all his life for Grandma. It was his reason for living—at least that's how I saw it. Uncle Bill did a few things for himself, sure enough, like going to the races and buying a new car every year. But he hovered around the family like a guardian angel. And if Grandma had said to him, *You know, Bill, I'd like to have a big mink coat and a necklace full of diamonds*, you could bet your rent money he would have found a way to buy them for her. Not that Grandma would have placed much stock in such foolishness as diamonds and furs. Flannel and angel brooches were more her style.

"Do you want to come with me and see where your mama works?" he asked. "Afterward I'll take you for a ride around town and we'll go buy that new purse."

"You bet!"

I enjoyed going anywhere with Uncle Bill. Two things were certain. You were going to have a good time and you were going to laugh a lot. It was as natural as sweet air after a rain shower.

I climbed into the new cherry-red Chevy Impala. As Uncle Bill cruised south down Waughtown Street heading toward Indura Mills, I read the street signs: JUANITA STREET, FRANCIS STREET, and now BERTHA STREET. *Hey that's nice*, I thought. *Mama works in a place where the streets are all named after ladies who work at the mill. But where's Sallie Street? Mama deserves a street named after her more than Bertha does.*

Although I'd never been to the mill, I had seen Mama's skill with a sewing machine. Whenever she added another patch to my jeans, she'd say, "There now, maybe you'll get some more wear out of them until they're too small for you." I marveled at how she found ways to get one more year out of old clothes that most people wouldn't have considered good rags.

We turned down Bertha Street, which was lined with little houses with big yards full of maple trees, dogwoods, and azalea bushes. *What a weird place for a factory—right here in the middle of a neighborhood*, I thought as Uncle Bill pulled up in front of a single white door. There, sitting among all those houses with their pretty yards, was the factory where Mama worked. I asked Uncle Bill why the mill was in the middle of the neighborhood.

"The mill owners used to build houses around their mills so the workers could walk to work," he said. "Shoot, honey, the South is full of places just like this one."

Uncle Bill didn't want to go inside; he didn't like talking to strangers, and he couldn't read a lick. "Shoot," he'd say, "they look at me like I ain't got good sense." He was afraid he might have to read something, like a sign he didn't recognize. He called them *don't-come-in-here* signs.

"Here, honey, you go take these things to your mama. I'll wait right here for you."

I walked into the mill. On my left was a small office with a glass door, but I didn't see anybody there. To my right was a big wooden door with a big black handle and no windows. I could hear what sounded like a thousand giant bees buzzing on the other side. Mama and Grandma wanted me to be an independent, self-sufficient young man, at least that's what they told me, and though I wasn't exactly sure what that meant, if Mama and Grandma wanted me to be that, it must be good. So rather than wait for an adult to show up, I opened the door.

The thousand bees became a million, and their agitation had increased to a deafening roar. I started to shut the door and run back to Uncle Bill and make him do it, but I knew he wouldn't. I thought about Mama working with no lunch or cigarettes, which I was sure were in her purse, not to mention the Juicy Fruit gum she carried; she chewed a lot of it. I stepped into a huge room crammed wall-to-wall with sewing machines. Black women, white women, old and young, in five long rows sat on gray metal stools hunched over their whirring sewing machines. *No wonder her back hurts all the time*, I thought. None of them looked up at me. I stood for a minute looking for the back of Mama's blond head. I'd recognize her long hair if I could see it. There she was, halfway down the third row, leaning over her sewing machine, working fast, like the place was on fire.

I saw her flip the lever on the machine and remove what I figured was a petticoat and throw it into a big box beside her. *My God, how does she stand this noise all day? Sitting on those little stools must hurt her butt as much as her back.* There was stuff flying through the air, little bitty things falling on the floor and piling up like snow. I figured it was cotton from the petticoats. I walked down the aisle between the rows of sewing machines and headed toward Mama, my feet kicking up the cotton snow with each step. As I passed their machines, women looked up and smiled or winked at me. Some of them moved their mouths but I couldn't hear what they were saying above the din.

When I reached her, I shouted, "Hey, Mama, here's your lunch!"

When she didn't turn around, I tapped her on the shoulder, and she jumped like I'd stuck her with a thumbtack. She spun around on her stool with a look that at first said *Now what?* but the moment she saw me, her face lit up. Her mouth moved, but again no sound. She stood up, took me by the hand, and led me through the door and back into the office where it was quiet. "Thank you, sweetie, for bringing my lunch and purse." She leaned over and kissed me on the cheek. "Where's Uncle Bill? Was he afraid to come in?" she asked, half smiling.

I nodded and said, "God, Mama, how can you stand to work here every day? I mean all that noise and stuff flying everywhere, and those stools. Why don't you have a nice chair? No wonder your back hurts all the time."

She put her finger to her lips to hush me and pointed toward the glass room, where a man in a bow tie now stood talking to a colored man dressed in greasy overalls. The colored man looked familiar to me. He glanced over at us, smiled, and nodded. The man in the bow tie looked at us like we were trying to steal his Christmas ham.

Mama walked me outside and waved at Uncle Bill. He nodded and gave that big horsey smile of his. "Hey, Sis, I see he found you."

She turned back to me and said, "It ain't so bad, after you get used to it."

"It's awful in that place. I don't want you in there. You need to be working in some nice place where it's quiet and you can sit in a nice chair and listen to music and stuff, maybe answer a phone now and then. Why don't you get a job like that?"

She smiled, stroked my hair, and said, "My little worrywart. Now I got to go back to work. Mr. Billingsley ain't going to like me being out here talking to you when there's petticoats to sew. You be sweet and I'll see you after a while, and quit worrying about me. It's not that bad."

"Mama, who was that colored man standing in there? He looked familiar."

"That was Mr. Tucker. You remember him. You met him a while back. He does things around Grandma's house. He's the maintenance man at the mill now."

"Oh, yeah. He don't look the same in them greasy overalls."

"No, I don't reckon he does. I gotta go now, honey. 'Bye." She turned and walked back into the beehive. I wanted to cry.

12

Christmas

In a normal year during a normal Christmas, Mama put up our tree as soon after Thanksgiving as she could. As I left Larry's house after spending the night, Christmas was one week away, and still we had no tree. No tree and no presents. The lone decorations up at our house were the red plastic candles Mama put in the windows and the plastic Santa Claus face hanging on the front door. Larry's tree—a nice big one—was up, but his dad was working and mine wasn't. *Why is that?* I wondered. *They both drink too much and they are both mean, but Larry's dad is able to work.*

Last week I'd overheard Mama telling Grandma: "I'm afraid this won't be much of a holiday. We may not even be in the house come Christmas. If Jesse doesn't find a job soon, we won't be able to make the house payments." I heard what she said, but I didn't understand. Why would we want to leave our house?

I didn't know anything about money, or jobs, or house payments, but I knew I didn't want to leave our house or the neighborhood. This was my world. Grandma was a short walk up the hill, Larry was across the street, and my cousins were four blocks away. Everything I loved and knew was either in this house or close by.

With those thoughts racing through my head, I walked up the steps to our house. I opened the front door and saw a sight that triggered a happy "Yippee!" There, in front of the picture window, stood a small Christmas tree. Mama had set out all the decorations and waited for me to help. That was so like her. Decorating the tree was the sign to Santa that all was well. I stood admiring the little tree when Mama walked into the living room, a dish towel in her hand and a big smile on her face. "See, I told you we'd have a tree. Well, what do you think?" she asked.

"Wow, she's a beauty," I replied, giving Mama a big hug.

She wrapped her arms around my neck, kissed me on the cheek, and said, "We have your uncle Bill and Grandma to thank for it. So you thank them when you see them."

"I will, don't you worry," I said, wondering what we would have done, during this crazy time, without Grandma and Uncle Bill.

After a lunch of peanut butter and banana sandwiches, we started decorating the tree. We strung lights and hung red, silver, blue, and gold ornaments. Then we wound silver garland around the tree from top to bottom, careful to get it nice and even. If you did the garland right, even a little tree looked big. Then came my favorite part—the tinsel. Mama would take the silver icicles one by one and place them just so on each branch. For me it was more fun to stand back and throw them on a handful at a time. Despite her preference for having the tinsel hang perfectly, she let me do it my way. When we finished, Mama gave me the honor of placing the haloed, golden-haired angel on the top—a task that I considered the most important and most holy of tree decorating.

"Well, that's that," Mama beamed. "She's a beauty, don't you think so, sugar?" I nodded. "And that's not all," she added. "Tomorrow I'm taking you Christmas shopping."

I was wound up, as Grandma would say, "tighter than Dick's hatband" by bedtime. That night I dreamed Mama had quit her job at the mill and gone to work for Santa, sewing little outfits for dolls.

I woke up with this strange dream still clear in my mind. I couldn't wait to share it when I heard voices that snapped me back to reality. Dad was home, and he and Mama were arguing in the kitchen. I sat up in bed and listened, my heart aching with every harsh word.

"It's eight o'clock Saturday morning, I haven't seen or heard from you since Thursday, and when you do come home, you're still drunk!" Mama lamented.

"So what?"

"You promised to take Gene and me to Sears."

"I will."

"But you're in no condition to drive, Jesse."

"Who says?"

"What if the police stop us?"

"Do you want to go to Sears or not? If you don't want me to drive, you're free to take the goddamn bus."

"You know I can't take the bus today."

"Then shut up."

I wondered how Dad could be drunk so early in the morning. Uncle Bill and Grandma had to buy our Christmas tree because we were too poor, yet Dad always had money for liquor. *We're struggling to make ends meet and eating nothing but beans and 'taters, but Dad always manages to find money for booze.* There was a knock at my bedroom door.

"Gene, are you awake?" Mama asked.

"Yes ma'am."

"I can't make breakfast this morning. Aunt Goldie wants you to come over to their house for breakfast. Do you mind?"

"No ma'am." I knew she didn't have anything to fix for breakfast. She had used the last of the flour and milk to make biscuits and gravy the day before. Anyway, every Saturday Aunt Goldie made a huge pancake breakfast. And going over to her place would get me away from my drunken father. It would also give me the chance to brag to my three cousins that I was getting a brand-new bike from Santa.

I walked to Aunt Goldie's house and found her standing in the kitchen. The big oak table was piled high with link sausage, crispy bacon, and enough pancakes to feed Paul Bunyan. "Hey, sugar, I hope you're hungry this morning," Aunt Goldie said with a smile on her face.

"I'm always hungry for your pancakes."

Now, my cousins Tim, Jerry, and Denny were normal-sized kids, but they ate like they were convicts on a road gang. They wolfed down stack after giant stack of pancakes, and when my stomach was ready to bust, they were still up to their elbows in pancakes and maple syrup. After breakfast, we went into the living room to watch *Woody Woodpecker*. We kept the TV volume low because Uncle Ed was still asleep. He was the hardest-working man I'd ever seen. He held down two full-time jobs while Dad couldn't hold down one. Uncle Ed worked the day shift at RJR, which ended at 4 P.M., and an hour later he was already at work on the second shift at Hanes Hosiery Mill. He tried to make up for lost sleep on the weekends. If he wasn't in bed asleep, he was asleep on the couch or in his easy chair.

Uncle Ed's hard work and sacrifice meant his family had a nice house, car, and pickup truck. My cousins never lacked for anything. Their Christmas tree tickled the ceiling and was crowded underneath with stacks of presents. They didn't have to worry about losing their house.

Although I didn't want them to, my cousins felt sorry for me because they knew my situation firsthand. On far too many occasions Dad had made a drunken ass out of himself in front of them. They were never mean or cruel or made fun of me or my family because they were raised to be respectful.

"I hear you might be moving because your dad lost his job," Tim said to me. I just nodded. Bad news traveled fast.

13

The Grinning Maniac

When I got home, the fight over going to Sears was still in full swing. Mama had two choices: Let Dad drive us to Sears or fight all day. She let him drive. As we climbed into the backseat, I wondered, *Why doesn't Mama want to take the bus? Seems to me that it'd be safer than riding in a car driven by a drunk who walks like he has two left feet. We ride the bus all the time.*

Dad floored the old Chevy, pinning us to the backs of our seats as he roared up Urban Street and zoomed past the church. The car flew across Sprague Street ignoring the stop sign. He'd just about overshot Waughtown Street—where he was supposed to turn—when he jerked the wheel left. The old Chevy's tires screamed as the car leaned into the turn, sending one of the hubcaps rolling off in the opposite direction. He floored the car again and sped down Waughtown, racing through two more stop signs, blowing the horn, and cussing cars for being in his way.

"Jesse, please slow down or you're going to get us all killed!" Mama ordered.

"That won't be so bad, will it?" he sneered, making a sharp right onto South Main Street. "Then all our troubles will be over. No more bills, no more movin', no more drunken husband, and no more bitchy wife."

The car roared through the century-old Moravian village of Old Salem. Bewildered tourists, standing in front of the Krispy Kreme doughnut shop, found their peaceful morning coffee and hot glazed doughnuts interrupted by a smoking jalopy driven by a grinning maniac.

"Why have you been drinking so much, Jesse?" Mama asked. "And why in God's name are you driving like this?"

"Because I can."

"It's your drinking. It's ruining your life—and your family's. We used to own a beautiful house and now we're about to lose it. You had a good job and you've lost that, too. If it wasn't for my family, we wouldn't even be celebrating Christmas."

"It's my life," he said.

"No, it's our lives."

Glancing in the rearview mirror, he saw my terror. "Are you scared of dying, boy?"

"Yes sir."

"You got it all wrong, boy." He slammed on the brakes to avoid smashing into a pickup truck. Mama and I jerked forward, stopping inches away from smashing our faces into the front seat. "Dying ain't scary, boy. Livin' is. When you're dead, you don't feel nothin'."

I wondered what caused him to be so reckless with his life and ours. Did he believe his family considered him a loser, or did he consider himself a loser? Did he believe his family was ashamed of him or was he ashamed of himself? Whatever the reasons, whatever the cause, Dad knew just one way to silence his demons. He drowned them.

We reached Sears in one piece. The parking lot overflowed with the cars of Christmas shoppers, so Dad pulled the old Chevy into the underground lot. Before we left the car, he reached into the glove compartment, pulled out a bottle of Ten High bourbon, and took several swigs.

How can he drink so much liquor? I wondered.

To Mama's exasperation, he didn't put the bottle back in the glove compartment. Instead he stashed it in the left pocket of his bib overalls.

"Please leave it in the car, Jesse."

"Why should I? It's mine, ain't it?"

"What if the police catch you?"

"They won't."

Mama, knowing that he would make a scene, dropped the subject. She asked him to take me to the toy department and then meet her back at the entrance. "And don't create a ruckus," she pleaded.

As she walked through the sliding glass doors, I asked Dad, "Where's Mama going?"

"To the layaway department."

We put everything on layaway. "What's she getting in layaway?" I asked.

"Shut up."

We walked over to sporting goods and looked at the fishing poles. About ten minutes later he said, "See if your mama is finished. I want to get the hell out of here."

Moping, I retraced my steps to the entrance where they had agreed to meet. I turned around and saw Dad sitting on one of the display couches. He glanced around, then reached into his pocket and pulled out the bourbon. He wrapped both hands around the bottle and raised it to his mouth.

I didn't see Mama anywhere. *Should I go back and tell him I didn't see her, or just stand here until she comes along? Either way— if I don't come back with Mama or if I stay here and he sees me looking at him—he's gonna have a fit.*

Then I heard him shriek in agony. I looked over and saw him clutch the sides of his head with both hands. He pitched forward onto the floor as if someone had grabbed a new ax handle from the hardware section and whacked him in the head.

"Dad! Dad! What's the matter?" I cried, running to his side.

There was no response. He lay on the floor, staring up at the fluorescent lights. All of a sudden he began to jerk as if he had grabbed a live electrical wire. He turned blue and his eyes rolled back in his head. He clenched his teeth tight and he was making noises that sounded like bacon being fried. I had seen him have seizures before, but this one was bad, and I was scared.

"Please help me!" I yelled at onlookers, not knowing what to do. "My dad is dying! Please, somebody, help me!"

61

He was thrashing around now, his arms and legs jerking like he was possessed. I panicked. Crying and yelling out for Mama, I knelt beside him as his body continued to shake and twitch. A group of bewildered onlookers crowded around and watched. He was banging his head into the hard concrete floor so I tried putting my hands underneath, but each time my fingers got mashed. "Please help me!" I pleaded, tears streaming down my face. "Please help me!"

Someone came rushing through the crowd. "Don't worry, honey, I'm here."

"Mama!" I cried with relief.

In an instant she was kneeling beside me, a small pillow in her hand. She placed it under his head and then pulled out a flat rubber stick from her purse. "Grab his head," she said. I held his head while Mama tried to insert the piece of rubber into his mouth. She grimaced as he chomped down on her fingers. She tried again. This time she succeeded and then she cradled his head on her lap.

"Is he dying?" I asked.

"No, honey. He'll come to soon. His spells look worse than they are. He'll be all right."

A few seconds later Dad's body stopped its violent jerks and twitches. He fell into a deep sleep and lay on the floor for several minutes. When he opened his eyes, he was disoriented and irritable. "Where the hell am I?"

"At Sears, you just had a spell."

He looked around and saw a few people staring at us. "Let's get out of here," he said, staggering to his feet. On the way to the parking lot, my father, oblivious to the stares from curious shoppers, snarled out at Mama, "Why did you drag me to Sears in the first place?"

We climbed into the car, but before Dad started the engine, he reached into the pocket of his overalls for the bottle of Ten High.

"Please, Jesse, don't," she pleaded. "It's the liquor that makes your spells so bad."

"So you're a damn doctor now?"

"Your doctor said the medication to control your spells won't work if you keep drinking."

Dad gunned the engine and pulled out of the parking lot, squealing the tires.

"It's my life," he said, tipping the half-empty bottle to his thin lips. After draining it he said, "Aw, shit. I forgot to get them damn tires pumped up. Remind me to borrow a hand pump from Ed when we get home."

Mama grew pale. "Jesse," she whispered, "hush, don't talk like that. Gene is in the backseat." From the look on her face and her whispering, I knew this wasn't a conversation she wanted me to hear.

My curiosity got the best of me. "What tires is Dad talking about, Mama?" I couldn't help asking. At first I figured he meant the car tires, considering how many times they squealed on the trip over. *They must need some attention; maybe low air in the tires is why he's driving so slow now. But then he wouldn't use a hand pump for the car tires; he'd just stop at a gas station.* No one answered my question, and the car picked up speed as we headed on down Fifth Street.

"What tires is Dad talking about, Mama?"

"Honey, just hush, we'll be home in a minute. Then you can help me wrap Grandma's Christmas present." For whatever reason, I couldn't stop asking Mama about the tires. Getting nowhere with her, I turned to Dad.

"What tires, Dad?"

I don't know if it was the effects of the seizure or the bourbon, or his annoyance at my questions. Or maybe, just maybe, it was in fact what he himself had said many times, he just didn't give a shit. Whatever it was, as the car came to a stop at a red light he turned his head and said, "Your goddamn bicycle tires, that's what tires I'm talking about. I forgot to get them pumped up at Sears. Are you happy now?"

I was not happy. What did he have to pump up bicycle tires for? Wasn't Santa bringing me a new bike on Christmas Day? Wouldn't the tires already be pumped up?

"I thought Santa was supposed to bring me my bike."

"Yes, he will, honey, he will," Mama said. Then she turned and said, "You shouldn't have done that, Jesse. He's just a child. And children are supposed to believe in Santa Claus."

He glared at her. "Screw Santa Claus! It's time he stopped believing all that foolish bullshit." Glancing at me in the mirror, he said. "You're a big boy now. There ain't no such thing as Santa Claus. That's a lie storeowners made up so they could sell more crap every Christmas. Your bicycle is right behind you in the goddamn trunk. We went to Sears to pick it up."

It was as though he'd turned around and hit me between the eyes with a two-by-four. *What does he mean, there is no Santa Claus? Everyone knows there is a Santa Claus. I had my picture taken with him last year, right there in Sears.* The bike I was going to get wasn't supposed to come from Sears layaway. It was supposed to come from Santa in his sleigh. The sudden realization that Santa wasn't real crushed me, and I cried like I had never cried before.

Mama yelled at my father, "You bastard! I begged you to keep his bicycle a secret. You just couldn't resist ruining his Christmas, could you? How can you be so cruel to your own son?"

"He'll get over it."

But I didn't get over it. When we got home, I was still crying. The bike in the trunk might have been the one I wanted—a light blue Schwinn Flyer with a bell on the handlebars and a small headlight on the front fender—but it wasn't from Santa. I refused supper, retreated to my room, and tried to cry myself to sleep.

Later Mama came in, sat on the edge of my bed, and laid her soft warm hand on my head. She explained the tradition of Santa Claus. I understood what she meant, but I'd never forgive my father for his callous heart.

She began singing,

Que sera, sera
Whatever will be, will be

With her angelic voice filling up my room, I drifted off to sleep.

I dreamed that night that it was a bright Christmas morning and I was sitting in the living room in front of a warm fire. It had snowed overnight, and the sun's rays made the fresh snow glisten like diamond dust. There was a knock at the door and I opened it to find Santa Claus standing on the front porch. Behind him stood his sleigh, piled high with presents. "Merry Christmas, Gene. Here's your present." Santa said, my new bicycle sitting beside him.

"Merry Christmas, Santa. So you are real."

"Sure I'm real," Santa said with a chuckle, "for as long as you believe in me."

14

The Magic Bike

I woke up to the aroma of Maxwell House coffee. I lay in bed listening for the sound of fighting. Instead I heard the sound of Mama's slippers sliding across the kitchen floor. There was no yelling, no cussing, so I knew Dad was still asleep. I threw the covers back, sat up, and looked out the window. The sky was steel gray and fog clung to the ground, muting the colors of the trees and grass.

On all other Christmas mornings I would have jumped out of my bed and run into the living room to see what wonders Santa had left me. Did he like the milk and cookies? Did he leave me a note telling me to mind my mama and daddy? But this year I knew the answers to those questions. I slid from the bed and walked into the kitchen. Mama was sitting at the end of the table, drinking a cup of coffee, a Pall Mall burning in the ashtray in front of her. When she saw me, she put down her coffee and opened her arms, an invitation for me to jump into her lap. When I climbed up, she folded her arms around me and squeezed me tight. "Merry Christmas, my most special little boy."

"Merry Christmas, Mama."

She kissed me on the cheek, her soft golden hair brushing against my face like angel fingers. "Let's go see what Santa's brought for the sweetest boy in the world."

I started to protest, to say that there was no Santa. Mama read my mind. "Don't," she whispered with a smile, her golden-green eyes twinkling. I knew then that she was not going to let the joy of Christmas die; that just because Dad said Santa didn't exist didn't make it so.

The joy and magic that I had thought was gone forever returned in that moment, given to me not by a fat old man with a snow-white beard but by a woman who refused to believe that life itself was not magical. We walked into the living room hand in hand, and there sitting beside the tree was my new bike. I found out later that Uncle Bill and Grandma had given Mama the money to get it out of layaway, but it was a magic bike even so. I ran to my room, dug Mama's secret present out of my toy box, and handed it to her. "Merry Christmas, Mama."

"My goodness, what in the world could it be?" she asked, the surprise evident in her voice. She unwrapped the present like it was the Holy Grail, and when she held up her new purse tears came to her eyes. "Gracious, honey, it's beautiful, it's perfect, I love it, and I love you."

"Well, Uncle Bill bought it for me to give to you. It's from me and him, but it was my idea."

"Well, it's the nicest present I've ever gotten. Thank you, honey, you're so sweet. And that uncle of yours, if he ain't the sweetest man God ever put on earth I don't know who is."

Mama helped me roll my bike across the tiny front porch, down the four steps, and onto the cold grass. It was a magnificent machine, blue like the Carolina sky on a warm spring morning. Its chrome fenders sparkled and shined even in the steel-gray light of this winter day. The tall, wide whitewall tires grabbed onto the ground like tiger paws. The seat was dark blue with white piping, and it was as soft and cushy as one of Grandma's pillows. A headlight rested on its front fender; a bell was perched on the gleaming handlebars within easy reach of my right hand. Red tassels hung from the white grips on the ends of the handlebars, making the bike look fast even when it was sitting still. On the white chain guard in bold red letters was the name FLYER.

We led my bike into the backyard and pushed it halfway up the slight hill. To me the gentle slope now resembled Grandfather Mountain, a place I'd visited with Uncle Bill and Grandma. I mounted my bike, settling into its soft seat and placing my feet on the pedals. For a moment it trembled. I turned my head to reassure myself that Mama was still holding on to the rear fender. She was there, holding it steady as my magic steed and I bonded for the first time. "Okay, let's roll her down the hill a little," she said. "I'll hold on. Don't worry. We'll go slow."

When I gained my balance, the bike responded and moved forward, the chrome handlebars wiggling back and forth. We picked up speed now, and Mama was walking fast in order to keep up. At the bottom I turned my head to make sure she was still holding on. Mama yelled out, "Watch where you're going! I've got you."

We reached the bottom, and I pressed back on the pedals. I jumped off and went back up and rode down again and again, Mama holding on each time. I kept going farther up the backyard mountain, increasing the speed on the ride down. I pushed my new bike to the precipice of the mountaintop. I mounted up once more, turned to Mama, and said, "You ready?"

At first the handlebars bucked in my hands, wiggling from side to side. Little by little the magic came to me and all at once, we were one. We gathered speed as we ripped down the mountain, and then we were flying. Just like in my dreams, my magic bike had let go of the ground and was now gripping the sky. I screamed with delight as my bike and I flew down the hill. When the ride ended, I turned to Mama: "How'd you like that?" Then I realized she was still standing at the top of the hill, a big grin spreading across her face.

"You did it! You did it all by yourself!"

The winter of 1960 refused to make room for spring, and in late February snow lay high in shady places. Snow in the South is a welcome thing, at least to an eight-year-old boy. A few days of sledding down hills, having snowball fights, building snowmen, and, of course, missing school made life for us kids worth living. Snow in Dixie doesn't last long. A snowfall gives way to warm sunny days when the snow melts and leaves no trace except for the pictures in a photo album. But this winter brought no such relief. I was itching to get on my bike and ride with Larry, but in this weather that was out of the question.

On a Saturday morning during this period of my winter blues, Mama told me we had to move. I was devastated. Christmas and New Year's had come and gone without any talk of moving. The passing time had lulled me into believing that we wouldn't have to be uprooted. The approaching spring and thoughts of endless days on my bike with my best friend by my side had given me a false sense that our financial woes were somehow behind us.

But fueled by his drinking, Dad seemed unwilling or unable to climb out of his black hole. Mama, with no time for spring daydreams, had been hunting for a new place for us to live. She found an apartment on Sprague Street, just a mile or so from our house. But to me, it might as well have been on Mars. It was closer to Mama's work, which meant she'd be able to catch the city bus in front of the apartment and ride it to within a block of Indura Mills. Since Dad's old Chevy was either broken down with no money to fix it or being used to "job hunt" in all the local pool halls, catching the bus was important.

I'd still be going to Forest Park Elementary, so Larry and I would see each other at school and church, but it wouldn't be the same as being neighbors. Larry and I had grown up together and played together every single day, but now that would change. A gloomy cloud had drifted over our lives, and I blamed Dad for its arrival.

The first week of March, a few days after my ninth birthday, Uncle Bill showed up with a truck and helped us move. I hated our new home from the start. The apartment was on the bottom floor of a run-down, two-story brick building. It had no front yard, and the backyard was a concrete parking lot, filled during the week with the run-down, oil-leaking cars of piss-poor factory workers.

I missed our home on Brookline Street. The baseball games and hide-and-seek with my friends, the flowering azalea bushes, the dogwood and maple trees, and the fragrant smell of honeysuckle drifting in through the open windows had made it a child's paradise. Now that was just a memory.

Outside the apartment building there were no trees, just light poles and telephone lines. There were no flowers or birds, unless you counted the crows digging through the garbage bins. The aroma that most often drifted in through the open windows of the apartment—if you could stand the steady drone of cars, trucks, and buses rumbling by—was the putrid smell of half-eaten cheeseburgers and chili dogs rotting in the garbage cans behind the beer joints and diners that lined the street. To make matters worse, the neighborhood was too much of a temptation for an alcoholic father who needed to find a job.

After the move, my biggest source of comfort became the public library two blocks down the street. I had my own library card, and to me it was like a driver's license that allowed my imagination to time-travel anywhere in the world. At nine years old, I was reading at a fifth-grade level.

Though she'd never finished high school, Mama was an avid reader. For her, reading meant the same thing it did for me—an escape. Like her love for games, puzzles, and music, books were another passion of hers that she had passed on to me. On the day she took me to get my library card, she said, "I wanted to go to college and become a nurse but I had to quit school to work. What do you want to be when you grow up, honey?"

I'd never thought about it. The future seemed no farther away to me than the next day. I almost said a meter reader, but then I recalled how miserable my father had been at that job and changed my mind. "A truck driver," I said. "Like Uncle Bill."

Mama pondered this for a while and said, "You know Uncle Bill can't read."

"Yeah, I know. It bothers him, too. How's he able to drive a truck? What about all those road signs you gotta read to know where you're going?"

"Well, he has a good memory. He memorizes the shapes of the signs and the roads he needs to take. When he gets back from a trip, Aunt Goldie or I fill out his logbook."

"Is he simpleminded like people say he is?"

She gave me an intent look. "Who told you that?"

"That's what Dad says sometimes."

"That's not true," she said. "Don't believe everything your father says. Not being able to read doesn't mean a person is simpleminded. My daddy—your grandpa—couldn't read, but he was one of the smartest people I ever knew."

"I love Uncle Bill an awful lot. He's about the most gentle and caring person I know. He's always doing nice things for other people. He's not mean like Dad."

"So you still want to be a truck driver when you grow up?"

"Maybe I'll be a race car driver. Uncle Bill says they make a lot of money. And we need money, don't we?"

"We do, but money isn't the most important thing in life."

"What is?"

"Being happy and kind and thoughtful to others," Mama said without hesitation.

"You're the kindest person I know, Mama, because you love Dad even when he's mean."

"It's not an easy thing to do, honey. But I took a vow to love your father through thick and thin. It's thin right now, and that's a fact. But I keep hoping and praying that things will change for him. I was raised by your grandpa and grandma, just like Aunt Goldie and Uncle Bill were, to be kind to people and to look for the best in everyone. Grandma would tell us that even though we were dirt-poor, if we had kindness and charity in our hearts, we were richer than kings and queens."

15

Untainted Love

We had been in the apartment for several months. Mama was working more hours than ever trying to keep our heads above water. She'd step off the afternoon bus from that old beehive of a mill, dead tired every day. After school I stayed away from the apartment as long as I could just to avoid Dad. He didn't care where I went.

I'd go to the library and sit in the back room reading. The librarian, Mrs. Whiteside, a tiny woman with hair the color of beach sand, had come to expect me. She got me hooked on reading Mark Twain. I loved *Tom Sawyer* and *The Adventures of Huckleberry Finn*. I couldn't help but be swept up by these stories. I related to the characters as if they were members of my own family. Aunt Polly, who believed it was in a boy's nature to get into mischief, was like Grandma Pearl. While Tom captured my imagination, it was Huck whom I most identified with. He was the son of the town drunk, and because of that, he was his own man, free to come and go as he pleased.

Huck's relationship with the runaway slave Jim fascinated me. Huck was a southern boy—at least that's how I saw him—though he did live in Missouri. I figured he had been born in the South and been forced to move away because his old man was a drunk like mine. He'd been taught—the same as I had—that colored folks were someone else's property and less than human. But on that raft, floating down the Mississippi River, he discovered that Jim was a good man and a good friend. And in the end, Jim treated Huck like his own son, and

Huck loved Jim. I wondered, as I floated down the river with them, if Dad had ever read *The Adventures of Huckleberry Finn*.

I hadn't noticed at first, but there seem to be a change in Dad. He started telling me to "be careful" whenever I left the house. His mood was brighter. And I no longer saw the usual pile of Pabst Blue Ribbon beer cans. In fact, I didn't see any.

I didn't want to get too excited about this change. From time to time my father had these "sober spells," as Grandma called them. He would just stop drinking as if the taste of booze didn't appeal to him anymore. During these sober spells Mama and I wouldn't let our guard down because we knew that if history was any indication, he'd soon be back to his old alcohol-drenched self again.

One evening while Mom, Dad, and I sat around the small silver-and-blue dining table eating stewed potatoes, collard greens, and corn bread for supper, he made a surprise announcement: "I've found a job."

"That's great news, honey," Mama declared, smiling. I hadn't heard her call him that in a long time. "What's the job?"

Dad took a drink of water and replied, "Running a spot-welding machine in an awning plant."

"How much will they pay you?"

"Enough for us to get by on."

Hoping against hope, I asked, "Will we be able to go back to our old house, Dad?"

"We might, son," my father said. "If I work hard enough."

"Wouldn't it be wonderful to go back?" Mama said. "Gene misses his cousins and friends. And I miss seeing Mama. So when do you start?"

"Next Monday."

"Will you be able to get the car fixed and drive me to work?"

"Yeah, I'm fixing the car this weekend and I go right by the mill on the way to work."

A week after my father began work at the awning company, Mama made his favorite supper—meat loaf, mashed potatoes, collard greens, and corn bread. Dad loved corn bread; on nights when he was sober and at home watching *I Love Lucy* or *The Honeymooners* his favorite snack was leftover corn bread crumbled up in a glass of buttermilk. He ate it with a spoon like it was ice cream.

He came home from work late that evening, tired but sober. After he took a bath and changed, we sat down to supper. Mama said grace and we began eating. Halfway through the meal, she said, "Barney Todd was here this afternoon." She said it with some reluctance in her voice.

"What did he want?" Dad asked, taking another slice of corn bread from the cast-iron frying pan.

"He wants to know why you don't stop by his place anymore."

"What did you tell him?"

"Nothing. I told him I'd tell you he came by."

"Well, next time you see him, tell him I don't have time. I'm too busy."

I sat straight up in my chair and blinked. Did he say he didn't have time for his favorite drinking buddy?

The next day Barney stopped by again. This time Dad was home. The two sat in the living room while I was in the kitchen watching Mama cook, but I was eavesdropping on the men's conversation.

"I'm giving it up, Barney," Dad told him. "I'm working again. I don't have time to go hopping from beer joint to beer joint anymore. It hurts my family."

"I hear you, Jesse. I need to give it up myself."

"Yeah, you do."

"I know. My business is booming, and I need to concentrate on work. Say, how about coming to work for me?"

There was a long silence. Mama stopped stirring a pot of beef stew and we both listened, waiting for Dad's reply. "I hope he says no," I whispered. She squeezed my hand and nodded.

"Thanks, Barney," Dad said. "But I'm happy working for the awning company."

Mama breathed a sigh of relief and smiled at me. Dad and Barney working together could have been a disaster. They'd known each other for years, and I'd never seen them together when they weren't drinking. Nothing good could come from them being together all day, every day.

"The pay is good. And my boss says that I'm a good worker and that if I stay with the company long enough, I might get promoted to supervisor."

"I'm glad to hear that, Jesse," Barney said. "And I wish you all the luck in the world. But I hope that won't prevent us from going fishing or coon hunting from time to time."

"If I can find the time."

That night, after Mama tucked me in, I prayed that Dad would stay happy with his job, and that this time he would stay sober forever. The prayer became a ritual. I don't know if the prayers or the steady job helped, but he remained dry. He even attended church with us on Sundays. And to my extreme delight, from time to time we started going fishing again.

On most Saturday afternoons Dad and I would visit Grandma Cheek. After Grandpa's death, she had sold the farm and built a little two-bedroom brick house across from Aunt Lucille and Uncle John's place. Her new home was closer to town but still out in the country. For me, the best part about it was it had two little farm ponds just down the hill within easy walking distance. During our visits with Grandma, Dad would do a few things around her house. He'd mow the grass or fix a leaky faucet, whatever needed doing. And then we'd take our cane poles and walk down to the ponds and fish. We'd catch a mess of bluegills, clean them on Grandma's back porch, and take them home to Mama. She'd roll them in cornmeal and fry them up along with homemade french fries, coleslaw, and hush puppies—a meal that would have made old Huck proud.

Mama was more relaxed and happier than at any other time I could remember, and there was laughter in the house again. One Friday evening Dad came in from work and told Mama he wanted to take me to Topsail Beach for a weekend of fishing. "Can I come along?" she asked.

"No, honey," he said. "This is just for me and Gene. You and me will go somewhere special on our tenth wedding anniversary. How about that?"

"I'd love it," she said, and kissed him.

It was like a dream come true—a glimpse into the past, a peek at young love before it was tainted by alcohol and heartache. It brought tears to my eyes.

"What's the matter, honey?" Mama asked.

"I wish we'd stay this happy forever," I said.

"We will, son," Dad said, giving me a hearty hug.

16

The Spots Are Runnin'

We packed our fishing gear into the trunk of the old Chevy and finished just as darkness filled up the summer sky. After hugs and kisses for Mama, we headed for Topsail Beach. The last time the family had made this trip had been the summer of 1953 when I was two years old. My photo album has a black-and-white photograph of Mama holding my hand as we posed on the pier. Her biggest memory from that trip was a broken leg. She'd stepped in one of the cracks between the boards on the pier while chasing me and broken her leg.

As we drove along Dad said, "Son, I love you and your mama more than anything in the world. Your mother is the best thing that ever happened to me, that is until you came along. Now you two are the most important things in my life. I ain't gonna drink no more, I swear. I want you to be as proud of me as I am of you. If I stop drinking, you think you can be proud of me again?"

His brown eyes, often cloudy and dull from liquor, were now clear and bright. "I'm proud of you, Dad, and so is Mama. We love you, and if you stop drinking we'll be happy forever."

We arrived at the beach in the wee hours of the morning. The full moon and the millions of stars reflecting off the calm Atlantic Ocean made it hard to tell where the sky ended and the sea began. We checked into a small motel about a block from the pier. The air was filled with the distinctive smell of salt water and the low marshland that lined the coast of North Carolina.

We were both tired from the long trip, but I wanted to walk out on the pier and look down at the ocean before we went to bed. Dad took my hand as we crossed the seashell-paved street and reached the pier. Walking out onto the weathered, wooden structure, I noticed how vulnerable it seemed, jutting out in the water exposed to the forces of the mighty ocean. Through the gaps in the pier's planking—the same ones that had broken Mama's leg—I could see the sand and water below. "I ain't going to break my leg or fall in, am I, Dad?"

He laughed and patted my head. "No, I don't think so. That was just a freak accident that happened to your mama. Just make sure you don't run on the pier."

An old man sitting in a folding chair, his feet propped up on an ice chest, looked up as we approached. "How they bitin'?" Dad asked.

"Like they ain't got good sense," said the grizzled angler. "I'm a-catchin' 'em two at a time as fast as I can go. Shoot, I ain't even got the line in the water right now, just so's I can catch my breath." The old man laughed at his own words.

"Well, don't catch 'em all," said Dad.

The next morning Dad shook me awake at dawn. "Wake up, sleepyhead. The fish are waitin' for us."

We sat down in a little diner across from the hotel to eat breakfast. I was gulping down my food, in a hurry to get to the fishing. "Slow down there, boy, or you're gonna choke. The fish ain't gonna mind if you take time to chew before you swallow. Did I tell you what happened to this preacher I know."

"No sir, I don't think so."

"Well, last week this Baptist preacher was coming home late after visiting one of his bedridden parishioners. It was late, and the night was as black as a witch's heart. Anyway, this preacher was driving down this old country blacktop when he noticed old Junior Thompson's white Ford Fairlane in his rearview mirror. Now, old Junior had obviously been heavy into the happy juice again, as the Ford was swerving from one side of the road to the other. The pastor—watching his rearview mirror instead of where he was going—ended up running his own nice new Buick Skylark right into the ditch. Well, old Junior stops his car, walks up to the pastor, and says, 'You all right there, Pastor?' The pastor replies, 'I'm fine, Junior, I've got the Lord riding with me.'

Old Junior looks around the car and says, 'Well, you better let him ride with me, you're gonna kill him.'"

"That didn't really happen, you made that up," I said, laughing.

"Well, it's funny anyway. Come on, let's go catch us a mess of fish." We picked up our gear and headed for the pier. What a glorious day. There wasn't a cloud in the sky, and a cool breeze blew off the emerald-green ocean. The rhythmic sound of waves folding over onto the sandy beach sounded like music to me.

"I bet the spots are running today, son."

"What are spots, Dad?"

"Spots are sorta like bluegills."

I remembered how much fun I'd had catching bluegills at the farm ponds behind Grandma's house. The bluegills weren't real big, but they were fierce fighters. Dad—holding his hands about a foot apart—had said about them then, "If they were this big, why, they'd pull a full-grown man in and drown him." They were good to eat when Mama wrapped them up in cornmeal and fried them in bacon grease.

"Why are they running? They don't have legs, do they?" I asked, seeing in my mind's eye these tiny weird fish with little legs and feet.

My father burst out laughing. "It's not that kinda running, son," he said. "Certain kinds of fish stay together. They call that a school. And spots are one of those. They move into an area hunting for little fish to eat, and that's what running means."

We walked out onto the pier. As Dad started getting our gear ready for fishing, he reached for a thermos he'd brought along and took a swig. *Oh my God*, I thought. *He's drinking again.* He must have seen the crushed look on my face, because he asked, "What's the matter, son?"

"Nothing," I said, not wanting to ruin our fishing trip.

"Well," he said, smacking his lips in satisfaction, "let me show you how your new fishing rod works." He'd bought me a new, shiny, green Zebco 202 for this trip. It had two hooks and a weight shaped like an Egyptian pyramid. "You don't have to throw it like you do when you're pond fishin'. Just push this button"—he pointed to it—"and let the line fall into the ocean and sink to the bottom. Once it hits the bottom, reel it up just a bit." Again, he showed me how.

On the first try, I felt something tugging on the line. "I got one! I got one!" I squealed, suppressing the urge to jump up and down on the pier.

"Reel it in," he said.

I did and was amazed to see that it wasn't one fish, but two—and they were bigger than a bluegill. I grinned with pride and so did Dad. He took the silver-colored fish off the hooks and turned one sideways toward me. Pointing to the back of the fish's head, he said, "See that black spot right there? That's why they're called spots." He threw the fish into the ice chest. "Good job, son," he said, patting me on the back. "Now let's see if we can catch two more just like 'em." He baited the hooks, and I pushed the button and let the hooks fall into the ocean with a *clomp*. I cranked it up just a little, and again the end of the little pole jerked and I felt the tug. Wham, just like that, I'd caught two more fish. "Great job," said Dad, "you're a natural-born fisherman."

"Thanks, Dad. You're a natural-born teacher." We both laughed.

After these last two fish went into the ice chest, he took another swig from his thermos. My joy faded and I started pouting. *Why does he keep drinking? He'll be drunk pretty soon and then get into a bad mood, and our fishing trip will be over.*

Seeing me sulk, he asked, "What's the matter, son?"

"Aw, nothing," I said. This time he saw my eyes staring at the thermos in his hand.

"You want some?" he asked.

"No."

He laughed, making me wonder what he thought was so darn funny. "Come on, try some. It won't hurt you."

He held the thermos up close to my mouth, laughing. I was about to push his hand away when something struck me as odd. It didn't have that godawful boozy smell that reeked from his breath when he was drunk. It was the smell of fresh-brewed coffee.

"I had my thermos filled up when we ate breakfast this morning." He smiled at the suspicious look on my face. "And, no, there's no liquor in there. You don't believe me? Just take a swallow."

I took a sip, then another. It was nothing but warm coffee with lots of cream and sugar. Mama drank her coffee black, and in good times made fun of the way Dad fixed his. "Why don't you put some coffee in that cream and sugar, Jesse," she'd kid him. With a wink, he'd reply, "I like my coffee the way I like my women—blond and sweet."

"I'm sorry, Dad," I said, figuring I'd hurt his feelings. "I thought you were drinking."

"No need to be sorry, son," he said, patting me on the shoulder. I noticed tears welling in his eyes. "I'd have thought the same thing if I was you. Now, let's get back to fishing."

I caught fish for hours until our cooler overflowed. As the sun began to set, we headed back to the motel.

"I'm proud of you, son."

"Thanks, Dad. I had a great time. Can we do this again?"

"Sure, we'll be coming back again before you know it."

Then it struck me. His line had never once gone into the water during all those hours by the pier. He'd been content to watch me fish.

New Dad

Good memories tend to take the place of bad ones, and it was that way around our house now. The old memories of a father too drunk to care were being crowded out by new ones of a kind father. He liked his job and hadn't missed a day of work since he'd started. I hadn't seen him take a drink in two and a half months, and Mama and I were both happy and proud of him.

The start of the new school year wasn't far off, and I dreaded it. This year school would consist of half days, with half the kids attending in the mornings, the rest in the afternoons. They—whoever *they* were—said it was due to overcrowding. I wouldn't have minded—I mean, half as much school was a good thing—except Larry had been assigned to the afternoon and I'd been assigned to morning. The opportunities to see my best friend would be limited to church now.

One Saturday morning I was watching *The Lone Ranger* in the living room, and Mama was busy washing the breakfast dishes. Dad was in the bedroom getting ready to leave for work. Since getting back from our trip, he had volunteered to work Saturdays.

"By the way," Dad told Mama, "I want us to go to Lucille's tomorrow afternoon because we haven't seen the family since Daddy died, and John and Lucille want to start having the get-togethers again. Lucille wants you to cook."

"But, Jesse," she protested, "I work all week and I'm tired on the weekends. On Sundays I just want to come home from church, fix us a nice supper, and rest. Lucille doesn't work. Why can't she cook?"

"Because you're a mighty fine cook, Sallie," he said, trying to humor her. "The best."

"Well, I appreciate that, Jesse, I do. But would it be too much trouble for Lucille to call and ask me if I feel like cooking for twenty people or so instead of telling you that she wants me to cook?"

This sounded to me like a fight was brewing. I knew she was right. Dad's family treated us like heel hounds. But when it came to saying anything bad about them—unless he was the one doing the saying—his reaction was predictable. His smile faded. "What have you got against my family? You cook when we get together with your family and you don't complain."

"That's because I offer to cook; they don't order me to. And Goldie and Mama both help. Also, when we get together with my family it don't end in a big argument, at least not anymore." What she was tiptoeing around was the fact that since he'd stopped drinking, there had been no fights or arguments with the Andersons.

"The honest to God's truth, Jesse, is I don't enjoy these get-togethers anymore. Not one bit. And neither does Gene. I mean, haven't you ever noticed the way they treat us? I'm just there to cook and clean up. It ain't right. I don't want to start a fight over this because things have been going so well between you and me. Why don't you go and me and Gene will stay here. I'll even cook so you can take the food with you."

"I'm not going alone, damn it. You're my wife and Gene is my son. You're coming with me whether you like it or not. So you'd better just make up your mind right now that we're going, and you're cooking." With that, he stormed out of the apartment.

"Are we going to Aunt Lucille's then?" I asked Mama.

"We have no choice, honey."

After walking to the corner store to buy the things she needed for the get-together, we went to work in the kitchen. I peeled potatoes for the potato salad while Mama began frying chicken. She had the radio tuned to WTOB and was singing along to "It's All in the Game" by Tommy Edwards, "Chances Are" by Johnny Mathis, and one of her favorites, "You Send Me" by the great Sam Cooke. No matter who was singing on the radio, Mama could fall into harmony faster than you could say the word. She had just put the potatoes on to boil when Uncle Bill showed up.

"Well, whattaya think of her?" he asked me, bobbing his big head toward the sleek car parked out front.

"Wow! Is that a new one?"

"Yeah. Ain't she a beauty? I picked it up this morning. That's what you and I are gonna ride in when we go to the race in Martinsville, Virginia."

"When?"

"Tomorrow, if it's okay with your Ma and Pa."

"Hot-diggity-dog!" I yelled, throwing my arms around him.

Mama walked up and hugged Uncle Bill's neck. "My goodness. Is that your new car?"

"Yeah, ain't she a beauty?"

"Sure is. I bet that set you back a pretty penny."

"You don't even want to know, Sallie," Uncle Bill said, dropping his eyes. He was a sensitive man. And the fact that his sister and nephew lived from hand to mouth didn't sit well with him. He was responsible for getting us a lot of things that we'd have otherwise gone without, and it was a sore spot between him and Dad. "I don't want his damn charity," Dad had said many times. Mama, out of a sense of pride and knowing that Uncle Bill was taking care of Grandma, would let him help just so much.

"Well, whatever it cost," she said, "you earned it."

Uncle Bill brightened. "So, do you and Gene wanna go for a ride with me?"

"Sure we do," Mama said.

She turned off the stove and we followed Uncle Bill to his newest new car. It was a black Pontiac Bonneville convertible. The wings standing vertical on the rear fenders gave the powerful-looking car the illusion of flight. And with Uncle Bill, who was a lead foot, flight was not out of the realm of possibility. As we were cruising along Waughtown Street headed toward Five Points, Uncle Bill said, "Sallie, I promised I'd take Gene with me to the race in Martinsville tomorrow. Is that okay with you?"

"I don't mind, but Jesse wants us to go see his ma and them."

"Shoot," Uncle Bill said. "Why does he want to see his mama all the time?"

"Look who's talking."

Uncle Bill flashed an embarrassed smile. He knew he was a mama's boy.

"Please let me go, Mama," I pleaded.

"But your dad will be mad," she said.

"Let me talk to him," Uncle Bill said.

"I don't think that's a good idea," Mama said. "It ain't like you two are Dean Martin and Jerry Lewis. I'll talk to him."

"Thanks, Mama," I said.

Uncle Bill came to Five Points, an area where Sprague and Waughtown Streets and three other roads converged. He turned north and headed out on Highway 150 toward the rural town of Kernersville. Once out in the country where there was little traffic, Uncle Bill pushed his new car.

After about fifteen minutes on the open road, Mama said, "We'd better head back, Bill. I got to finish all that food for the infernal get-together tomorrow. If I don't, Jesse's going to bust a gut."

As we got out of Uncle Bill's shiny new rocket ship, he said. "I'm going to Union Cross to look at a house I'm thinking of buying for Ma. I'll come by and see about the races after a while. You know, we'll have us a grand old time, honey." He broke out in a full-faced grin and drove off.

Back home later that day, Dad told Mama, "Gene ain't going with Bill, and that's final!" I stood behind my bedroom door and heard every word they said. I didn't want to go to Aunt Lucille's. My cousins John-John and Melissa were at the bottom of my want-to-see list, and they felt the exact same way about me. They didn't like me and I didn't like them. In my mind I figured Dad was doing this to spite Uncle Bill. It had nothing to do with me, except its effect on me.

Mama, bless her heart, pleaded my case. "Jesse, please let him go. You and I can go to Lucille's."

"Hell no. He's my son. If that brother of yours wants a son, why don't he get married and have one?"

"Why are you being so stubborn about this? It ain't like Gene don't see your family all the time. This is a big deal to Bill and him. You know how crazy they are about the car races."

"No!" Dad then stormed out the door. When I heard the old Chevy backfire and then pull out, I emerged from my room.

Mama looked at me and said. "I'm sorry, honey. I tried."

"I know you did, Mama. It's all right. I didn't expect him to let me go."

When Uncle Bill showed up about an hour later, Mama broke the news to him. "Well, if Jesse don't take the cake then I don't know who does." He looked at me and said, "Don't worry, honey. They'll be a lot more races you and me can go to."

"That would be great, Uncle Bill. I can't wait. I'm sorry I can't go with you tomorrow, but you have a good time."

Uncle Bill shook his head. "Shoot, honey, I ain't going to that race tomorrow, not without you."

18

Old Dad

When I got out of bed Sunday morning, I found Dad sleeping on the couch still in his work clothes. He'd fallen off the wagon all right, and he smelled like he'd landed in a vat of Ten High bourbon. As I walked toward the bathroom, Mama came out of her bedroom. She motioned for me to follow her to the kitchen and whispered, "Don't say nothing to your father if he wakes up. He was drunk when he got home, and he's going to be in one of those moods."

I was crestfallen. *One of those moods* meant the so-called new improved Dad had become his old soused self. This sober spell had lasted longer than its predecessors, but it ended the same way all those others had, with a headlong sprint back into the bottle.

We dressed for church and left him asleep. We walked the half mile to Urban Street Baptist Church. Getting to see Grandma and Larry was worth the walk. Larry and I sat in the corner of the Sunday school classroom, ignoring Mrs. Renegar's lesson, catching up with each other on the past week's events.

When church let out, Grandma, Mama, and I walked over to the little corner store that was owned by a church deacon. He opened it as soon as church ended. We sat out front on the old wooden bench and drank Cokes.

I asked Grandma, "Where's Uncle Bill?"

"Well, now, where do you think he is? He's in bed, of course, snoring loud enough to wake the dead." He did, too. Boy, if you didn't close his door, his snoring would shake things off the wall. Despite constant urging, Grandma could not get Uncle Bill to go to church. Oh, he'd go on special occasions—Easter, Christmas, and Mother's Day, for sure—but that was about it for him despite the fact that he and his family had attended this church for too many years to count. He still considered most of those folks strangers. And he was no good around people he didn't know.

"Tell him I said 'hey' when he wakes up."

"I will, sugar, I will."

Mama and I left Grandma at the corner. She headed down Devonshire toward her house, and we headed up Urban toward hell. When we walked into the apartment, Dad was sitting at the kitchen table with a cup of coffee. "Y'all get your clothes changed and let's get going," he said without looking up. He didn't speak at all during the trip to Aunt Lucille's. When we arrived, he pulled the Chevy under the shade of a pear tree, got out, and without a word slammed the door. Rather than go inside Aunt Lucille's house, he walked across the gravel road to Grandma's new home.

"We shouldn't have come here, Mama," I said.

"I'm beginning to think the same thing."

"Can I play outside?" The day was sunny and warm.

"Okay, honey, but stay close. I'll call you when we're ready to eat, and don't worry, we'll get through this. We'll just stick together." I helped her carry the food to Lucille's porch, and then I sauntered down the gravel road to the neighbor's soybean field. Brown and mowed down, the field was several hundred yards from Lucille's house. I would have preferred to walk on down to where the road ended in the woods where it would be impossible for my cousins to find me, but Mama had told me to stay close.

I found an old broomstick by the road, one of John-John's old horses, I figured. I picked it up and started hitting rocks into the field. I was Mickey Mantle the "Commerce Comet," bottom of the ninth, bases loaded, two outs, game tied. Up went the rock. I swung. "It's a long fly ball to straightaway center field," announcer Phil Rizzuto yelled out. "It's back . . . way back . . . it could be . . . it is . . . a home run . . . Holy cow, the Yankees win the World Series." I could—and wanted to—repeat this fantasy for hours at a time.

I saw my father come out of Grandma's house, leading her across the road toward Aunt Lucille's. "Hi, Grandma," I shouted.

"Hey, Gene," she called and waved.

"What are you doing outside by yourself?" Dad asked.

"Playing baseball."

"Why don't you play with your cousins?" asked Grandma.

"I don't know where they are," I said, not wanting to tell her the real reason. Dad helped Grandma into the house and then walked to the backyard to join the rest of the men. I followed him from a safe distance. They were pitching horseshoes down in a little gully behind the house. Lucille's husband, John, had built the horseshoe pit so that the men would have a place to get away from the women. The minute I realized the men were drinking as they played, I sensed trouble brewing. Sure enough, one of the men handed Dad a Schlitz. He hesitated for a split second before accepting it. I watched him gulp it down and then ask for another.

A short time later Aunt Norma yelled out the back door, "Supper's ready." To avoid my cousins I took my plate outside and headed down toward the horseshoe pit. Sitting on a root and leaning against a dogwood tree, I watched the men pitch horseshoes and drink. I lost count of how many cans of beer Dad drained. Disgusted with him, I returned to the gravel road and continued to be The Mick, swatting home runs. John-John and Melissa skipped down the road and watched me. I tossed a rock into the air, took a swing, and hit what would have been another game-winning home run had my cousins not been there to spoil the play-by-play. I tossed another rock into the air and socked it. It flew behind me and slammed into John-John's leg. He screamed in pain. I ran over to him and said, "Gosh, I'm sorry, John-John. Are you all right?" I looked at his leg. There was no blood, just a slight red spot where the rock had hit him. But John-John kept howling and took off toward the house. "I'm going to tell my dad! I'm going to tell my dad!"

"Our daddy's gonna beat your white trash butt," Melissa sassed at me.

"It was just an accident," I said, ignoring the insult. "And I said I was sorry."

"Uncle John's gonna whip you good," said Spencer, one of Aunt Millie's redheaded children. He was standing at the edge of the yard as John-John ran by, his damaged leg working fine. Soon poor little John-John was limping across the yard, his giant father John holding his hand. Uncle John was six foot six inches tall and resembled one of those giants from *Gulliver's Travels*. Trailing behind him was my Lilliputian father, Schlitz in hand, birthmark glowing red.

"Gene!" my father yelled. "Get your ass up here right now!" I dropped my broomstick and trudged toward him. "Did you hit little John-John here with a rock?"

"Yes sir," I said in a remorseful voice, head bowed. "But it was an accident, and I said I was sorry."

"That's a lie," John-John whimpered. "He meant to hit me. He said so."

"No, I didn't."

"He did, too," Melissa chimed in. "Spencer and I saw him do it."

"That's right," Spencer said, nodding.

"So you're lying to me, huh?" my father said, his speech slurred and his birthmark glowing.

"I swear I didn't hit him on purpose, Dad. He was standing behind me and I fouled off a rock. It didn't hit him hard."

"Are you going to whip the boy or do you want me to do it?" demanded Uncle John.

"I'll do it," Dad said. He grabbed me by the hand and started dragging me toward the house.

"It was an accident, Dad," I kept saying as he hauled me through the screen door and into the kitchen. "I didn't mean to hit him, honest."

"That don't matter," he said. "You shoulda been more careful with them damn rocks."

"I'm sorry," I pleaded.

"It's too late for sorry," he said as we entered the back porch leading into the kitchen. I caught a glimpse of Mama washing dishes. *Thank God,* I thought.

"What's going on?" Mama asked, looking at my father, who was still holding me by the arm with one hand and a beer in the other one.

"Gene hit little John-John with a rock, and I'm going to whip him for it." He made it sound like I had chased John-John around the house throwing rocks at him.

"I didn't mean it, Mama, I'm sorry. It was an accident. I swear it was."

"His cousins say he did it on purpose."

"Tell me what happened, honey," Mama said.

"I fouled off a rock and it fluttered behind me and hit John-John." She looked at my father and said, "It sounds to me like it was an accident. And Gene has apologized. Why are you going to whip him?"

"Because he needs his ass beat."

"If he needs a beating, I'll give him one. You're in no condition to do it."

"No, I'll do it."

By this time the entire Cheek clan was crowding around us to watch the circus.

"No, I insist," Mama said. "It would give me great satisfaction to whip him. He's been bad anyway, and I want to be the one to put a stop to it. Give me your belt."

I gaped at her in disbelief.

"All right," my father said, removing his rawhide belt and giving it to Mama. "Remember to whip him good."

"Oh, I will!"

My cousin John-John sat on his dad's knee with a smug look as he watched Mama pull me into the bedroom and shut the door. "Mama," I protested, "it was an accident. I didn't mean to hit him. Honest I didn't." I noticed a flicker of a smile on her face. Strange, I'd never seen her smile before when she was about to whip me.

"I believe you, honey," she whispered. "Now listen to me. What we're about to do is just between you and me, understand? You can't tell anyone." Bewildered, I nodded. "I'm going to take the belt and hit it hard across this pillow," she said. "When I do, you scream as loud as you can, like I'm peeling the hide off your butt."

"Yes ma'am," I said, awed by the brilliance of her plan and choking back a laugh.

"Now, this ain't funny," Mama said, again reading my mind. "If your dad finds out, he'll have a fit and you and I will both have hell to pay."

She picked up a plastic-covered throw pillow and placed it on the bed, drew back the belt, and began to whack it. With each whack, I howled, "Please, Mama, stop! I won't do it again!" I yelled, trying hard to suppress a laugh. "I'm sorry."

After rapping the pillow a few more times, she stopped, leaned toward me, and whispered, "Now rub your eyes hard so it looks like you've been crying. Stay in here a minute or so and when you leave, rub your eyes again, sniffle, and walk straight out the door. Got it?"

I nodded. Mama struck the pillow one more time, and I forced another yell. Then she left the room. I stood behind the closed door, doing my best not to laugh. I sniffled loud and rubbed my eyes hard for a minute. Figuring the proper time had passed, I walked through the living room and out the front door. I threw a quick glance at my cousins. They were gloating.

19

Slipping Away

By the summer of 1960 my dad was feeding the beast with a new vigor. He didn't fall off the wagon, he jumped, and his return to a life of drinking was swift and complete. The months of sobriety and the memories of the happy family we'd been were gone. He lost his job at the awning company, so he went to work for Barney. With the start of school a month away, Dad took a strange and sudden interest in my future. "I want Gene to start coming to work with me."

"What for?" Mama asked.

"He's old enough to work."

"For God's sake, Jesse, the boy is nine years old."

"That's old enough. Barney's son ain't that much older. And he's been helping him for years now. It'll be good for Gene to work a little and we'll get to spend more time together."

"But Gene wants to go to vacation Bible school at church, so he can see Larry. He can stay at Mama's. It'll be good for him."

"I don't give a damn about Bible school. It won't hurt him to work. I was helping Daddy around the farm when I was his age. Besides, he already spends enough time with your mama. She's spoiling that boy and teaching him craziness."

Mama was at a disadvantage: It's hard to reason with an unreasonable man. She was not going to win this argument, she'd tried before and it always ended in defeat, cussing, and blood and bruises. So she did what she had to do. She hammered out a compromise.

Bible school was still two weeks away, so until then, I went to work as a drunk plumber's helper's helper.

Dad's attempt to groom me to follow in his meandering footsteps began on Monday. On our way to our first job, Barney's twelve-year-old son Eugene and I sat in the back of his father's orange International pickup while our fathers passed around a bottle of Ten High bourbon and a Nehi Orange soda as a chaser. Eugene was a big, strong man-child with his father's blazing red hair and a temper to match. He cussed like a sailor, was as tough as a marine, and chain-smoked Winstons because, as Eugene liked to sing, "They taste good like a cigarette should."

"How can they work with all that liquor in 'em?" I asked Eugene.

"Wait and you'll see."

That day we were going to fix a busted pipe that had flooded the cellar of a farmhouse owned by an older couple outside Kernersville. The man was half blind, and his wife was feeble with rheumatism. When we pulled up to the job site, I overheard Barney tell the customer that he'd brought a large crew with him because it was a big job and he wanted to do it right. The old man said he appreciated the effort and would pay whatever it took. I glanced around wondering where the rest of the crew was. Eugene lifted the cellar door, and a million crickets scampered for higher ground.

"You boys go on down there and see if you can find that leak," Barney ordered from the shade of a hickory tree, my father at his side.

From the looks of the knee-deep water, I didn't figure finding the leak would be too hard. Down the half-rotten wooden steps, we sloshed our way into the cellar. The soaked red clay floor sucked at our shoes with each step. When we found the leak, Eugene yelled up to his dad, telling him what he needed to fix it. Eugene knew what to do. He had been the sober hands and eyes for his drunken father long enough to be well versed in plumbing repairs. Eugene did all the work and I helped him by fetching tools and supplies.

Meanwhile our fathers leaned against that old tree passing the bottle. Soon they figured it was lunchtime and left, saying they'd be back in a while. We fixed the leak and started hand-pumping the red water out of the cellar. Our fathers made it back several hours later with fresh bottles of Nehi and Ten High for them and a couple of bologna sandwiches for us. The job of pumping the cellar dry took several more hours to finish. It would have taken a lot less time if they had helped us crank the pump instead of pulling on the bottle.

As we drove away, Eugene whispered to me, "That was an easy job. Those old folks paid way too much for that little bit of work."

"Our dads must have made a lot of money on this job."

"Yeah, but they won't keep any of it. They'll turn right around and spend it on liquor and gambling. They'll both be broke before we get home."

Instead of heading home, Barney drove us to their favorite haunt—a pool hall in Kernersville. Our fathers spent the next few hours drinking and shooting pool, losing money by the handful to two hustlers who were drinking Nehi Orange soda instead of Nehi Orange and Ten High bourbon. Eugene and I sat outside in the bed of the pickup and talked about the New York Yankees and The Mick. "You like Mickey Mantle a lot, huh," Eugene asked me.

"Oh! Heck, yeah, he's the greatest ever, he's leading the league in homers again, and the Yanks are six games in front of the Orioles."

"Yeah, I like Mickey, but I don't like the Yankees much, I'm a Cardinal fan."

In 1960 all of the Cardinal and Yankee games were heard on local radio stations. North Carolina was divided, half for the Yankees and half for the Redbirds. As Eugene talked on about Stan "The Man" Musial, he pulled out his pack of Winstons and offered me one. I shook my head. "No, Mama says I shouldn't smoke."

"But she does."

"Yeah. But she don't want me to start. She says it's a terrible habit, and she wishes she'd never started."

She'd started smoking as a teenager and become addicted to Pall Malls. "I thought it made me look grown up and sophisticated," she had told me.

I didn't want Eugene to think I was a mama's boy, so I told him, "I'll try one. I reckon it won't kill me."

"It's real easy," he said, handing me a Winston. "And smoking will make a man out of you. It'll make you tough." Eugene looked to be both of those things, so I took the cigarette and placed it between my lips like I'd seen Humphrey Bogart do in the movies. Eugene flicked a lighter and lit my Winston. Head tilted back, I took a big drag and inhaled, causing my lungs to revolt. I hacked and coughed as Eugene roared with laughter. I went home more than a little green.

My career as a drunken plumber's helper's helper ended one Saturday afternoon while Mama and I were at Grandma's. Dad and Barney went on a job by themselves without supervision. They got drunk and were run off the job site by the customer. Taking their troubles to the poolroom, they proceeded to get drunker, and ended up by beating each other bloody in the parking lot, which prompted Barney to fire Dad. As Dad told it later, "Barney had the nerve to say I was bad for business and a bad influence. Can you believe that shit," he said through his swollen lip. I could believe it, but having to pick "the bad influence" between those two would have been a tough call.

Dad was back to being unemployed. Mama's tiny paycheck wasn't going to pay the bills, so it didn't take long for the landlord to tell us to vacate the premises.

"Where will we go, Mama?" I asked.

"I don't know, honey," she said. "I don't know."

"Can't we move into Grandma and Uncle Bill's new house?" Uncle Bill had bought Grandma a new three-bedroom brick house with a full basement and a carport out in the country in Union Cross.

I could tell this was something she had thought about, but it wasn't an easy thing for her to talk about. "If I could just love him a little more, and give him a little more understanding, he could stop drinking and be the man I married again."

"Mama, I don't think Daddy's ever going to stop drinking. It ain't your fault he drinks, it ain't nobody's fault, he just drinks." I'd seen her endure my father's alcoholism and abuse, and stoically go on keeping it all inside hoping somehow he'd change. "He ain't ever gonna change Mama, never. He keeps sinkin' deeper and deeper, and gettin' meaner and meaner."

She stood in the kitchen, her back turned to me. She was crying. "I guess you're right; I've done all I can do. Maybe it's time we moved out on our own, me and you. I know your uncle Bill would let us move in with him and your grandma."

"When will we leave, Mama?"

"Soon, honey, soon."

But soon didn't come soon enough. A week before our eviction date, I was in my bedroom reading *House on the Cliff*, a Hardy Boys mystery by Franklin W. Dixon, and Mama was in the kitchen cooking fried okra, stewed potatoes, and fried fatback, when Dad came home. I could hear them talking. "Bobby found me a great job," he told her.

"What's the job?" There was a note of skepticism in Mama's voice.

"I'm going to be a foreman at a dairy farm," he said. "The job comes with a big house where we can stay rent-free. We'll have all the room we want and then some. There's even a backyard where Gene can play instead of being cooped up here going stir crazy."

"Where's the house?"

"In Kernersville."

"Kernersville?" Mama cried. "But that's way out in the country."

"So what? It's not that far."

"But Gene will be starting school again soon."

"They've got schools in Kernersville, Sallie."

Two days later Uncle Bobby showed up in his Ford pickup to help us move to Kernersville. Mama had quit her job at the mill the day before, and I'd said good-bye to Larry. I had walked to the library to turn in *House on the Cliff*. Mrs. Whiteside told me she was sad to see me go, and as I walked out the door, she added, "Now, you promise to keep reading, Gene." I gave her my word and walked off toward another new beginning, this time in Kernersville.

20

A Place Where Hope Dies

With our hopes and Dad's promise of a happier life packed in among the boxes, my father pointed the old Chevy toward Kernersville about twenty miles away. As rolling hills, dairy farms, and tobacco fields sped by my backseat window, the hand of dread tightened its grip on my stomach. Mama sat in the front seat, her eyes staring out at the countryside.

When we reached Kernersville, Dad stopped the old Chevy at the blinking stoplight that divided the tiny farm town. On my right sat the feed store, a tin-roofed, whitewashed wooden building with a large porch. On the porch, and to the left of the front door, sat a group of old men dressed in faded blue overalls playing checkers and drinking Coca-Cola. Above the porch hung a red, white, and blue plywood sign that read RED'S FEED AND SEED. Covering the front of the building, and hanging at odd angles, were rusty tin signs reading DEKALB CORN, BURPEE SEED, and RED MAN CHEWING TOBACCO. To the right sat the one-room post office built from the same white clapboard siding as the feed store, a big hand-painted sign hanging above the door reading KERNERSVILLE, NC. Off to my left, and across the street, sat the lone gas station. A tiny Shell station built in the shape of a big shell and painted bright yellow.

A few miles outside town my father turned the car onto a washed-out, rutted driveway to a dilapidated farmhouse that looked more like an abandoned building than the nice house I had envisioned. My hopes of a new start evaporated.

The run-down house sat surrounded by sun-dried corn standing brown in red dirt fields. Hay fields and gray-green soybeans stretched out as far as I could see. Not a single house except our farm shanty was in sight. An unpainted weathered barn squatted on the other side of the driveway. I almost laughed out loud when I pictured the big bad wolf saying, "I'll huff and I'll puff and I'll blow your house down." He wouldn't have had to blow too hard; a sneeze would have blown down the barn. Uncle Bobby backed his pickup next to the sagging front porch and turned off the engine. I grabbed a box and walked into the farmhouse.

Old straw and cornhusks littered the cracked and yellowed linoleum floor. In one corner vines had grown in through a broken windowpane and had climbed their way up the wall and onto the ceiling. The front room, despite numerous windows, was as dark as a mine shaft. It was as though the sun refused to shine into this place. In the middle of the room stood an old oil-burning furnace on a rusted-out drip pan. The vent pipe was lying on the floor, covering much of it with fine black soot. A single, naked lightbulb hung from the soot-stained ceiling.

At the far end of the living room were two tiny bedrooms, one to the left and one to the right. At one time my room, the one on the right, had been a porch. Its windows, which made up the outside wall, had sheets of plastic covering them. The door in the corner, which led outside, was nailed shut.

The kitchen was the real gem of our new home. Big chunks of the gray linoleum floor had been torn out or worn out, leaving holes that exposed a grimy wood floor beneath. The cabinets all slouched at odd angles on the wall, causing the doors to hang open by gravity. The countertop, which rolled up and down like a mountain range, was covered in brown grease, as was the rusty stove. And as further evidence of how far we had toppled, off to the right of the kitchen was the lone bathroom, which had a rusty sink and a claw-foot tub to match, but no toilet; that was fifty feet out the back door.

We finished unloading the boxes from Uncle Bobby's truck. Without knowing what to say, he got into his pickup and disappeared from sight.

"My God, Jesse," Mama exclaimed as soon as she'd recovered from shock. "Whatever possessed you to bring us here?"

My father stood silent in the middle of the floor, staring at the derelict surroundings as though he were lost. Without a word he walked out the door, got into his car, and drove away. Mama and I stood dumbfounded in the place Dad had described as a "new beginning." To me, it was the place where hope had died.

Relief from the isolation came a week later when Uncle Bill and Grandma visited us one godawful hot afternoon. The old farmhouse, exposed in the middle of a cornfield with no trees for shade, was as hot as a tobacco barn. Uncle Bill and Grandma stood in the living room unable to believe their eyes. "It's not right what Jesse's doing," Grandma declared. "Y'all shouldn't be living like this. It's just not right."

"Why don't you and Gene move in with us?" Uncle Bill ventured. "The new house has plenty of room."

"I can't just pack up and leave Jesse."

"Why not?" Uncle Bill asked.

"He's my husband. He'll change."

I was stunned. "He'll never change," I blurted out. "I want to go live with Grandma and Uncle Bill. I hate this place."

"Things will get better, honey," Mama said.

"No they won't!" I stormed out.

Mama followed me outside and found me sitting near the edge of the cornfields hugging my knees to my face and sobbing.

"Don't cry, honey," she said.

"I want to go live with Grandma and Uncle Bill."

"I want to live with them, too, honey. But your dad needs us. Let's give him another chance. He's a good man inside. He's just going through a rough spell." She was holding on to something I had let go of a long time ago—the hope that Dad would change. She might as well hope that a twister would whisk our house away and in its place plop down a mansion. At least that had a better chance of happening than Dad straightening up for good.

Mama gave me a hug. "Listen, honey, let me talk to him one more time. I'll give him one month to stop drinking. If he doesn't, we'll move in with Grandma and Uncle Bill. Is that a fair deal?"

I wiped my tears and nodded.

Two days later, while we were playing Monopoly in the living room, the owner of the dairy farm paid us a visit. He sat on the couch, holding his bent and dusty straw hat in his gnarled hands. "Is your husband home?"

"No."

"That's funny," the farmer said. "I told him to meet me here."

"What happened?" asked Mama, sitting down in the rocking chair across from the farmer, waiting for the ax to fall.

"Well, ma'am, I found him passed out in the fields. He told me that he'd had a spell."

"Is he okay?"

"He's okay. But I'm afraid I have to fire him."

"Fire him?"

"Yes ma'am. I'm sorry."

"Didn't he tell you he suffered from spells?"

"He told me, and I ain't firing him for that. When I found him passed out next to the tractor, it wasn't from no spell. No ma'am. He was drunk. I could smell the liquor ten feet away. And the people who work under him told me he drinks on the job." The farmer paused, turning his hat over and over in his hands. "I run a business, ma'am. This dairy farm has been in my family for generations and I take great pride in it. When Bobby told me that his brother was a hard worker who had fallen on hard times and needed a chance, I was willing to give him one. Especially when I heard that he had a wife and child to support. But I can't keep a foreman who drinks on the job. Sorry, ma'am. I hope you understand."

"I understand," Mama said, fighting back tears.

"Now you take what time you need. I ain't kicking you and that little boy there out onto no street. No ma'am, I ain't gonna do that."

When the farmer left, Mama broke down. "I don't understand Jesse. I just don't understand him at all." I wrapped my arms around her as we both wept. My father returned home late that evening. Even though it was well past my bedtime, I stayed up just in case she needed me.

"So what are we going to do, now, Jesse?" Mama said as soon as he walked through the door.

"About what?"

"Where are we going to live?"

Dad gave her a bewildered look. "Where are we going to live? Here, of course."

"Is that so?" Mama said in a sarcastic tone.

"What the hell are you talking about, Sallie?"

"I'm talking about you being fired. Mr. Jonas came by this afternoon and told me he'd fired you for being drunk."

"The lying son of a bitch," he yelled. "He has no right to fire me. I wasn't drunk. I had a spell."

Mama looked my father straight in the eyes and said, "I've had it, Jesse. I've had it. I'm leaving you."

"Go ahead," he said. "I don't care."

"I can't live with a drunk anymore. God knows I've tried to help you. But you refuse to change. Come to think of it, I should have left you a long time ago."

"Why don't you leave now, you fat bitch?"

"Gene and me need a ride to Mama's. We can't walk in the dark."

He wagged a finger in her face. "If you're leaving me, find your own way to your mama's. I ain't taking you nowhere." He turned, stormed out the door, and drove off.

Mama flashed a brave smile at me and asked, "Do you think you can walk with me into town, honey?"

Without hesitation, I replied, "Yes."

She grabbed her purse, and we both set out in the moonless night to find a pay phone. To my nine-year-old legs, it felt like we walked a hundred miles, and Mama winced with each step. There were no streetlights along this old blacktop country road, no sidewalks either, just knee-high grass and unseen gullies full of creeping, crawling critters.

"Mama, are we going to move in with Grandma?"

"Yes, honey."

By the time we got to town, the big yellow Shell station was closed. It had a phone booth, though, and Mama called Uncle Bill.

"He's not home," Mama said to me after hanging up the phone. "He's gone to the store. Grandma says she'll send him over to get us as soon as he returns. So let's just stay put, honey."

We'd been sitting on some Pepsi crates near the back of the station for over an hour when I saw headlights coming toward us from the direction of the dairy farm. "That doesn't look like Uncle Bill's car," I said.

"Maybe it's your dad looking for us. Let's hide in the woods."

We ran into a stand of trees behind the gas station. The car slowed as it approached. I saw my father's face for a brief moment, but he couldn't see us. The car then roared off. We emerged from the woods and once more stationed ourselves near the rear of the Shell station.

About ten minutes later Uncle Bill pulled into the gas station in his car. He was furious. "Where's that no-good son of a bitch?"

"Watch your mouth, Bill," Mama said.

"Where is he?"

"He left the house a while ago. Now he's driving around looking for us."

"I know where you can find him," I said.

Uncle Bill looked at me. "Where?"

"The pool hall."

"Let me take you home first," Uncle Bill said, fuming. "Then I'll go find the bastard. He'll be sorry he was born before this night is over."

"Don't hurt him, Bill," Mama pleaded as we drove to Union Cross. "Just leave him alone. He's a sick man."

"Sick or not, he had no right to drag you and Gene to the middle of nowhere and then abandon you."

"But we're safe now and that's what matters."

"Well," Uncle Bill said, his anger abating. "I'll let it go this time because you asked me to. But if he shows his face at my house, I'll kick his ass so bad his mama won't recognize him. I should have done that a long time ago. I should have taught the son of a bitch a—"

Mama interrupted him. "Bill, let's not talk about Jesse anymore, please. I'm so tired."

Uncle Bill drove us back to the farmhouse so we could pick the few possessions we cared most about—my bike and toys, our clothes, family pictures, and the jewelry box that Dad had bought her when they were courting.

"Don't worry about the rest," Mama said when Uncle Bill told her he was willing to make another trip to pick up the furniture. "He can have it or throw it away. I don't care."

During the ride to Union Cross, I said, "Are we leaving for good, Mama?"

"I hope so," Uncle Bill said.

"I don't know, honey," Mama said. "I don't know."

21

Little-Boy Heaven

What a joy it was to be living with Uncle Bill and Grandma. To me, their new house was paradise. Our home in Kernersville had been dark, dumpy, and depressing. The house in Union Cross was the opposite—full of warmth, laughter, and the spirit of love.

No more walking around on eggshells. No more looking over my shoulder, worried about what kind of mood Dad was in. No more fights between Mama and Dad.

I thought of a quote from the great pitcher Satchel Paige in a book I'd read earlier that summer about the Negro Baseball League. He had said, "Don't look back; you never know who might be gaining on you." Well, in this house, no one was gaining on me.

The brick rancher was perched on a small hill on a quiet, dead-end, red dirt road about five miles outside Winston-Salem, just off Gum Tree Road. Behind the gigantic yard, as far as you cared to walk, were woods and fields that rimmed a treeless hill. I discovered the hill the day after we moved in and thought that come winter, it would be a great place to sled. Across the dirt road was the Union Cross Freewill Baptist Church. It's amazing how much fun an empty church parking lot can be to a kid on a bicycle.

The back door, which was under a carport, led into a kitchen and dining area that featured a shiny linoleum floor, natural hardwood cabinets, and windows that filled up with the morning sun. The house had three bedrooms—one each for Mama, Uncle Bill, and Grandma. I was tickled when Grandma announced that I'd be sharing her bedroom, sleeping in the spare twin bed, which was covered with enough color-ful quilts to keep me warm during another ice age.

I was happy for Mama when she got her old job at Indura Mills back. Though I hated her working in that awful place, it was what she knew, and she needed to make some money. Uncle Bill, who left on Monday mornings and returned Friday afternoons, was letting her use his new car while he was on the road. She looked great behind the wheel of that black Bonneville.

The day after we had settled into our new surroundings, we drove to Union Cross Elementary School, where I enrolled in the fourth grade. Riding in that car next to Mama, with the window rolled down, my arm hanging out in the warm summer air, was one of the best days of my life. I felt like this was a new beginning for us. Our old life was becoming distant and far away, and by believing this was so, I thought I could make it so.

The next Monday morning Mama dropped me off at the school bus stop just up the dirt road from our house. I was dressed in new clothes from head to toe, courtesy of Uncle Bill. I wore dark blue slacks, a button-up gray shirt, and shiny black penny loafers with new dimes peeking through the slits. A little bench with a roof to keep out the rain stood at the corner where the bus stopped. Two boys and a pretty blond-headed girl dressed in a bright yellow flowered dress and white buckle-up shoes were waiting for the bus.

"My name is Elizabeth, but everyone calls me Beth," said the girl, who looked about twelve. "What's your name?"

"My name is Gene."

"Well, nice to meet you, Gene. These two dullards here are my brothers Jake and Aaron. I'm in the sixth grade, and Jake and Aaron are in the fifth. They're twins, just not identical." Beth flashed a big perfect smile.

Jake and Aaron, who seemed to take no offense at their sister's remark, nodded in my direction and said nothing. I replied in kind and fumbled with my notebook, trying hard not to stare at this charming girl.

"We live right there," she said, pointing at a big green-and-white farmhouse. "That's our farm. Daddy grows tobacco. You just moved in, didn't you?" Without waiting for a reply she went on. "You need to come up and play. We got a basketball hoop inside the barn. We got a fort made out of hay bales in the loft, and that's where we have corn-cob fights. It's a hoot at our place, isn't it, boys?" Her brothers nodded.

"Well, thanks. I'll do that."

As the yellow bus pulled up, she added, "Everybody's welcome at our house."

I thanked her again and told her I'd come up and play, as we all climbed into the bus. Jake and Aaron went to the back together, neither saying a word. Beth ambled over to a chunky girl, joined her, and started talking. I walked to the nearest seat I could find and sat down, my face as red as a pickled beet from too much attention from a pretty girl.

Union Cross School was much nicer than Forest Park School. Though they were built at around the same time, Union Cross had been remodeled and upgraded. My fourth-grade teacher was Miss Andrews, a petite young woman with dark hair and captivating golden-brown eyes.

The best things about my classroom were the tall windows that allowed the room to fill up with sunlight. At Forest Park the windows were narrow and situated just below the ceiling. They let in sparse sunlight and a little fresh air, but they weren't fit for daydreaming. But the windows in my new classroom rose halfway toward the ceiling and looked out over a green pasture surrounded by tall oak trees. They were the perfect daydreaming windows.

I saw Beth once that day as I was on my way to lunch and she was returning to class. She smiled and waved; I just blushed and looked down at my shoes. The first day of school was over before I knew it.

Grandma was sitting in the kitchen, a bologna sandwich and glass of milk waiting for me, when I came in the door. "Hey, honey, what'd you learn in school today?" I told her all about my day, and the little blond girl and her twin brothers who lived on the corner. "That must be Eli Johnson's children," she said. "The Johnsons are fine people. Eli and his wife, Camellia, brought down some fresh butter and eggs when me and Bill first moved in."

I wolfed down the sandwich without chewing, I couldn't wait to change my clothes, jump on my bike, and ride up and down the dirt roads, exploring my new surroundings. And if I was lucky, maybe I'd see Beth again.

My bike had been leaning against a wall for almost a year now, and was ready to break free and fly again. From the dead end to the intersection, the dirt road was about a mile long and passed just three houses. Half a mile from the end of the road I snooped around an old gray wooden building. It was too small to be a barn. Springwater flowed through it into a basin like a sunken bathtub in the middle of a cement floor. The basin was full of goldfish, big ones. It was cool and dark inside, and the floor and walls were covered with crickets. I asked Grandma about it later, and she said it was an old springhouse where people used to keep things cold before there were refrigerators. I started taking leftover bread with me when I left the house to feed to the goldfish. All in all my new home was a boy's paradise, a perfect place to play and explore and ride a bike.

That night, worn out from discovering new trails and roads, I had one of my favorite recurring dreams: The night is lit by a full moon. I jump up several times, each time getting lighter and rising higher until I can stay suspended in the air at treetop level like a kite. I can move around at will with no effort. I'd just think, *Boy, it'd be great to be over there*, and I'd drift over there. In my dream, my ability to fly left my friends' faces covered in looks of wonder and envy.

22

Sugar and Spice

The third week in September 1960, Uncle Bill hailed me as I was zooming by the house on my bike. "Honey, stop a minute and come here. I want to show you something."

I pushed down hard on the right pedal and turned the handlebars hard left. Leaning the bike, I put my left foot on the ground and slung the bike into a power slide, stopping in front of him. "How'd you like that move, Uncle Bill? That's just like the motorcycles at the fairgrounds."

"Yeah, honey, that was just like 'em. Here, I want to show you something." He pulled two tickets from his shirt pocket and showed them to me. "We're going to The Lady in Black."

"The what?"

"That's what the drivers call Darlington. I guess it's because widows wear black, and Darlington's a tough and fast racetrack."

"We're going to a real stock car race?" My eyes got wide. "Wow! When?"

"This coming Saturday. I asked your mama a week ago, and she says it's fine."

Wrecks and stuff, I thought. *I don't want to see no one widowed, but a few spins and fender benders will be all right.* "I can't believe it! We're going to the races! Thanks, Uncle Bill." My joy knew no bounds as I peddled my bike up the dirt road as fast as I could go. At the corner I saw Beth and her brothers walking toward their barn. I rode across the field and pulled up next to them. "Hey, Beth," I said, nodding at Aaron and Jake. "What are you guys doing?"

"Were gonna have a corncob fight. Want to be on my side?"

"Sure, that sounds like fun. My Uncle Bill just told me we're going to the race in Darlington, so I'm celebrating." Beth looked at me, her blue eyes as deep as indigo. She was wearing a pair of jeans rolled up at the bottom, a red North Carolina State sweatshirt with WOLFPACK written across the front, and a pair of brown-and-black saddle oxford shoes. She smiled and said, "My favorite driver is Glen Jarrett. Who's yours?"

"I like Fireball Roberts. That's who Uncle Bill likes, too."

"Oh, I see—a couple of Chevy boys. Glen Jarrett drives a Ford. I'm a Ford girl myself. You know, F-O-R-D, First on Race Day."

Wow, I thought. *She's pretty, she's smart, and she likes racing. This is some girl.* Of course, I didn't have much on which to base that assumption. She was the first girl I'd ever carried on a real conversation with. I wasn't about to argue the pros and cons of GM versus Ford with her. She was too pretty and too smart for me to argue with. We went into the big barn, which was three times as big as Grandpa Cheek's barn. Its loft ran on both sides and along the back. Beth and her brothers had made two forts by piling hay bales along the sides of the loft. There were tunnels to crawl through and holes to peep through, and places to stand up and throw corncobs.

We gathered up corncobs from a big pile in the corner of the barn. With our buckets full, we climbed the ladder, the twins going one way, Beth and I going the other. We crawled through the tunnels, positioned ourselves at different ends of our fort, and started bombarding the twins with cobs.

The twins fired back, all of us yelling out, "Got ya!" and "Ouch!" Beth could throw better than me; she was no ordinary girl. When our corncob ammo ran out, Beth and I climbed down; tired and out of breath, we plopped on top of the hay bales. The twins started shooting basketball at the other end of the barn.

"Your daddy doesn't live with you, does he?" Beth asked me out of the blue.

I turned red and looked down at my shoes. "No, he lives with my other grandma."

"Is he a drunk? Is he mean to you and your mama? Does he beat you?" I didn't answer right away but I could tell by the inflection in her voice that she wasn't being nosy, just concerned. She picked at the straw bale and continued, "My daddy drank a lot, and he was mean to us, and he beat my mama. But about seven years ago he got saved and quit drinking. He's the best dad in the world now."

Beth's words flew all around me. How did she know these things about me?

I fought back the tears. *I can't cry now. Not in front of a girl.*

Beth put her hand on mine and said, "Don't give up hope. Some people change." With that, my new friend got up and walked toward her house. She turned and said, "See you later, Gene. I got to help with supper."

I tried to speak, but my throat felt like I'd swallowed a watermelon, so I waved at her, jumped on my bike, and rode off to have a good cry.

Uncle Bill and I left for the Darlington racetrack first thing that Saturday morning. I'd been to Darlington once before, but not to see a race; I'd been there with Uncle Bill. I was around six, I guess, and my cousin Tim was playing a Little League football game in South Carolina. Uncle Bill and I had gone to see the game, and we stopped in Darlington.

You'd think being as shy as he was Uncle Bill wouldn't know any-one, but he knew almost everyone. The track was closed, but he some-how knew the guard on duty. They talked together for several minutes, and Uncle Bill talked the guy into letting him drive around the track. He was driving a rocket ship back then, too, a midnight-blue Chevrolet Impala. He opened it up pretty good around the track, not like he wanted to I imagine, but with me in the car and the guard watching he took it easy. Heck, I was thrilled. How many kids could brag about rid-ing around "The Lady in Black"?

Glen Jarrett won the race, lapping the rest of the field by seven laps. It was a good old-fashioned butt whipping, and I figured I'd hear about it from Beth. She didn't say a word until I brought it up Monday morning while we were waiting for the school bus. And all she said then was, "Did you have a good time even though your guy didn't win?" When I told her I'd had a great time, she just smiled that smile that could defrost a freezer and said, "Well, that's all that matters."

One week after the race, Dad came by the house. He'd been coming by from time to time to see Mama and me. When he came, I tried to avoid him. This time I was in the yard working on my bike. The chain had come off, and I had the bike upside down, trying to fix it. He parked his car at the church and walked over.

"Hey, you want me to help you with that?" he asked.

"Sure. I can't seem to get the blasted thing to go on," I said without looking up.

Dad walked to his car and came back with his toolbox. "This ought to help," he said, pulling out an adjustable wrench and a pair of vise grips. "Here, you hold this and let me loosen up the wheel." I held the vise grips, and he loosened the nut and slid the rear wheel forward. He slipped the chain back on the cog and tightened the wheel. "There," he said. "She's good as new."

"Thanks, Dad," I mumbled.

"Listen, I'm on my way up to the Union Cross National Guard station. There's a big softball tournament up there this weekend and I thought you might like to go."

He'd been having another sober spell, and his manner and tone were relaxed. He was dressed in a pair of pressed khakis, a dark blue pullover, and polished wing-tip shoes. His hair was cut shorter than usual, and he was clean-shaven. He looked nice, like the Dad of old.

I had spent the previous ten days thinking about what Beth had said while we sat on the hay bales. I hadn't figured out what caused her to say those things to me. Maybe it was something about me, something just she could see. She hadn't said another word on the subject though I saw her almost every day, including the day I helped her, the twins, and their dad hang tobacco, tied onto long sticks, in their barn for curing. Mr. Johnson had paid me fifty cents.

Now, as he righted my fixed bike, I stared at my father. His bright, engaging smile disarmed me, blocking any of the bad memories that still prowled in my mind. "Sure, I'd like to go to the ball game. Let me go ask Mama."

Of course she said yes, so Dad and I headed to the National Guard station to watch some of the best fast-pitch softball players in the country.

"I didn't know you liked softball," I said to Dad.

"Oh yeah. I used to play fast pitch for the City Beverage Company before you were born and before I started—" He paused and glanced out the car window before finishing his sentence. "—drinking so much." As we came up the hill, the lights around the softball park lit up the now darkening sky. The stands were packed, and we found two seats in the bleachers down the first-base foul line.

While Dad went for peanuts and drinks, I watched the players take infield practice. Their uniforms were much more colorful than baseball players wore. These guys were good, too, slick fielders who whipped the ball around with amazing precision. Dad returned with fresh-roasted peanuts still warm in the brown paper bag and two Dr Peppers. During the game, I loved listening to the chatter on the field: "Hey now, kid, let's see what you got." "Throw that old seed by him, kid, whattaya say."

Meanwhile Dad was yelling at the umpires. "Hey, ump, where's your Seein' Eye dog?" or "Hey, blue, you gotta be kiddin' me. My grandma could have made that call. He was safe by a mile." Each time he'd slap me on the leg, and we'd both laugh our heads off.

During the drive home, Dad asked me, "Do you know what Alcoholics Anonymous is, son?" I shook my head no, so he explained it. "I'm an alcoholic. I'm ashamed of it, but it's a fact nonetheless. I don't know how I got to be what I am, drinking all the time, yelling, cussing, getting angry, and hitting your poor Mama, and you, God forgive me. But here I am, and that's what I am, an alcoholic. They say it's a sickness, and I suppose they're right, but calling it a sickness don't make it right. I go to meetings at AA—that's what they call Alcoholics Anonymous—five nights a week and I've been going for a whole month. Just got my thirty-day badge night before last." He pulled it from his shirt pocket and showed it to me. "I ain't touched a drop in over a month now. I know that don't mean much, and it shouldn't, not to you anyway. Having to see me day in and day out in all kinds of drunken states, a month ain't much, no sir, but it's a start, son. It's a start."

Dad had never admitted such things to me. He'd said he was sorry before, but never admitted that he had been wrong. I gathered a new understanding and respect for him that night; I saw a side I had never seen before. And he was right—a month ain't much, but it was a start.

23

Cotton Candy and Pinto Beans

During October in the Piedmont, the leaves begin to turn a thousand shades of red, yellow, and orange. It's during this season of warm days and cool nights that the Dixie Classic Fair comes to Winston-Salem. Next to Christmas, it was Mama's favorite happening. She planned and saved for it like it was something bigger than just a fair.

We didn't go every year, at least Mama didn't when money was tight. The Forsyth County school system considered the fair an educational experience and took all the schoolkids. This year she had saved some money and announced we were going to the fair. And to top it off, we were going with Larry and his mama, Becky.

I'd seen Larry just twice since I left the apartment. He and I had helped each other through some bad times, and bad times make people close. I missed my best friend, and I worried about him.

Larry and his mom came to pick us up around 6 P.M. in their burgundy Buick Skylark. It was great to see my old friend again. He'd grown taller and was thinner, but there was more sadness in his eyes.

As we headed to the fair, Larry and I sat in the backseat talking and eavesdropping on our mothers' conversation.

"You don't know how good it is to be doing this again, Sallie," Becky said.

"This will be just like old times," Mama said. "We're all together again. Talking to each other on the phone just ain't the same as going to the Dixie Classic Fair."

"Larry's missed Gene so much."

"Gene's missed Larry, too. Now that things are better in our lives, we'll see more of each other."

"Is Jesse still going to AA?"

"Yes, he goes five nights a week and he's been sober now for two months."

The car stopped at a red light. Becky said with a sigh, "John's drinking has just gotten worse. We fight all the time. It's affected Larry so much that his schoolwork is suffering. He tells me all the time how much he hates his father."

"Gene's said that same thing many times."

"Larry's even threatened to shoot his father," Becky said in a whisper. Larry heard his mother's comment and said, "That's right, Mama. I'll shoot him dead if he don't stop hitting you. I know where he keeps his shotgun. I'll shoot him dead."

"Hush, Larry," Becky said. "Stop talking about guns. You scare me sometimes."

I felt sorry for Larry. My life seemed to have turned the corner and was heading for better days, but his was still the same old mess. "Maybe your dad can start going to AA with my dad," I said to Larry. "Then he'd stop drinking and they'd become good friends and we'd see each other more often."

"I wish he would," Larry said. "But he's hanging around with that stupid no-good Barney Todd."

Mama heard what Larry said. "Is that true?"

Becky sighed. "Yeah, ever since you moved, Barney and John have become real close."

"But they couldn't stand each other."

"Well, Barney says it was all because of Jesse. Now he comes by just about every day, and they go off drinking. When John gets home, all hell breaks loose."

"I think Barney had a lot to do with Jesse's drinking. I'm so glad he's rid of him."

"I wish John would do the same."

As bad as Barney was, I didn't think he was the reason our fathers drank so much. Misery loves company, and miserable drunks enjoy each other's miserable company. If they weren't drinking with

Barney, they'd be drinking with someone else; both our dads had proven that.

I changed the subject and told Larry about Beth and her untalkative twin brothers, the corncob fights, and the hanging of tobacco. Larry seemed to force a smile. So I tried another tack. "How about Big Mama? Has she taken the frying pan to Frank's head?"

Larry burst out laughing, and his mood changed. He started singing, "Gene and Beth setting in a tree, K-I-S-S-I-N-G."

I punched him on the arm before he could finish. "She ain't my girlfriend, you nitwit," I protested. "She's older than me. We're just friends like me and you." Pointing to where I punched him in the arm, I added, "And don't rub it or you're a baby." We laughed. It was good to see my buddy again.

After we arrived at the Dixie Classic Fairgrounds, we wandered with our mothers from exhibit to exhibit. We had no interest in seeing quilts or canned peaches, but it was the order of things. Larry and I loved to make fun of our mamas and the "old lady" things they wanted to do.

Larry, impersonating his mama's voice, said, "Oh, look at that quilt. Don't you just love the pattern? That would be such a nice gift for an expecting mother."

Then, in a falsetto voice, I chimed in, "Oh, yes, quite so. And look at this precious handmade doily. Isn't that just too cute." Our mothers turned around and swatted at us. Faking anger, Mama warned, "Boy, if you don't shut up, I'm going to kill you dead."

An hour later the women began dragging, so they found a comfortable place to sit, bought a cup of coffee and a bowl of pinto beans, and sat down. I never understood the pinto bean thing. You'd think Mama had eaten enough pintos at home. When I asked her about this, she said, "Why, boy, these are Dixie Classic beans made by the Lions Club. They don't get no better than that." They just looked like regular beans to me.

Larry and I were after more exotic foods, and we stuffed ourselves with cotton candy, candy apples, fried apple pies, fried chicken, and fried pork rinds with hot sauce. Meanwhile we tossed rings at Pepsi bottles, threw darts at water-filled balloons, shot at stars with a BB gun, and rode everything that moved.

Our mothers were dead set against us riding the "grown-up" rides, like the big Ferris wheel, the Tilt-A-Whirl, the Zipper, or the swings that spun so fast, riders were whipping by parallel to the ground. But we had a foolproof plan—we tried to get them to ride with us.

"Come on, Mama, don't be chicken," I said, flapping my arms and squawking like a chicken.

"No, honey," she said. "I don't feel like throwing up all over the place. I'm tired."

"Me, too," said Becky.

"Well, then, can we go on some rides by ourselves?"

"Well, I guess so."

Larry and I let out a whoop and jumped up and down. Worked like a charm every time. "Remember where we are," Mama said, handing me some money for tickets. She and Becky were seated at a picnic table that we had dubbed the "command post" near the entrance to the Ferris wheel. "And check in from time to time, you hear?"

"Yes ma'am," Larry and I said in unison, and off we went.

We were riding the Tilt-A-Whirl for a second time when Larry said, "I think I'm going to throw up." When our moon-shaped car stopped spinning around, we staggered off the ride. Larry made it a few steps before he collapsed onto the ground and spilled his guts on the grass.

I was dizzy and disoriented like Larry but I didn't throw up. We had no idea how to get back to the command post and began wandering through the crowds, lost. We were getting scared when I heard a voice say, "Hey, Gene."

I turned and looked up and was startled to see a colored man. Beside him stood a wiry black boy who looked a bit younger than me. I wondered how he knew my name.

"You are Gene, aren't you?" the man asked.

"Yes sir."

"Don't you remember me?"

"No sir."

"I'm Cornelius Tucker. We met at your grandma's house, and another time at the mill when you brought your mama her lunch and purse."

"Oh, yeah, now I remember."

"Who's your friend?" Mr. Tucker asked.

"This is Larry, my best friend." Then I looked at the boy with Mr. Tucker.

"Oh, this is my son," Mr. Tucker said. "Everyone calls him Goot." Seeing the confusion on my face, he added, "Don't ask me how he got that nickname. No one can remember."

We all smiled and Larry and I said hi to Goot, who seemed to be pretty shy.

"You're not here by yourselves, are you?" Mr. Tucker asked me.

"No sir. We came with our mothers. But we can't find them."

"Where'd you leave them?"

After I described the place, he said. "That's way on the other side. Follow me." Staying right behind him, we weaved through the thick crowd. We found our mothers sitting at the command post, worried to death. It turned out that they'd been taking turns looking for us. "Thank you, Mr. Tucker," Mama said.

"You're welcome, ma'am," he said. "How's your mama doing?"

"She's fine, Mr. Tucker. Thanks for asking."

"Well, you tell her I said hello, and I guess I'll see you around the mill next week." With a slight bow and a tip of his fedora hat, he led his son back into the throng.

"Where do you know that colored man from?" Becky asked while driving us back home. I could tell from the tone of her voice that she thought it odd that Mama knew a black man. After she explained meeting him at Grandma's and seeing him at work, Becky asked, "What does Jesse think about your knowing a Negro?"

Mama then told of the day my father went berserk when he found her and Mr. Tucker sharing Grandma's couch.

"I'm not surprised Jesse reacted that way," Becky said. "John would kill me if he ever saw me talking to a colored man, let alone walk into a room and find me sitting next to one."

"Jesse hates coloreds when he's drunk," Mama said, adding, "but then he hates everyone when he's drunk." Larry and I, eavesdropping in the back, got a good laugh out of that one.

"It doesn't matter to John," Becky said. "Drunk or sober, he hates

118

Negroes. He won't even let me drive through Colored Town alone." Becky lowered her voice to a whisper, but still I was able to hear what she was saying. "If you want to know the truth, I think he belongs to the Klan."

"What makes you say that?"

"Well, sometimes he leaves at night and says he's going to meetings. And one time I found this white uniform with a hood in his closet. When I asked him if he belonged to the Klan, he told me to mind my own business."

24

Some People Do

The last week of October 1960, Mama dropped a bombshell. She'd just returned from an outing with my father. "Your dad is going to move in with us, honey," she said.

I turned off the TV. "Why?"

"Well, he misses us and he needs us. He's still going to his AA meetings every night, and he hasn't touched a drop of liquor now in three months, and he's working full time at the gas station. I talked to Grandma and Uncle Bill about it, and they think we should give him another chance. What do you think?"

I didn't know what to think. It was true Dad had changed, but he had changed before, and sooner rather than later he'd revert to his old drunken self again. It seemed to me that we were all better off when he wasn't around. He had started drinking right after I was born. Maybe being a full-time father and husband was too much for him. Maybe the responsibility of having a child was more than he could take. Yet I wanted to believe Beth's words: *Some people do change*. Maybe Dad had changed, but it wasn't easy for me to believe that.

"What if he starts drinking again?" I asked.

"I don't think he will honey, I believe he's licked alcohol. And he misses you."

"I hope you're right, Mama."

Dad moved in on a Saturday, bringing his few clothes and a new respectful attitude toward everyone. There were no fights and no arguments. He tried his best to be a good husband, father, son-in-law, and brother-in-law. He shared in the warmth, laughter, and love that filled Grandma's house. We went fishing and rabbit hunting. He helped me with my homework and showed pride in the progress I was making at school. I was happy to have him back in my life, but the ghost of the old Dad still lingered nearby.

Fall gives way to winter and winter to spring. With each changing season, Mother Nature presents signs of that change—the first frost, the first snow, the first blossom. Like the changing seasons, Dad began displaying subtle signs of change.

By early spring he was sitting in front of the TV on nights when he should be attending his AA meetings. Grandma would ask him, "Jesse, aren't you going to your meeting tonight?"

"Not tonight, Pearl. I don't feel good. I have a bad headache," he'd reply. When Grandma pressed the issue, he'd mutter under his breath, get into his car, and drive away, coming home the next afternoon.

Dad was getting irritable. He became withdrawn and moody, spending more and more time away from the house. Mama saw the signs as well, and her smile and cheery disposition began to fade.

One Saturday afternoon we went to Grandma Cheek's for supper. We arrived early so Dad could work on the tin roof of her tiny barn. While Mama and Grandma were cooking, I was outside watching Dad. He had a half-pint bottle of Ten High bourbon, which he was trying to hide in the side pocket of his overalls, and a Mountain Dew with him. From time to time I'd catch a glimpse of him pulling the half-pint out and taking a swig.

To secure himself and avoid falling from the steep roof, he had tied one end of a thick rope around his waist and the other end to a tree on the other side of the barn. It was a pretty stupid way of making sure you don't fall, if you ask me, but no one did. As the afternoon wore on, I noticed he was getting drunker, sloppier, and more careless. In total disregard, he'd stand up and walk on the slick, sloping roof like he was walking across the living room floor.

"Be careful, Dad!" I shouted up to him after I saw him struggling to catch his balance.

"Shut up," he snapped. "And quit staring at me. Go somewhere and play."

I lowered my head, shoved my hands into the pockets of my overalls, and shuffled toward the gravel road looking for something to do. *Why did Mama let him back into our lives? Why did I think he could change? Some people do and some people don't or can't. I wonder which Dad is—the one who doesn't want to change or the one who can't.*

After wandering around in the warm spring sun for an hour, I went back to see if supper was ready. I looked up at the barn, wondering if Dad had finished his work. To my horror, I saw him facedown, folded over the edge of the roof like a closed book. His legs were dangling over the side and thrashing in the air. From the looks of things, as he'd slid down the roof, the rope had slipped up his waist, and at the last second, he'd grabbed on to it with his left hand. His weight and gravity had pulled the rope as tight as a guitar string around his armpit and his neck. His left arm was pointing straight back up the roofline with his hand clinging to the rope. Somehow, he'd gotten his right arm free, and was trying to use it to liberate himself from his predicament, but the rope was cutting off his air and he was fading fast. Terrified, I raced toward the house, screaming, "Dad's dying! Dad's dying!"

Uncle Bobby, who had shown up while I had wandered off, came running out of the house. Together we managed to untie the rope from around the tree. By this time Dad was motionless. There seemed to be no way of lowering him without making matters worse. Uncle Bobby decided the best hope Dad had was for us to let go of the rope. He hit the ground like a sack of potatoes with a sickening thud and lay motionless. Uncle Bobby removed the rope from his neck and tried to revive him. I thought for sure he was dead.

Mama and I wrapped our arms around each other and cried. The rescue squad arrived within minutes and was able to revive him. They loaded him into the ambulance and took him to the hospital. Mama went with him but I didn't want to. Uncle Bobby took me back to Union Cross and then headed for the hospital. A little while later Mama called, saying nothing was broken and he would be fine in a few days although he had to spend the night in the hospital. The doctors said had he not been drunk, the fall could have killed him.

Had he not been drunk, he wouldn't have gotten himself into the mess in the first place, I thought. *I'm done with him. He'd tried to hang himself right in front of me; that's the way I see it. Shoot, I should've stayed in the woods a little longer, and he could've had his wish.*

Dad had a fiery red rope burn around his neck that didn't fade for months. I heard people say that I helped save his life. To me, that wasn't something to be proud of.

The hanging episode marked the resumption of my father's self-destruction, and this time he didn't try to hide it. In a matter of days he lost his job at the gas station. Though drinking had almost killed him, he didn't give it up. On the contrary, he drank even more. The arguments intensified, and those arguments were hardest on Grandma, whose weak heart couldn't tolerate the stress.

One afternoon the three of us went grocery shopping for my tenth birthday party, which was in a few days. At the store, they began arguing when he picked up a case of Budweiser.

"Put that back," Mama ordered him. "I'm not using my hard-earned money to buy you liquor."

"I'll pay you back as soon as I get a job."

"No!"

He cussed as he put the case back on the shelf.

I hated him with a new intensity. It was the end of the line, and Mama and I were hanging from it.

On the way home he kept cussing her, calling her his usual assortment of filthy names as I steamed with every word. Mama remained quiet, her face covered in contempt and rage. When the car pulled into the driveway, she turned to him and said, "I want you to pack your things and leave right this minute. And I never want to see your drunken face again."

"So you're kicking me out, is that it?"

"Yes."

Without warning, he punched her in the face. "Get out of my car, you bitch!" he shouted.

As she stumbled out the door, I saw blood trickling from her nose and mouth. As I sat in the backseat, all those years of hate and anger came to a peak and I was no longer afraid of him. At ten years old, I felt like I was more of a man than he was. Glaring at him with hate that must have been unmistakable in my eyes, I said, "If you ever hit Mama again, I'll kill you. Do you hear me? I'll kill you if you ever lay another finger on her." At that moment, I'd never spoken truer words.

He glared back and said, "You get the hell out, too." I did, and my father drove off.

I celebrated my tenth birthday in a subdued mood. Despite lots of presents, including a basketball and a basketball hoop from Mama and plenty of friends, including Larry and Beth, I was depressed. The last fight between Mama and Dad was still vivid in my mind. I shuddered at the thought of how much fury his drunken cruelty had raised inside me.

Beth and I sat under the carport as Larry and his mama drove off and the silent twins headed up the road toward their farm. Aunt Goldie and my cousins had left already.

"How could I love Dad and hate him at the same time?"

"You hate what he is, and you love what he was. You hold on to those memories of what he was." I looked at Beth and started to cry. She put her arms around my shoulders and let me cry.

"I'm sorry I ever told you about my daddy," she said. "I asked you to hold on to false hope, and now you're hurt worse than ever. I'm so sorry, Gene. I didn't mean for it to hurt you."

"No, what you told me was true, and I needed to hear that. Somehow, you always say the things I need to hear. How do you do that? How is it that you can see right inside me?"

"From the first time you walked up to that bench to catch the bus, I could see right inside you. There's something special about you, and I could see that. But there's darkness and pain, too. I don't like seeing or knowing these things, but I do. I always have. It's a curse."

Beth kissed me on the cheek and said, "Happy birthday." She got up and walked up the road toward her house. I watched her, wondering where this girl had come from. *Is she an angel or some magical person? I don't know, but whatever she is, I love her.* I started to yell out to her, but she was too far away. I wanted to tell her that what she had was not a curse.

A few days after my birthday, Mama said to me, "I noticed you weren't having all that much fun on your birthday, honey. What's the matter?"

"Oh, nothing," I said. I was leaning against the carport, staring into space as storm clouds gathered in the distance.

"Something's bothering you, I can tell."

"It's about Dad," I said.

"What about him?"

"You won't take him back again, will you? I mean, you ain't gonna let him hurt you no more, are you?"

"No, honey, I won't take him back."

"Even if he comes here with presents?"

"Not even then. I've learned my lesson."

"Promise?"

"I promise. As a matter of fact, I'm going down to the courthouse to file separation papers tomorrow."

25

The Man of the House

The following day while Mama was at the courthouse, Grandma, who was in bed and not feeling well because of her heart condition, called me into the bedroom. "I want to talk to you for a minute," she said. "I'm proud of you, honey. You're a good boy."

"Thanks, Grandma." I knew the compliment wasn't the reason she had called me.

"But there's one thing I want you to promise me."

"Anything, Grandma."

"Now that your mama has decided to leave your father, promise me you won't hate him for what he's done."

That caught me off guard. *Why is she asking me to make such a promise? Has she been talking to Beth? No, I know better than that. But how does Grandma know I hate Dad?* "But he's not a good man, Grandma."

"He has plenty of good in him, honey. Otherwise I wouldn't have let him marry your ma."

"If he's so good then why does he drink?"

"He drinks because he's weak," Grandma said. She reached for her medication on the nightstand and asked me to bring her a glass of water, which I did. She took a small white pill with a small sip.

"But I hate him," I said. "He's mean."

"Mean he is," Grandma said. "But you shouldn't hate him for it. People who hate other people are miserable people. There's enough hate in this world already, honey, especially here in the South. White people hate the coloreds and the coloreds hate back."

This was not the first time I had heard such words from her. Grandma was a southern lady whose skin was the color and texture of old parchment, but she was no run-of-the-mill southerner. I'd never heard her utter an unkind word against another human being based on color. While the rest of the white world around me screamed and cussed at every slight advancement and freedom the Negroes eked out, Grandma held fast in her beliefs. As far as she was concerned those beliefs hung on one irrefutable fact—her God was color-blind, and so by grace was she.

She continued to speak to me in that calm, soothing voice. "I grew up around colored people, and we were all just poor back then, not black or white. Most of my playmates were colored. I ate with them in their homes and their parents treated me like one of their own. I ain't ashamed of that and there ain't nothing wrong with it, neither, despite what other folks might think. They are people just like we are. There's good and bad in all people. How can I hate the colored, knowing God sees us all the same? I won't do it.

"I've taught your mama not to hate them, either. And I don't want you to grow up to hate. You shouldn't hate your dad or anyone else. People who hate are miserable, honey, believe me. If you want to be happy in life, stay away from hate. It will eat you up inside. Hate hurts those who are hated, but it destroys the one who hates.

"You think about it like this: They don't have no control over the color of their skin no more than you decided to be white. You were born that way and so were they. God decides who's who in this world, and that includes what color we are and who our daddies and mamas are. He's got a plan. Whenever I see a person who is hated, or mistreated, or down on their luck, I say to myself, *There but for the grace of God go I.*"

Grandma paused and took a sip of water. Then she held my hand. "I love you, honey. A lot of things have happened to you that shouldn't happen to any child. There's nothing you can do about that. The Lord must have wanted it that way. But I want you to be happy for the rest of your life. I don't know how much longer I'll be around, and it would hurt me if I died knowing that you were full of hate."

"You ain't dying, Grandma, are you?" I said, panicking.

Grandma flashed a weak smile. "No, honey. There's still a lot of life left in this old body. I just wanted to talk to you because now that your dad is gone, you have to protect your mama. And to protect her, you can't be full of hate. Be full of love, not hate."

"I'll protect her," I said.

"I know you will, honey," Grandma said, patting my arm with her cold hand. "Now I'm a bit tired. Let me sleep a little and then you and I will play Chinese checkers."

Grandma went to sleep and I left the bedroom, confused by what she'd said about loving those who deserved to be hated, including— according to the rest of the world—the coloreds. But I trusted her, and whatever she said was gospel to me. And the nearness of what Grandma and Beth had both said was not lost on me, either.

I was proud she'd asked me to protect Mama. At ten years old and my father gone for good, I felt I was old enough to do that.

A few days after I became—at least in my own mind—the man of the house. I was brushing my teeth before bed when Mama came to the bathroom door and said, "I have a big surprise for you, honey."

"What is it? I love surprises."

"Tomorrow someone is coming over to put up your new basketball goal."

"Oh, that's great!" I roared. I loved basketball. I listened to all the Wake Forest games on the radio and I played whenever I got the chance. But to be good, to be real good, you had to practice. And practice meant you needed your own hoop.

"I love you, Mama," I said, giving her a hug. I could feel my eyes watering.

"I love you too, honey. I know how much you want to practice, and if having your own goal makes you happy, then that's the most important thing in the world."

The next day I was up at the crack of dawn. I went to the carport and waited in the cool morning air, staring down the dirt road. Around eight-thirty I noticed a car approaching, trailed by a cloud of dust. It was a gray-blue Chevy Bel Air. I was relieved that it wasn't Dad's old Chevy.

The car pulled into the driveway and a colored man got out. It was Mr. Tucker. I wanted him to know I remembered him this time. "Hello, Mr. Tucker."

"Hello, Gene. Nice to see you again," he said in a gentle voice, holding out his hand.

I shook it without hesitation. "Nice to see you, too."

"Where do you want me to put the hoop?"

"I'll show you," I said.

He went to the trunk of his car and retrieved the same toolbox I'd seen him carrying at Indura Mills. Grandma came to the door and said, "Well, hello, Mr. Tucker. It's been a while."

"Yes, it has," he said. "The last time we saw each other you were still living on Devonshire. How have you been, Mrs. Anderson?"

"Fair to middling, Mr. Tucker. These old bones are still holding up."

"This is a real nice house you got," he said.

"Yes it is, isn't it?" Grandma said. "It's much quieter than Devonshire Street was. The city is growing so fast that the traffic is getting bad."

"So, you enjoy living out here in the country?"

"Yes, I sure do. I was raised on a farm and didn't know how much I missed the country till I got back to it."

"Your daughter asked me a couple of days ago if I could come and put Gene's basketball goal up," Mr. Tucker said. "Is she home?"

"Yes. She's in the kitchen making breakfast. She tells me you're working at Indura Mills these days."

"Yes ma'am. I do maintenance work for them."

"Well, I sure do appreciate your coming all the way to Union Cross."

"It's a pleasure, Mrs. Anderson. I guess I'd better get started. Gene looks like he's straining at the bit. Nice seeing you again and you take care of yourself."

"Nice seeing you, Mr. Tucker," Grandma said. "You take care, too."

I led Mr. Tucker to the back of the house and showed him where I wanted the post mounted.

Soon I heard the screen door slam and Mama came around. "Hello, Mr. Tucker," she said. "Thanks for coming."

"Hello, Mrs. Cheek."

Turning to me, she said, "Gene, come and eat breakfast."

"Yes ma'am."

"Would you like to join us for breakfast, Mr. Tucker?"

"Thank you, Mrs. Cheek, but I've already had mine."

When I came back outside after breakfast, Mr. Tucker had finished mounting the post and was now working on attaching the hoop.

"So how's school?" Mr. Tucker asked.

"Fine, sir," I said. "I'm in fourth grade now."

"What do you want to be when you grow up?"

"I don't know yet."

As I watched Mr. Tucker work it was obvious he knew what he was doing. As he worked, we continued talking. "Mr. Tucker, Mama says you can fix almost anything at the mill."

He smiled and said, "Well I appreciate the kind words. I guess I'm what you'd call a jack of all trades and a master of none. I learned most of it from my daddy. He was a handyman and a painter, and I helped him from the time I was about your age until he passed away."

"My grandpa was a painter," I said. "Grandma said he was a good one."

"Yes, I believe your grandma told me that your grandpa was a house painter. I bet he was good. Knowing your grandma, she's not one to say things that aren't so."

"Grandma says she knows the truth when she sees it."

Mr. Tucker laughed out loud and slapped his leg. "Yes sir," he said, "I believe she does at that." He finished up what he was doing and carried his small stepladder and toolbox back to his car. I followed him. "Why don't you get your mama so she can check out our work."

He had included me by saying *our work*, though I hadn't done anything but watch, but what he said made me feel good. "Yes sir, I'll go get her."

Mama came to the edge of the carport and looked at my new basketball goal. "Oh, it looks real fine, Mr. Tucker," she said, and then handed him some money.

"I hope Gene enjoys it," he said, putting the rest of his tools into the trunk.

"I'm sure he will."

I grabbed my basketball, dribbled, and shot a line drive that clanged off the rim. Mr. Tucker closed his trunk, walked over to me, and picked up the ball.

"Follow through when you shoot. That's important. Your hand should look like this when you shoot the ball." He shot, holding his hand out, sort of pointing it at the basket. The ball went in with a swish, nothing but net. He picked up the ball and spun it on his finger, then tossed it to me. "Here you try it." I tried it, but I couldn't get it to stay on my finger.

"You'll get better with practice," he said, "Don't forget that practice makes perfect."

"I won't forget."

Mama and I walked Mr. Tucker to his car and then watched him drive away. Then I turned to her and said, "Mr. Tucker sure is nice."

"Yes, he's about as nice a man as you'd ever want to meet. He's always smiling at work and goes out of his way to speak to everyone."

She headed back into the house while I began practicing everything Mr. Tucker had showed me. I stopped for lunch and supper and that was because Mama made me.

26

Dying Inside

My father came to get his belongings, but he picked a bad time. Uncle Bill was home from the road and was fast asleep. Mama warned Dad to be quiet as he gathered his things.

"Bill knows you hit me. So please, Jesse, don't wake him up. He says he'll kill you this time."

Dad was drunk again. "I ain't afraid of that retard. If he wakes up and wants to fight me, I'm ready."

He stomped around as if he was looking for trouble; the fact that Uncle Bill was here and asleep wasn't going to change that. I felt sorry for him. I wanted to cry for this man who was trapped in a hell that he couldn't escape. I knew he didn't want to be the man he had become. I wanted to grab him and shake him, and yell out over and over, *Dad, Dad, snap out of it!*

But I knew he wasn't going to snap out of it. I'd known it for a long time. I just never wanted to admit it. No amount of shaking or pleading or calling out his name was going to rescue him from this hell. It was his hell. He had paved the road to it and there was no bringing him back.

"Where are my damn shoes?" he yelled.

"They're in the bag already. Please, Jesse, keep your voice down. Bill is just down the hall."

"I don't give a shit! Where's my damn razor?"

"Everything is in the bag," Mama whispered. "Just go."

"What's the big hurry? You're mighty glad to be getting rid of me, ain't you?"

My heart stopped beating when I saw Uncle Bill's towering figure in the doorway. He was dressed in striped pajamas, and there was a confused look on his face. He wasn't sure what had stirred him from his sleep, but when his head cleared and he saw my father standing there, Uncle Bill exploded. "What the hell are you doing here, you son of a bitch!"

Before Dad could say anything, Uncle Bill flew over the couch and was on top of him, his large hands closing around Dad's neck. Dad struggled to breathe as his face turned blue. He wasn't fighting back; he just lay there. I saw it then for what it was. *Dad wants to die. He wants Uncle Bill to kill him. He's committing suicide right before my eyes.*

Uncle Bill had gone crazy, and his face had contorted into that of a maniacal stranger. His lips were pulled back, showing his clenched, crooked teeth, and his eyes were wild with hate. I knew Dad was in serious trouble. No matter what my confused feelings were toward him, I didn't want him to die. My voice was paralyzed from shock and I couldn't cry out to Uncle Bill to stop. Instead I watched helpless as he continued to choke my father.

Screaming at Uncle Bill, Mama and Grandma tried to pry his strong fingers from Dad's throat. "Don't kill him, Bill!" Mama pleaded. "Please don't kill him!"

"Bill, listen to your sister!" Grandma pleaded. "Don't kill the father of her child." Uncle Bill's face lost its wild look. He loosened his powerful grip, stared at me, and mumbled, "I'm sorry, honey." With that, he staggered into the bathroom across the hallway and threw up.

His face a nasty purple, Dad lay on the floor gulping for air and rubbing his bruised neck.

"You'd better get out of here before he comes back," Mama warned him.

Without uttering another word, he got up, grabbed his bag, and staggered out the door. Seconds later his car cranked up, and he sped away.

I started crying and threw myself into Grandma's arms. While holding me and stroking my hair, she whispered, "There, there, honey, don't cry. It's all over now. Everything will be all right. This is the end of it."

Mama sat on the couch, trembling and sobbing uncontrollably. I went to her and put my arms around her. She jerked back when I touched her. The trauma of her life with my father had found its high-water mark. She was in shock. The fear and despair and all those frightening nights she had borne the brunt of his abuse so her precious son wouldn't have to, poured out of her in one instant. She laid her head on my shoulder. "Oh, Gene. Oh, Gene, I'm so sorry. Oh, God! Oh, God! Oh, God! My precious son, what have I done to you?"

The next morning Grandma woke up weak and feeling poorly. She was pale, and her usual spunk was gone. At first I blamed Grandma's low spirits on the tension that still lingered from yesterday's fight. It had left us all drained. The darkness of what had happened stained everything and everybody in the house, but Grandma had suffered the most from those terrible few minutes. She came into the living room where I was watching TV and lay down on the couch.

"Are you okay, Grandma?" I asked.

"Yes, honey," she said.

"Can I get you anything? Are you hungry? Thirsty?"

"No. I'm fine."

When Grandma fell asleep, I turned off the TV and went outside to shoot basketball. I was worried about her. I wished I could do something to make her feel better, to forget those terrible things that had happened yesterday. *She'll be all right in a little while—I hope.*

A little while later Uncle Bill came outside and stood next to the basket, tossing me the ball while I shot free throws. "I'm sorry about what happened yesterday, honey," he said. "I'm so sorry."

"I know. It's okay, Uncle Bill. It wasn't your fault. Mama warned Dad not to wake you up. You were just trying to protect us."

"Well, it shouldn't have happened. I'm sorry you saw me like that. I'd never do anything to hurt you or your mama. I love you both. You know that, don't you, honey?"

"Yeah, I know. And we love you, Uncle Bill."

He continued watching me shoot baskets. Uncle Bill had never played sports; he had worked since he'd been about my age so he could take care of his family.

The gray skies started to drizzle and the drizzle turned to rain, but I kept shooting, determined to get three baskets in a row.

"Lunch is ready, honey," Mama said.

"I'm coming," I shot one last basket and watched it swish through the white net.

"Say, you're getting pretty good," she said.

I beamed. Walking into the house, I noticed that Grandma wasn't on the couch. "Where's Grandma?" I asked, sitting down at the kitchen table before a steaming bowl of homemade vegetable soup and a bologna sandwich with mayonnaise, lettuce, and tomato.

"In her bedroom," Mama said.

"Is she all right?"

"She's fine, I think she just needed a little rest."

I finished my soup and sandwich and headed back to the living room. On the way I passed Grandma's bedroom. The door was open a crack, so I peeked in. I was relieved to see Grandma sound asleep on the bed. Half an hour later I was in the middle of watching a Roy Rogers movie when I heard Uncle Bill scream out, "Sallie! Sallie! Oh, God! Come here! Hurry!"

"What's the matter?" Mama asked from the kitchen.

"It's Mama!" Uncle Bill said in a panic-stricken voice.

I heard pots and pans drop and Mama's footsteps rushing toward Grandma's bedroom. I jumped up, ran to her bedroom, and found Uncle Bill weeping beside Grandma's bed. "Mama, Mama, please wake up," he said in a pleading little child's voice, tears streaming down his face.

My mama reached for Grandma's wrist and felt for a pulse. "Quick, call an ambulance," she said to Uncle Bill. Mama focused her attention on Grandma's still body. Uncle Bill remained frozen.

"Bill, please call an ambulance! Tell them to hurry!"

Uncle Bill snapped out of his trance and rushed to the phone. Looking up at Mama, I saw the tears flowing down her face. I opened my mouth to speak but no words came out. I wished I had magical powers that could make Grandma wake up. I wanted her to open her loving blue eyes, to move her right arm that had caressed my cheek so many times, but it was now limp in Mama's hand.

Uncle Bill came back. "The ambulance is on its way," he said. He took one look at Grandma and busted out crying again. He placed his hands on my shoulders, and the dam broke. I started crying, and I'm not sure when I stopped, or if I ever stopped. Each passing minute seemed like an eternity as we waited for the ambulance. I stood motionless, rooted to the floor of Grandma's bedroom, praying for any sign of life from her still body.

At last two paramedics rushed down the hall and into the bedroom. I stepped aside so they could squeeze the stretcher in through the narrow doorway. They asked us to wait outside and then closed the bedroom door, leaving Uncle Bill, Mama, and me in the hallway, holding each other and crying.

When the paramedics came out of the room, one of them said, "We have to get her to the hospital."

Mama turned to Uncle Bill. "Stay here with Gene and call Goldie and have her meet the ambulance at the hospital. I'm going with Mama." She turned and followed the paramedics outside, holding Grandma's hand every step of the way.

As I stood in the carport watching the ambulance speed away through the blur of my tears, I wondered if I would ever see my beloved Grandma again.

She died before she reached the hospital.

Uncle Bill was never the same after Grandma's death. He blamed himself, convinced she'd died from the stress created from the fight with my dad.

"It wasn't your fault, Bill," Mama told him. "You were trying to protect me and Gene."

Uncle Bill was beyond comfort. For days he brooded over Grandma's death. He wouldn't eat and he didn't go to work. He sat on the couch staring at her picture, whispering to himself, "I'm sorry, Mama, I'm so sorry."

Grandma's death fell on me like a millstone, and it ripped my heart out. I didn't think I could survive without her. She had been my guardian angel, and I had worshiped the ground she walked on. Every word she'd ever spoken to me had fallen on my eager ears like it was from an angel, and they were burned into my memory.

She'd showered me with love when I needed love. She'd comforted me when I needed comfort and was discouraged. She'd surrounded me with kindness when the rest of the world offered nothing but hate and pain. And she'd blessed me with her wisdom when I had none of my own. Her belief that we must treat people as we want to be treated wasn't just words to her; it was the way she lived.

I remembered her plea to "take care of your mother" and treasured her final words of advice to "be full of love, not hate." She had known, as she always knew, that one day I would need those words. Her words to me, and her example, would become the most important things in the world to my own survival.

Like Uncle Bill I cried for days, unable to stop, my heart ravaged by sadness and despair. Without Grandma the world was a cold, loveless ball floating in space. Why would God, whom she had served and honored in her life, take her away from us? She was just sixty-one years old.

Her funeral took place at the Urban Street Baptist Church, where she had been a member for more than thirty years. She had buried a husband and baby son, had raised three children two blocks from the church, and now had come home one last time. The Reverend Renegar, who'd known Grandma for more than twenty years, stood in the pulpit and cried as if his own mother had passed away.

He told the packed church, in between sobs—not trying to hold them back—"The likes of Pearl Anderson won't be seen on this earth again until the Blessed Savior comes back. She was one of those rare people who grace us on earth. She was kind, caring, giving, and loving toward her fellow man. She was a true follower of Christ."

Rain fell in waves as we followed Grandma's casket to the cemetery on Sprague Street. God and the angels in heaven were crying for our loss, and the gray sky reflected the sadness in my heart. I knew our lives would never be the same without Grandma, and I dreaded facing the future without her.

Less than a month after Grandma's funeral, Uncle Bill called Mama and me into the kitchen and said, "I don't know how to say this." He bowed his head as if he was praying. He couldn't look at us.

"What's the matter, Bill?" Mama asked.

"Now that Mama's gone, I can't live here anymore," he said. "I bought this place for her. Now that she's gone, it's just don't seem right to stay here."

"But we're still family."

"Yeah, I know," Uncle Bill said. "And we'll always be family. But I have to sell this place."

Mama was stunned. "Sell the house?" she stammered.

"Yeah, someone has already put a bid on it. So I'll be moving out at the end of the month."

"Where will you go?" Mama asked.

"I'll rent a room."

"Well, it's your house, I can't stop you, and I understand how you feel. Gene and I will just have to find a place of our own."

"I'm sorry, Sallie. This ain't our house. It was Mama's house, and every time I look around, I see her—in the rocking chair, in the kitchen, in her bedroom. If I stay here it's going to eat me up inside."

"I understand, Bill. There ain't no hard feelings over this. You're a good brother and you were a good son to Mama. You took care of her and gave her everything she could possibly want. You've been so good to Gene and me, I owe you a lot."

"I'll still take care of you. You can always count on me."

"I know we can," Mama said.

Uncle Bill hung his head and asked, "Any idea where you'll be staying?"

"I'll start looking for a place tomorrow."

Later I trudged out of the house, my tears splashing onto the muddy road. I had to say good-bye to another angel. Twice in a month I had said good-bye to someone I loved. Grandma was gone forever, and now I was pretty sure Beth would be, too.

We stood at the edge of a cornfield in a cold drizzle. "I hate that I have to go," I told her. "I'm sure gonna miss you. You're a good friend, the best." My words tumbled out between the sobs. Beth didn't cry. She hugged my neck and purred, "This isn't good-bye, Gene Cheek. It's just *see you later*. I ain't saying good-bye to you. If we never see each other again, this still ain't good-bye. I'm not saying those words to you. We'll see each other again, somewhere, sometime, some-how." She kissed me on the cheek and said, "See you later." She walked a few steps, turned, and said, "I love you, Gene Cheek."

"I love you, Beth Johnson." As I watched her walk away, I tried to memorize every thread she was wearing, from her dark blue pedal pushers and pink shirt to her white socks and tennis shoes. The silent twins opened the screen door for their sister and waved to me in uni-son. I waved back, dying inside.

27

On Our Own

In the late spring of 1961 we moved into a two-bedroom duplex near the corner of Urban and Waughtown Streets. The apartment was just a few blocks north of Grandma Pearl's old house and our dream house on Brookline Street. And like our old apartment on Sprague, which was just two blocks north, it was surrounded by gas stations, diners, beer joints, and pool halls. I could stand in the yard, throw a rock, and hit one of the pool halls where I'd sat on a Pepsi crate and watched my father pave his road to hell.

The apartment was small and run-down, but it was all Mama could afford on what she earned at Indura Mills. That first night in our new apartment I cried myself to sleep, missing Grandma and a certain blond girl. Despite an occasional bout with sadness and our ever-increasing poverty, we spent some of our happiest times together that summer. We were a team now, and it was the two of us against the world. When she wasn't working, she devoted all her time to me. Uncle Bill continued to let us use his car while he was on the road, and after school let out for the summer, we took advantage.

We took a picnic basket full of fried chicken, potato salad, and homemade lemonade to the fairgrounds with Larry and his mama. We spent all day cutting up and laughing, just waiting for it to get dark so we could watch the Fourth of July fireworks show.

We went to Crystal Lake, a swimming lake with white sandy beaches, where for twenty-five cents you could swim all day. We'd pack a lunch and eat under the pine trees on a picnic table.

When we didn't have extra money, which was more often than not, we'd stay at home and watch TV, play games, or read books.

I hadn't seen my father since the day Uncle Bill almost killed him. He made no effort to contact me, and that was fine by me. I didn't want to see him anyway. After his separation from Mama, he moved in with Grandma Cheek and agreed to pay twelve dollars a week in child support. In the months since that agreement was signed, he had yet to pay the first nickel.

A new school year started in August, and every day I walked five blocks to Hill Middle School where I was enrolled in the fifth grade. Hill was a new school with all the modern wonders, great food in the cafeteria, and its own running track. What it didn't have was Beth or Larry, and I missed their smiling faces. My teacher was a plump, silver-haired lady named Mrs. Clodfelter who would have rather been home watching *As the World Turns* on TV.

Mama, whose shift at Indura Mills ended at four o'clock, made it home just about the same time as I did every day. Some days I'd take my time walking home, going by Grandma's grave on Sprague Street just to talk to her and let her know we were okay.

I was happy, and Mama seemed to be also. I missed Grandma Pearl, but each day it got a little better. I missed Beth and the silent twins, but I kept holding on to what she'd said: *One day, we'll see each other again.* I made new friends with the kids in the neighborhood, and although they weren't Beth or Larry, they were somebody to play with.

Not far from the apartment was the Red Shield boys club, where I played basketball in a gym for the first time and learned to swim. I went back to the library, where Mrs. Whiteside was still the librarian. She recommended more books like *Treasure Island* by Robert Louis Stevenson, *Robinson Crusoe* by Daniel Defoe, and *Twenty Thousand Leagues Under the Sea* by Jules Verne.

We didn't eat like the Rockefellers, but we got our fill. Pinto beans and stewed potatoes graced our table almost every day. To a southern boy, eating pinto beans with a small piece of fatback and 'taters stewed with a little farm-fresh butter was not a sign of poverty; it was a sign of good taste.

With corn bread or Johnny cake—biscuit dough baked in a black iron frying pan—beans and 'taters were as good as eating gets. Add fresh-sliced farm-grown tomatoes or cantaloupe and we're talking high-on-the-hog eating.

Mama was standing at the stove working her culinary magic one day when I asked, "Are you happy, Mama?"

"Yes, honey, I'm happy," she said, adding a little butter to the potatoes. "Are you happy?"

"I miss Grandma and my friends an awful lot, but I'm happy. It's nice just the two of us. No fighting, no yelling and cussing."

"Well, if you're happy, I'm happy."

One afternoon I came in from playing football with some of the neighborhood kids. I was sitting on my bed reading *A Connecticut Yankee in King Arthur's Court* by my favorite writer, Mark Twain. Mama's room was across the tiny hall from mine, and I could hear her talking on the phone. It sounded like she was crying. I opened my door just a crack and listened. Her words were coming between muffled sobs.

Worried, I walked to her doorway. Mama turned and looked at me. Tears flowed from her red eyes and down her wet cheeks.

"What's wrong?" I asked.

She held up one finger as if to say, *Just a minute*. "I have to go," she said into the phone. "Gene just walked in. I'll call you back." She hung up.

"What's wrong, Mama?" I asked a second time. "Why are you crying?"

She wiped her eyes with a tissue and said, without looking at me, "There's nothing wrong, honey. Why don't you go read your book?"

I refused to budge. "Well, something's wrong," I said. "You're not crying over nothing. Is it Dad? Did he upset you again?" We hadn't heard from him, but if she was crying, it was a good possibility that he was somehow connected.

"No."

"What is it then?"

She didn't answer. Instead, she got up from the bed and walked to the living room. I followed right behind her. She sat down on the couch and lit one of her Pall Malls. Puffing on it, she looked at me and then started shaking her head from side to side.

"What's wrong, Mama?"

She knew I wouldn't leave her alone until she told me why she was crying. I had seen enough of her tears to last a lifetime, and I knew she didn't cry over nothing. She took another puff, the remnants of her lipstick leaving a red ring around the unfiltered cigarette. She exhaled, picked the tobacco off her lip, and said, "Well, the person on the phone is a friend of mine. He's someone I've been seeing for a little while." She took another puff, and exhaled.

"You mean a boyfriend?"

"Well, I guess so."

I was shocked. I didn't know she was seeing anyone. When did they meet? And why was she keeping him a secret from me? I figured this guy, whoever he was, had done something that made her cry, and already I didn't like him. "What did he do to make you cry?"

She glanced down at the cigarette in her hands. "It's kinda hard to explain. I don't know how."

"Mama, I'm ten years old. I'll be eleven soon. I know about boyfriends and stuff." *Why is this so hard for her? We never had any problems talking about things before. There's more to this story, more than she's telling.*

She was searching for just the right words, and was having a hard time finding them. "You know about boyfriends and girlfriends, huh?" she asked, stalling.

"Uh-huh. It's when the boy gives the girl Valentine's cards and chocolate and flowers and other junk, and they hold hands and go to movies, stuff like that."

She laughed.

"Is he nice to you?"

Mama was stuck in place and didn't want to talk about it, but I pressed on. Her reluctance to talk about him, whoever he was, made me more determined to know every detail about this secret boyfriend.

"He's a wonderful man," she said, blinking back her tears. "The nicest and kindest man I've ever known."

"If he's so nice and kind, then why are you crying?"

"He thinks we should stop seeing each other. He's worried that you won't approve, and he doesn't want to hurt you."

"I don't get it," I said, convinced there was more to it than that. "If he's nice and you like him, then why does he think I won't approve?"

She looked down at her hands folded in her lap. I'd never seen her so sad or anxious. She cleared her throat and said, "Because he is a colored man."

28

And So It Begins

You could have knocked me over with a feather. It was 1961; we lived in Winston-Salem, North Carolina, in the heart of Dixie. I knew to the southern man there was no greater sin than race mixing. The prevailing views of most white southerners concerning blacks were not news to me. I knew that the majority of the white world—including my father—considered blacks less than human. I knew these things because I listened and I read. In fact I was always the first to read the morning edition of *Winston-Salem Journal and Sentinel*.

Every week in the headlines, man's hatred toward his fellow man was evident, even to a ten-year-old boy. "Freedom Riders Attacked by White Citizens in Anniston Alabama." "200 Arrested in Anti-Integration Riots." "29 Arrested in Greensboro Sit-In." Even in school, the tension of the world around us and ever-increasing unrest were evident. We were shown what to do in case of a nuclear attack. We'd bend over at our desk and put our heads between our knees. On the playground we called it "Bending over and kissing our ass good-bye."

I knew that colored folks were freed from slavery by President Lincoln, but it didn't seem that the news had made it this far south. Now almost a hundred years to the day after the Emancipation Proclamation was signed, a different form of slavery, called Jim Crow, ruled. Under Jim Crow laws, Negroes had their own water fountains, restrooms, schools, and neighborhoods. Generations of North

Carolinians had taken such laws for granted. With my own ears I heard Pastor Renegar bellow down from the pulpit at the Urban Street Baptist Church, "These laws are in place because they enforced God's will by keeping Negroes and whites—for the good of each group—segregated from the cradle to the grave."

I remember Grandma talking about the civil rights movement. A few months before she died, we were watching the news on Channel 12. A Negro man, Carl Wesley Matthews, was arrested for staging a sit-in at the whites-only lunch counter of the local Kress's five-and-dime store. "Now there's a young man with courage," said Grandma. He returned days later and was joined by black students from Winston-Salem State Teachers College.

"Just a bunch of troublemakin' niggers," grumbled Dad, and when the TV cameras showed white students from Wake Forest University joining the sit-in in Winston-Salem, he said, "Well, whattaya expect from a bunch of rich nigger-lovin' Yankee kids." The TV reporter described how angry and fearful the demonstration made most white people. The southern world was scared and confused; Negroes like Matthews were threatening the fabric of the South. "Hogwash," said Grandma. "All these people want are the same rights everyone else in America has."

Grandma believed that Matthews and other students were doing the right thing. "This is the United States of America," she said. "The home of the free and the brave, and what's good for one is good for all. And if it ain't that way now, then it needs to be made that way now!"

It was one thing to desegregate lunch counters, but it was quite another for an ivory-skinned woman to have a colored man as a boyfriend. That was something most white people would consider a mortal sin.

I didn't know what to say to Mama. Racist remarks that I had heard over the years coming from Dad and even Uncle Bill swirled in my head. You could stand on any corner of an all-white neighborhood of this city, or hundreds of other cities, and hear hate spewed at coloreds as if the words were the gospel of Jesus Christ. Of course, nothing I'd ever heard read from the Bible supported any of this hate.

Grandma told me that many churchgoers used "some twisted version to suit their own twisted beliefs."

News of lynchings could be found in the newspaper every week. I read those stories, and thought about them. They seemed—to me anyway—to be in some far-off place with people who weren't like those of us in Winston-Salem. Yes, there were state laws against interracial marriages, but we didn't just hang people from trees because they were a different color than us. Did we?

"Do you love him?" I asked her.

She smiled. "Yes, honey. I do love him."

"Does he love you?"

"Yes."

I thought on this for a long time. I looked at my thirty-one-year-old mother and saw a light in her eyes that I hadn't seen before. For the first time I realized how hard it had been for her to keep this secret from me, and from everyone else.

She couldn't tell Aunt Goldie about it. She couldn't tell Uncle Bill. She couldn't tell her friends. And Grandma was gone. Had Grandma been around, Mama would have confided in her, and Grandma would have understood and tried to help. After all, it was Grandma who'd taught us all to judge people by the content of their hearts, and not the color of their skin. It's one thing to say you believe something; that's easy. To look on something from a distance when it doesn't affect you takes no effort. I was standing face-to-face with it now, and mere words wouldn't be enough. Action would be required. I was confused. I thought about Grandma and what she would expect of me. She would expect me to do the right thing. I wasn't sure what that was, but I knew what my heart told me.

I was Mama's confidant now, the one person in the world she dared to share this deep and frightening secret with. I didn't realize at the time that she was exposing herself to danger, real danger, by falling in love with a Negro. I didn't understand the dire consequences of interracial love, or the depth and breadth of racial bigotry in the South, or the blind yet directed hatred that simmers in people's dark hearts. To me it boiled down to one simple issue: Mama loved me, I loved her, and she loved this man. I'd heard it said in church: "You have to walk it like you talk it." On the playground we said, "Put up or shut up." Either way it's what I had to do; it's what Grandma would expect.

"If you love this man and he loves you, then the color of his skin doesn't matter," I said to Mama.

Her face regained its color. She took a long look at me and said, "I knew you would say that. I knew it."

29

Secret Friend

Who was this man? I wondered. How did they meet? It seemed to me this man was taking a great risk. I remembered Grandma talking about Emmett Till, a fourteen-year-old black boy from Chicago, who was visiting his relatives in Mississippi when he was beaten to death for just whistling at a white woman.

"Where did you meet this man, Mama?" I asked.

"I met him at work."

"What's his name?"

"Cornelius Tucker, the man who put up your basketball goal last year."

"Mr. Tucker from Grandma's? Why, I like Mr. Tucker. He seemed nice each time I met him. When did you and him, start to— you know—become friends?"

"It was shortly before your Grandma died," she said. "We had talked at work before, but not too much, people always looked at us funny. It's dangerous for us to be seen talking at work. We could both be fired."

I was flabbergasted. "You mean they would fire you just for talking?"

"You better believe they would, so we're always careful about it. We had a long conversation when I went to his house and asked if he'd put up your basketball goal. Then when your Grandma died and he found out she'd passed away, it hit him hard and he cried."

"He must have liked Grandma a lot," I said.

"Yes, honey. He said she was one of the kindest women he'd ever known. Grandma made a big impact on a great many people, black and white. Tuck said that had he known, he would have come to the funeral. That's how much he cared about her. But I don't think Uncle Bill would have let him in the church."

"Why not?"

"Because Negroes aren't supposed to attend the funerals of white people, honey. And white people aren't supposed to attend the funerals of Negroes."

"Well, that's pretty stupid, don't you think? I mean anyone ought to be welcome in church. If he wanted to go to Grandma's funeral, he should have been able to."

"Yes, honey, everyone should be welcome in church, but not everyone feels the way you and I do. We had the benefit of being around your Grandma. Not everyone has such a wonderful person in their lives."

"Why does Uncle Bill hate coloreds so much? He was raised by Grandma, too."

"Well, I'm not sure your uncle Bill really believes all that you hear come out of his mouth. He's a man, a white man, and he's been on the road a long time driving his truck. He's met some pretty bad characters during all that time, and as sweet as your uncle Bill is, he's also just a big child in a lot of ways and easily led astray."

I knew she was right about Uncle Bill. He said some pretty awful things about colored people. He wasn't as vocal as Dad was, but he was a prejudiced man. In his heart he was a good man; you could see that in him. But he wasn't the sharpest tool in the shed; Grandma herself had said that. "He means well, but he gets confused easy."

"Well, Mama, Grandma thought Mr. Tucker was a good man. And if you love him, well then, I know he's a good man."

Her distress vanished and she relaxed. It was plain to me that my approval of her relationship with Mr. Tucker had been so important that she had allowed her happiness to hinge on it. I had the strong feeling that if I hadn't approved, they would have ended the relationship that night.

She looked happy for the first time in a long time, and I decided that come what may, I'd protect her secret and support her newfound happiness. A few minutes later I was sitting in my room thinking about all that had just unfolded. Mama had shared something with me that had taken tremendous courage on her part. She had known the risk she had taken in telling me this secret of hers.

If I had reacted in another way, it could have driven a wedge between us that would have been hard to remove. She had trusted me, she had believed in me, and that made me feel like a million dollars. Another factor was evident: This man meant a great deal to her.

Mama came to my door and peeked in at me, and in her eyes I could see that a great load had been lifted from her. "If I call him, will you tell him what you just told me?" she asked. "I want him to hear it from you. I want him to know what a special person my son is."

I didn't want to. I mean, what would I say? But seeing the look on her face when she asked told me that it was important to her, so I said yes.

"He'll want to hear it from you, and he'll want to thank you."

"Okay, Mama, but he doesn't have to thank me."

She stood smiling, and dialed his number on the phone.

"Hi, it's me," she said, blushing as she spoke. "I have someone here who wants to talk to you." She handed me the phone. "Here, honey, say hello."

"Hello, sir," I said. "This is Gene."

"Hello, Gene. How are you?"

"I'm fine, sir, and you?"

"I'm fine, too, thanks." There was a pause as a little nervousness passed between us. "Do you remember me?" he asked.

"Yes sir, I remember you well."

"Your mama thinks the world of you. She loves you a lot."

"Yes sir, I know, and I love her a lot."

"This is a pretty awkward situation we're in here. I want you to know that I wouldn't do anything that would hurt you or your mama. I was worried that you might get hurt by the fact that she and I are—" He paused, trying to find the right words. "—friends." He paused again. "I love her."

"Yes sir."

"You don't have a problem with the fact that I'm a black man? Because if you do, I'd understand." There it was, the million-dollar question. Mr. Tucker came right out and asked it, no beating around the bush, no stammering or hem-hawing, just right out.

"No sir. Like I told Mama, if the color of your skin doesn't matter to her, it doesn't matter to me. If she loves you, then that's all that matters."

There was another pause, longer this time. "You're a remarkable young man, Gene. Your Mama told me that from the beginning, and she was right. I look forward to getting to know you better."

"What should I call you?"

"Tuck. My friends call me Tuck."

"Okay," I said. The fact that Tuck considered me his friend made me feel like a man.

"Can I talk to your mama again?"

"Yes sir." I handed her the phone and walked downstairs to the living room to give her some privacy. Mr. Tucker, on those few occasions I'd met him, struck me as a good and decent man. But my father had started out that way, too, and look what happened to him. However, Mr. Tucker seemed to be genuinely good and I looked forward to getting to know him.

Mama came back to my room. "Tuck wants to give you a present," she said.

"When?"

"Tonight."

"Is he coming here?"

"No. That would be too dangerous. You'll have to meet him somewhere else, somewhere close by."

"Am I meeting him alone?"

"Yes, honey. I can't afford to be seen with him."

With plans for my secret rendezvous with Tuck made, I put on my coat and left the apartment. It was exciting. I felt like a secret agent going into the backyard of my enemies to gather information. There was a chill in the night air so I covered my nose and mouth with a scarf, which also served to hide my identity. I walked east toward Kermit's hot dog stand. I glanced around making sure no one was following me.

Anderson House, Devonshire Street.

Sallie, with Gene, 18 months.

Grandma Anderson.

Grandpa Anderson.

Sally Anderson, age 18.

Cornelius Tucker, age 19.

Gene, age 5, with Santa.

Gene, left, with Larry, 1958.

Gene, age 10.

Gene, Randy, Tuck, 1961.

Courthouse, Winston-Salem.

Sally, Tuck, Randy, Greg, 1980.

Christmas, Hickory, North Carolina, 1994.

Evergreen Cemetery, Winston-Salem.

As I walked, I wondered, *What gift does Tuck want to give me? Why can't he come up to the apartment? What would happen to him if he did? Is Dad hiding somewhere in the dark? And what would Dad do if he did catch me with Tuck?* At the corner I turned right and walked south down Urban Street to the corner. Then, following the plan, I turned around and headed back up the street. A car turned the corner and crept toward me with its headlights off. It had to be Tuck.

I was halfway up the block when the Chevy turned its headlights on. Seconds later it pulled abreast of me. The passenger's window was open. Heart pounding, I stopped and glanced at the driver. Before I could make out his features in the darkness, I heard a voice whisper, "Happy birthday. Catch." Something flew out the window.

I caught the flying object. It was a new leather football, an official NFL model. The driver didn't stop. The car continued down the road, turned right, and sped away. I looked at the football. Could things get any stranger than this? I thought. A man drives by in a car and throws a football to a kid standing on the street. He can't just park the car and walk up to the door and say *Happy birthday*. Just because he's a black man. God, that didn't seem right. In order to give a white boy a present he had to sneak around like he was stealing chickens.

30

Don't Forget Me

"How's your mama, son?" Dad asked.

"She's fine."

"Does she have a boyfriend?"

"No."

"You ain't lying to me, are you?"

This was the first time I'd seen Dad since he'd been kicked out of the house in Union Cross. He had moved in with Grandma but she had cramped his style so now he was living in a fleabag motel on Fifth Street in downtown Winston-Salem. I didn't want to visit him, but Mama had insisted.

"I ain't lying, Dad," I said. "She doesn't have a boyfriend. I'd tell you if she did." He stared at me. I wondered if he already knew about Tuck. I figured if he did, he would go crazy and not be so coy about it.

"I've seen her driving around in a fancy car," he said. "Where did she get it?"

"It's Uncle Bill's car. He lets her drive it when he's on the road."

"If she starts seeing anyone, you'll tell me, won't you, son?"

"Sure."

"I still love your mama," he said, his voice cracking with emotion. "I've made my share of mistakes. But she shouldn't have kicked me out. Do you think it was right for her to kick me out, son?"

"I don't know, Dad. You guys couldn't get along and you fought all the time. Maybe this is for the best." *My God*, I thought, *who is the adult here?* Why would he ask me a question like that? What should I say? The truth? *She should have dumped you sooner.* That's what I should have said.

"I've stopped drinking," he said. "Tell that to your mama."

He must think I'm stupid and too blind to see the empty bottle of Ten High sitting on the dresser. "I will."

"And tell her that I have a steady job that pays good, see?" He pulled out a wad of bills. I stared, wondering where he got all that money. He peeled off twelve dollars and handed it to me. It was his first child support payment.

"Thanks, Dad," I said.

"Keep an eye on your mama for me, you hear. Next time you visit I want to know if she's seeing anyone."

"Okay, Dad."

"And next Saturday, I'll take you to the movies. How would you like that, son?"

"That'd be great."

We didn't go to the movies the next Saturday. Instead we went to a pool hall next to the Pep Boys auto parts store on Liberty Street. He shot pool and drank beer while I watched and drank Coca-Cola.

Had it not been for Mama I wouldn't have visited him at all, but I knew we needed the child support. What Mama made at the mill paid the rent and put food on the table, but there was nothing left over. The new clothes Uncle Bill had bought me last year at the start of school were what I was wearing now. I'd grown a lot since last year; my pants were all high waters, and my shirts were too tight. Though he had money to drink with, Dad never offered to buy me any clothes.

I hung around the pool hall long enough to get the twelve dollars, and told Dad good-bye.

"I'll see you next week, son. Maybe we'll go to a ball game or something."

"Yeah, Dad, that'll be fine. I'll see you then." *Ball game, my butt. We'll end up in some pool hall just like this week, but at least I have the child support money, and that's all that matters.*

I walked toward the main bus stop in front of the Mother and Daughter Department Store. While crossing the street in front of the courthouse, I heard someone yell, "Gene! Gene!" On the opposite corner waving at me was my first love and her mother. I ran over and gave Beth a big hug. It felt so good to feel her fresh peach skin and golden hair.

"Boy, it's good to see you," she said. Beth was wearing a light blue pleated skirt, a white buttondown shirt, a dark blue sweater, and white-and-black saddle oxfords. She was Rapunzel, the most beautiful girl who ever lived.

"You have no idea how good it is to see you." I brought her and her mom up to date about where we were living and my new school.

Mrs. Johnson smiled at me and said, "Tell your mama I said hello." Turning to Beth, she said, "Beth, honey, I'm going to walk over to Woolworth's. Why don't you and Gene go in Kress's and have a drink and get caught up. I'll meet you back here in thirty minutes."

At Kress's, Beth and I sat at the counter, and I bought us both a Cherry Smash with Dad's money. We talked and talked about school, the twins, and the young couple who had moved into Grandma's old house. I wanted to tell Beth about Tuck, but I couldn't, though I knew she wouldn't care.

The time flew by and I saw Mrs. Johnson standing outside. "Well, Gene Cheek, I guess I better go," said Beth. "I told you we'd see each other again." She leaned over and kissed me on the cheek. "You're still my best friend and I still love you, Gene Cheek. I'll see you again soon." Her indigo eyes glistened like new snow in the moonlight. "Don't forget me, okay?"

"I will never forget you," I said softly. "I'd sooner forget my own name than to forget you." With that, she turned and headed toward the door. "I love you, Beth." As she disappeared around the corner I fought back the tears and wondered if and when I'd see her again.

31

First Visit

On the night of my first visit with Tuck, I was as nervous as a cat in a
room full of rocking chairs. *What will I say? How should I act? What
if I say the wrong thing?* I had met him a few times before, but this
was the first time I was meeting him as the man who loved my mother,
the man she loved in return. *I don't know what to do. Heck, Gene,
there's only one thing you can do—just be yourself.*

That night Mama and I left the apartment after dark, our faces
muffled by coats and scarves. We walked down Urban Street and saw
Tuck drive past us. Then he doubled back and stopped. We hustled
into the car and sped away.

Once we left the neighborhood, Tuck looked in the rearview mirror and said, "Hi, Gene. Are you a little nervous?" He watched in the
mirror as I nodded my head up and down. "Me, too, but don't worry.
Things will be just fine. We'll get to my house, and then we can relax,
watch some TV or play a game or talk, whatever you want to do."

"Okay," I said. He smiled and his droopy mahogany eyes twinkled
in a way that told me not to worry. I relaxed, but only a little. It's not as
if we were like everyone else. A black man with a white woman and a
white boy? Where could we go together that wouldn't trigger threats
and admonishments and probable violence? We couldn't eat at a
downtown restaurant or shop at the department store or stroll in the
park together.

We couldn't do any of those things. All we could do was go to
Tuck's home, which was a one-bedroom house on Vargrave Street, one

block from the all-black Winston-Salem State Teachers College. As Tuck drove the car up Stadium Drive, he kept checking his rearview mirror to make sure no one was following us. When we reached Vargrave, he slowed the car and glanced down the street. He didn't turn but continued on. We went to the next stoplight. In front of us was the backside of the Salem College campus, an exclusive, all-white liberal arts college for girls. We drove through the entrance to the Old Salem Cemetery and turned around, leaving the same way we entered. Then Tuck turned down Vargrave, pulled the car into the second driveway on the right, and turned off the lights. We sat in the car for a few seconds before getting out.

His narrow home was what some called a shotgun house. It was called that because you could stand at the front door and shoot a shotgun through the house and hit the wall at the back of the house. It had white clapboard siding, white windows, a dark green front door, and green-and-white metal awnings over each of the single windows that faced the street.

We climbed the cement steps to the small covered front porch and waited for Tuck to unlock the front door. I stepped into his living room, which was furnished with a brown rug with a multicolored pattern, a brown upholstered couch, two upholstered rocking chairs, a TV, a small table and lamp, and a small cherry wood hi-fi and a case with dozens of albums featuring Nat King Cole, Moms Mabley, Billie Holiday, Redd Foxx, and Ella Fitzgerald, among others.

In the bedroom, which was about the size of the living room, a double bed, night table, and dresser rested on gray-and-white linoleum.

The kitchen had blue linoleum, a large white sink, and a blue kitchen table with chrome sides and four blue vinyl chairs.

After Tuck showed me around his small but neat home, his charm and genuine warmth relaxed my tangled nerves. "Make yourself at home," he said. We sat down in the living room, Mama on the couch, Tuck and I in the two rocking chairs.

"You want to listen to some music?" he asked. He got up without waiting for a reply and walked to the stereo. "What kind of music do you like?"

"All kinds."

"Well, I'll put on some I bet you haven't heard before. You ever heard of Billie Holiday?"

"No sir, I don't think so."

A salty mournful voice filled up the tiny living room, and we started talking about the extraordinary circumstances surrounding his and Mama's relationship and how the majority of the world would see it.

"There's nothing we can do about that. But we will have to be careful, real careful."

A haunting song poured out from the stereo and filled up my head with pictures.

> *Southern trees bear a strange fruit.*
> *Blood on the leaves and blood on the roots.*
> *Black body swinging in the southern breeze.*
> *Strange fruit hanging from the poplar tree.*

My God, I thought, *this song is about lynching*. "Is this about what I think it's about?" I asked.

"What do you think it's about?" Tuck asked me.

"Well, it sounds like it's describing a lynching."

"That's what it's about. A man named Abel Meeropol, a Jewish schoolteacher from New York, wrote it. I'm sorry if it upset you. I forgot it was on this album."

"No, that's okay. It's just so terrible to think about someone doing that to another human being. They don't do that anymore, do they? I mean, not around here. People don't do that here, do they?" I stammered.

Tuck turned off the stereo and looked at me. "They still do it. Not as much as they used to. It wasn't that long ago when they'd drag a man out of his house and hang him in front of his family. But times are changing, and men like Martin Luther King and others have brought it to the attention of the country. Hating is one thing; that can be done from a distance. But good people of all colors—people like your grandma, God rest her soul—ain't going to stand for people killing other people just because their skin is a different color."

We played checkers and three-handed rummy for the rest of the night. Tuck had stocked his refrigerator with Dr Pepper and his cupboard with Lay's potato chips. As we sat around the blue kitchen table playing cards, we talked about his family. Tuck was divorced and the father of three children, two sons and a daughter. His oldest son, Ernest, lived in New York City. His youngest son, Goot, who I'd met that night at the Dixie Classic fair, lived across town with his Mama. And Tuck's daughter, Martha Ann, and her husband, James, and their three small children, Kathy, Madison, and Cheryl, also lived in town.

It was easy to see how Mama had fallen in love with this man. His manner was easy and light and his laugh was quick. He was the most intelligent man I had ever met. No topic of discussion bored him. He talked about sports, current events, philosophy, and his favorite subject, the Bible. Like Grandma, Tuck believed that the answers to most of humanity's problems were in the Good Book.

Later that night, as we drove back to our apartment, any doubts I had about him as a man or as Mama's boyfriend were gone.

32

Friend to Friend

Every Saturday night, after my afternoon visit with Dad, we went to
Tuck's. My visits with Dad had become predictable, and they always
ended the same old way: I'd get the third degree. Today's visit had
been no different. I was sick of it, and I was sick of him. But he wasn't
going to pay child support unless I showed up to collect it, so I went. I
came home from these visits in a foul mood; it was like Dad's own
mood was communicable, and I always caught it. When I came in this
Saturday and told her about his ranting and accusations, Mama was
scared to death. She was afraid that he might be watching and following us. She was afraid if he found out about Tuck, he might do something drastic, like hurt Tuck or her.

"You think Dad would do that?" I asked her.

"I don't think he would. But he knows people who would."

"Who?" I asked.

"He knows men who are in the Ku Klux Klan."

"The people who wear robes and hoods and burn crosses? Dad
knows them?"

"They do more than just burn crosses. The Klan is responsible for
the death of a lot of black men in this country. You remember that song
the other night, 'Strange Fruit'?"

I nodded.

"Well, the Klan's the ones who have done most of the lynching."

"Would the Klan kill Tuck if they found out that he was your
boyfriend?"

She nervously bit her lower lip. "I don't know, honey. I don't know. That's why we're so careful when we visit him."

In many ways I was already more comfortable around Tuck than I had ever been with Dad. Tuck treated me like a friend. He and I had talked more in the few months I'd known him than my father and I had in eleven years. With Tuck, the conversation was friend to friend. Conversations with Dad had been nonexistent or short and one-sided—angry words from his mouth to my ears.

Regardless of what questions I asked or the subject of our conversation Tuck was always honest and never condescending. That night our conversation proved the point.

We were sitting around the kitchen table playing Chinese checkers when Mama brought up my visit with Dad and the third degree I was getting. "I hate him. If it wasn't for the money I'd just as soon never see him again," I said.

Tuck pushed back from the table and looked at me. "You can't hate your father, Gene, you just can't do that. You can disapprove of his life, you can disagree with the things he says, but you can't hate him. Hate is a powerful thing, and it does more harm than good to the hated as well as those who hate."

"Grandma told me that before she died."

"Your grandma was a very smart woman, and I don't want you to think I'm preachin' at you, but I know a little something about hate. Your daddy can't help the way he thinks. Now, that ain't no excuse for the way he behaves, but it's true as true can be. He was taught to hate. Everyone learns it from someone else, no one's born hating, they learn it. I guess your dad learned it from his dad, and your grandpa learned it from his, and so on down the line. But your grandma put an end to the line of hate that was handed down; she did that by the kind of life she led. And it would bother her very much if you got caught up in all that old hate."

I looked down at the table, and then at Mama. She was near tears, and there was a look of worry on her face. I knew Tuck was right just like I'd known Grandma had been right. I looked at Mama again, and then at Tuck and said, "I know you're right and I know Grandma was right, but sometimes I can't help the way I feel. But I'll try not to hate him."

"Well, that's all you can do is just try, try to understand the short-comings your dad has. He's human like the rest of us, and we all have our shortcomings. Now, what do you say we ride out to Papa Joe's and get some ice cream?"

There weren't many places the three of us could go together. The one place we could go, without worrying about what the reception might be, was the black business district. It spanned the length of North Patterson Avenue and Liberty Street. It was where we went to do the normal things others took for granted.

At first some of the neighborhood people were wary. A black man with a white woman and child was an unusual sight regardless of where you lived. They stared at first, but when they got used to seeing us and recognized Tuck, they didn't give us a second glance. We became a regular part of the community.

Papa Joe's was on North Patterson Avenue. The owner, Papa Joe, was an ex–football player with hands the size of hubcaps. He was a fun, joking man who loved to laugh and expected everyone around him to do the same.

When we'd pull up to the window, he'd flash his gentle grin and say, "Hello, Sallie. I see you and Gene are slumming today." Mama would smile and reply, "Yeah, Joe, the ice cream place in Buena Vista is closed today." We'd all laugh, Papa Joe the loudest. Buena Vista was the richest section of town.

To get to Papa Joe's from Tuck's, we had to drive through town, including several white neighborhoods. For that reason, we never went until after dark. This night, on our way there, we were stopped at a red light. I was on the left side of the car in the backseat behind Tuck. Mama was in the front and had on a black scarf to cover her face and hair.

A 1960 white Plymouth with three young white men in it pulled up beside us. The man on the passenger's side of the front seat looked over at me, and then at Tuck. He leaned forward to get a closer look, trying to see Mama. When he realized she was white, his face turned red. He started pointing at us, yelling at his friends. All three men were now staring at us. The man in the backseat rolled down his window and yelled, "Hey, nigger, what are you doing with that white woman and white boy?"

Tuck didn't reply. He kept his eyes straight ahead and his hands on the steering wheel.

"Boy, I'm talking to you," the man said. "What the hell you doing with them?"

Again, Tuck didn't respond except to roll up the window. "Just stay calm and look straight ahead," he said to us as we waited for the light to change to green. The wait seemed like an eternity.

"Who are they, Mama?"

"I don't know, honey."

Tuck said, "Just a bunch of young kids acting foolish." When the light turned green, Tuck switched lanes and turned right onto East Sixteenth Street. The other car switched lanes and followed us.

"They're coming after us," I whimpered.

Tuck took a left turn. The Plymouth kept tailing us.

"Oh, my God," Mama said.

"Don't worry," Tuck said. "They can't do anything to us as long as we're in the car." Somehow he remained calm. It occurred to me that this was nothing new to him. Getting cussed and chased by white men was just a way of life for most black men in the South. Seeing Tuck with a white woman and a boy infuriated them more, but we were just a good excuse to do what was being done anyway.

Meanwhile Mama and I were both scared to death; this was a new experience for us. In a small way, I was getting my first glimpse of how it felt to be hated. Just as the car caught up with us, the light ahead turned red.

"Pull over, nigger!" the driver shouted.

Tuck glanced both ways and sped through the intersection, ignoring the red light. The Plymouth sped up and tried to run us off the road. Tuck took a sharp right turn. The tires squealed through the turn as he raced down the narrow residential street. Houses, hedges, and light poles flew by us in a blur. The Plymouth hung on our tail. "Oh, crap," Tuck said. "This can't go on forever. Their car is too fast for me to lose them."

"Oh, my God," Mama said, clutching the door handle as Tuck flew through another intersection. I was shaking with terror now. We were in the middle of God knows where. Behind us was a faster car filled with wild-eyed stupid kids who could be armed and might do anything.

Tuck knew he couldn't lose them, and he knew he couldn't let them stop us. Without signaling, he veered left and flew down Cleveland Avenue. He seemed to know where he was going as the Chevy roared down the narrow residential streets. We ripped through another intersection, and then I realized we were in Colored Town. I heaved a sigh of relief, hoping this would at least make the punks think twice. The white car pulled up beside us, trying to get in front of Tuck.

Mama gasped and gripped the door handle tighter.

"Don't worry," Tuck, said. "We're almost there." He made a sharp right and again floored the gas pedal, the engine whining and tires screaming.

"Where are we going?" Mama asked.

"To Martha Ann and James's house," Tuck said. "It's our only hope." A moment later Tuck turned off the headlights, swerved into a gravel driveway, and stopped behind a black pickup truck. Peering out the back window, I saw the Plymouth continue down the street. Just when I thought we were safe, the driver of the Plymouth slammed on the brakes. Smoke billowed from the screeching tires, and two men jumped out, leaving the driver behind the wheel, engine still running. The men started walking toward us.

As they neared the car, my heart pounded in my chest. In my mind I saw them dragging Tuck out of the car and beating him to death and then doing the same to Mama and me.

"Quick! Duck down," Tuck ordered. We crouched in the car out of view. Tuck began blowing the horn until lights came on in the little house. I peeked over the seat and saw a tall black man with broad shoulders appear at the door. It was Martha Ann's husband James, standing in his pajamas on the porch. *Thank God*, I thought, *those boys will think twice now.*

"What the hell is going on out here?" James shouted when he saw the two white men approaching our car.

"James, it's me!" Tuck yelled. "Get your gun!" James rushed back into the house.

"Get back!" one of the white men yelled. "The nigger's gonna get a gun!" The two men scrambled back into the car just as James appeared with his pistol in his hand.

"You boys better run home to your mamas!" he yelled, a note of delight in his voice.

"We'll get you one of these days, nigger!" the driver yelled as the car shot down the street and disappeared around a corner.

33

Shut Up, Boy

"Son, are you sure your ma doesn't have a boyfriend, a nigger maybe?"

Oh my God, here we go again. "Oh, come on, Dad, be serious," I said.

"Don't lie to me now," he snapped. He took a swig from a Pabst Blue Ribbon. Empties had been thrown around the cavelike room where the drawn blinds kept the sunlight out and his misery in. The room was hot and smelled like dirty socks, beer, sweat, and cigarette butts.

"I swear, Dad, I don't know what you're talking about." *Where is this coming from? He knows something. This is more than just some drunken talk about a boyfriend. I wonder if he knows someone who drives a white Plymouth.*

"If she left me for a nigger," he said, "I'll kill the bitch."

I boiled. I wanted to tell him to kiss my ass, and then get up and leave. But I thought of my conversation with Tuck. Besides, we needed the child support money, and I knew if I upset him, I wouldn't get it. As it was, he paid whatever he felt like, whenever he felt like it. As he continued giving me the third degree, I just kept denying everything. I figured if he knew anything for sure, he would have already done something. He wouldn't just be sitting around throwing out accusations. He would have the Klan on the case.

The phone rang. It was Uncle Bobby. He wanted Dad to come over and help him with something. Before I left, he handed me five dollars. "This is for you, son," he said. "Don't give any of it to that bitch."

"I won't," I said, though I knew I'd hand it to her the minute I walked in.

"I'll be leaving this dump soon," he said. "I'm moving back in with your grandma. Would you like to come live with us?"

I started to say what came into my mind: *Hell, no!* But I didn't want to make it worse than it already was, so I said, "But I like my school."

"There are schools where Grandma lives, too," he said.

"Well, let me think about it."

"Sure, son. Take your time. But tell that bitch that from now on I ain't paying no more child support. And tell her I'm going to kill that nigger she's with."

When I got home and told Mama what he'd said, we increased our already "Top Secret" precautions. That night we rode the bus downtown. After we walked past the parking lot of the City Market, Tuck pulled to the curb and we got in and rode to his house.

Tuck and I talked while Mama made supper. "You know, I love America. I fought for this country during World War II. When we were fighting against the Nazis, I figured that we were fighting for freedom. We believed that when we came back home we'd be treated as equals. But that didn't happen. In fact, in some ways it got worse. We couldn't even wear our uniforms in public when we got back. When I was discharged in 1946 the people at Fort Bragg told us not to leave the base in our uniforms because blacks were being beaten and stripped of their medals and even the buttons on their coats. Most people don't want to accept us as human beings; they can't see beyond the color of our skin. We're still faced with the same racist stuff we faced before we fought and died for this country."

"Will things ever change?"

"Yes, they'll change; people can only take so much. Everyone has a breaking point, and blacks have reached that point. We have a right to be treated like humans because we're Americans, too. That's what the civil rights movement is all about. And if we aren't given equal rights and treated like humans, I'm afraid there's gonna be trouble in America."

"What kind of trouble?"

"Black people might stop listening to Dr. King's nonviolent approach and start listening to Malcolm X. He's—"

Before he could finish his sentence, the front door flew open and two white policemen, guns drawn, stormed inside. "Don't nobody move!" ordered the taller of the two cops, aiming his gun at Tuck's head. I stared at them in shock. It was like a TV show, surreal. This didn't happen in America, did it?

"There must be some mistake," Tuck said, his hands in the air.

"Shut up, boy. Your black ass made the mistake."

Mama came to the doorway. "What's going on?" she asked.

"What are you doing here, nigger lover?" one of the cops said.

Mama was tongue-tied.

"Why aren't you with your husband?"

"I don't have a husband," Mama said.

The tall policeman said, "Don't you know it's a crime for you to be living with a nigger?"

"My son and I don't live here. We're friends of Mr. Tucker's."

"Yeah, sure, you're friends. And my partner and me, we're the Lone Ranger and Tonto."

"Do you have a warrant to come barging into my house?" Tuck said with a calmness that surprised me, considering the two policemen looked like they were ready to shoot us all. I was petrified, unable to fathom why policemen would act this way. If I hadn't been seeing it with my own eyes, I wouldn't have believed it.

"Don't get uppity with me now, boy," the cop snapped. "Don't you know we can arrest you right this minute?"

"On what charge?"

"Sleeping with a white woman."

"Did you find us sleeping?"

"Are you getting smart with me, nigger?" the tall policeman said, again pointing his gun at Tuck. "You know I can shoot you for resisting arrest?"

"I'm not resisting arrest," Tuck said. "I just asked you a simple question. Were you planning on shooting the woman and boy also?" The cop ignored the remark.

"Don't make them angry, Tuck. Gene and I were about to leave anyway."

"I'll take you home," Tuck said.

"No, nigger," the short policeman said. "We'll take her home."

As the two policemen led us toward the police car, I noticed Mr. and Mrs. Woods—Tuck's neighbors and friends—out in their yard looking toward Tuck's house. Tuck stood on the porch, mad as hell but helpless to do anything. As we were getting into the car, I caught a glimpse of someone hiding in the shadows. I looked again, double-checking to make sure.

On the way to our apartment, the taller policeman said to Mama, "You ought to be ashamed of yourself, bringing a white child to Nigger Town."

"Why should I be ashamed? I've raised my son to respect all people."

"That's no place for a white child," the policeman said.

"Why is that?"

"Niggers live there, that's why," the policeman said. "It's wrong."

Wrong? You want to talk about wrong? I thought. *You're the ones who are wrong. If you would just get to know these people, you'd see they're no different from anyone else. Hating them because of their skin color—now that's wrong.*

"How did you know we were there?" Mama asked.

"We got a call."

"Who called you?"

"That's confidential information," the short policeman said. I already knew the answer to that one, but I didn't say anything. The tall policeman then said to Mama, "And let me warn you—if we can prove that you and that nigger are more than just friends, both of you will be locked up for a long time." The policemen dropped us at the apartment and drove off.

As we took off our coats, Mama began to cry. "Why can't they just leave us alone? We're not hurting anyone. You'd think we were criminals."

"I know who made that call to the police," I said.

"Who, honey?"

"Dad. I saw him outside Tuck's house. He was sitting in Uncle Bobby's car. It was parked down the street a little way, but I saw him. I wanted to say something, but I was afraid the police would hear me."

She let out a heavy sigh. "I should have known. He's done it before."

"He has?"

"Yes." She then told me how, after their separation, she had stopped by Tuck's to ask him if he'd put up the basketball hoop for my tenth birthday. It was Easter Monday. While she and Tuck were talking, there had been a knock on the door. Tuck opened it and there stood my father, half drunk. He accused Mama of "shacking up with a nigger," and when she denied it, a fierce argument erupted. That attracted the attention of neighbors, so someone called the police. When they came, Dad walked across the street to Uncle Bobby's car, and they drove away. And the police made her leave.

When she finished telling me about that confrontation, I understood where all this "nigger boyfriend" talk was coming from. And now with this stuff today I dreaded the thought of visiting Dad again.

As if reading my mind, she said, "You don't have to go see your dad anymore if you don't want to, honey. He ain't gonna pay child support now, no way."

We needed that money more than ever. The day before Mama had received a warning from the landlord that she was behind in the rent, and if she didn't pay it, we'd be evicted. She could have paid our rent on time if we'd been getting the child support. But now Tuck was all the reason Dad would need not to pay it.

The financial pressure that we were under came to a head two days later when Mama came home from work crying.

"What's wrong?"

"I've been fired, honey," she said.

"Fired? Why?"

"Someone told the owner of the mill about me and Tuck."

"Was Tuck fired, too?"

"Yes."

"Do you know who told the owner?"

"Maybe the police. Maybe your dad. I don't know."

"You'll find another job, Mama, don't worry—a better job than working at that godawful mill."

She wiped her eyes with a tissue and, with a look of desperation on her face, said, "I hope you're right, honey, I hope you're right."

For a week she sat at the kitchen table first thing every morning, studying the want ads. She'd circle jobs and spend all morning on the phone. In the afternoon she'd take Uncle Bill's car on the interviews. On the eighth day she walked into the house, and I could see a weight had been lifted.

"Good news, honey. I got a job today."

"That's great, I knew you would. Where at?"

"At Kress's five and dime downtown. I'm going to be working in the cosmetics department. It's just part time to start and it doesn't pay what I was making at the mill, but it's a job and we'll get by somehow."

We didn't know it at the time, but Mama's firing was the opening shot in an all-out war that was about to be waged against us. Her firing sealed our fate concerning the apartment on Waughtown. We had been living from hand to mouth since we'd left Union Cross, and the time she went without a paycheck broke the camel's back. We had to move, and soon.

34

The Garden

Our day-to-day, hand-to-mouth existence was nothing new. Our life had been one step forward and two steps back for as long as I could remember. Since Grandma died, it was one forward and three back. No matter how hard Mama tried, we couldn't get our heads above the waterline. As bad as these days seemed, they were about to become even worse

One afternoon in January 1962, a few months before my eleventh birthday, Mama made an announcement that would change our lives forever.

"You know Tuck and I love each other," she began.

"Yes."

"Well, when two people love each other, sometimes they have a baby together."

"A baby?" I shouted. "You mean I'm gonna be a big brother?"

"Yes. I don't know if it's a girl or a boy, but you're going to be a big brother soon." I was thrilled, and all I heard was *you're going to be a big brother*. Nothing else registered, and nothing else mattered. I already considered Tuck a father figure. I respected him, I trusted him, and I loved him. As far as I knew, the diaper commercials were accurate: Someone wants a baby and the stork delivers it, with a free week's worth of diapers.

Not that it mattered, nor would it have made any difference to me, since I knew Tuck and Mama loved each other; it was evident in everything they did. But the mechanics of where babies came from and how they were created were lost on me. I just didn't know much about the birds and the bees.

"When will the baby come?" I asked, beside myself with joy and excitement.

"In a few months," she said.

"Can I help you take care of the baby?"

She smiled. "Yes, and you'll be a big help to me, and a wonderful brother."

As I chattered away about all the things I'd teach my baby brother or sister—fishing, catching frogs, riding a bicycle, going to baseball games—Mama listened and laughed. I didn't realize at the time how much courage it had taken for her and Tuck to stand by each other during this time. I also didn't realize the changes the baby would bring.

What was more remarkable, and something I wouldn't find out until years later, was that they did know the changes that a baby would bring. And yet they never considered not bringing this baby into the world. They didn't do what at the time could have been done: find a back-alley abortionist to end the pregnancy. That fact more than any-thing else should have proven to the world the depth of their love for each other, and the strength of their character.

Several days after Mama's amazing news, Tuck and his brother James rented a truck and moved us to a new apartment. It was in a new low-income housing project called Piedmont Gardens. The Gardens, as it was called, stood on the north side of town on Liberty Street. The housing project was the first racially mixed neighborhood I'd ever lived in. It had an equal number of whites and blacks living side by side on the same streets. There was one thing we all had in common: We were dirt-poor. Mama wanted to help move, but Tuck refused to let her lift a finger. He told her to stay home and rest.

Tuck, his son-in-law James, and I did the moving and lifting. After we'd moved everything in, James drove Tuck back to his house and dropped me off at the apartment. That night, after dark, we left the apartment on Waughtown Street for the last time. We caught the bus into Old Salem, and Tuck picked us up at the entrance to the old graveyard. After supper at Tuck's place, Mama wasn't feeling well. So

Tuck and I left her lying on the couch, her feet resting on a pillow, and drove back to the new apartment to unpack.

The two-story redbrick apartment with white trim and a tiny covered porch was the nicest place we'd ever lived in, except for the house in Union Cross. The living room had blue wall-to-wall carpet, a first for us. Next to the living room was a small kitchen with natural maple cabinets, gold-specked countertops, a stainless-steel sink, and new appliances. In the little dining area just off the kitchen, a sliding glass door opened onto a tiny cement porch and a sidewalk that ran behind each unit and joined them all together.

The apartment complex had a playground with swings, sliding boards, seesaws, and a cement basketball court, which was a good thing considering there wasn't much of a yard. A row of crab apples grown together like a hedgerow separated the tiny backyard from a large field that ran parallel to Liberty Street.

I stared out the back door of the duplex at the open field behind the hedgerow. It reminded me of the fields behind our house on Brookline, and it looked like a great place to explore. I was grateful to be living in such a nice neighborhood. The area around the apartment on Waughtown was a city neighborhood; this was a real neighborhood, and it was going to be a fine place to run and romp, and ride my old magic bike.

Tuck came and stood beside me. He saw the crab apples and said, "Come here and let me show you something." He took a long, sturdy, limber switch from the hedgerow and with his Swiss army knife sharpened one end. I watched, curious. He picked up one of the dark red-and-yellow crab apples that had fallen to the ground and stuck it on the sharp end of the switch. "Now, you have to be careful not to hit anything," he said with a mischievous smile. "These things can break a window easy." With that, he drew back the switch and, with a quick whiplike motion, launched the crab apple.

"Wow!" I said watching it sail out of sight. It was a new game and a new use for all those crab apples—and it was free. Tuck and I walked around to the car, grabbed the last two boxes, and carried them to the front door and up the stairs. Both bedrooms and the bathroom were on the second floor. Mama's was on the right of the bathroom, and mine was on the left. Once we finished with those last two boxes, Tuck said, "You and your mama should be happy here, don't you think?"

"Yeah," I said. "It's a nice place. The nicest place we've lived in except for Grandma's house in Union Cross."

"And when the baby comes, you'll help your mama take care of him, right?"

"I sure will," I said. We made sure everything was in its place, then Tuck locked the door and we walked to his car. "You must be hungry from all the hard work you've done today," he said. "Let's me and you grab a cheeseburger."

We drove to Papa Joe's and had cheeseburgers and fries and strawberry milk shakes. Tuck bought Mama a hot dog and fries and headed back to his house. "I hope you didn't mind having to change schools again."

"Nah, we weren't that far into the school year and I didn't know too many kids in my class." I'd moved so many times in the last few years that I was used to being the new kid and feeling out of place. It wasn't as big a deal as it used to be.

"Good," Tuck said. "Your new school is just a few blocks from the apartment. It's called Lowrance; it'll be a nice walk, not too far at all."

On the drive back to his place, Tuck stopped the car suddenly. "What's the matter?" I asked.

"Nothing," he said. "Somebody lost part of their load of firewood, and I'm going to get it. Free wood burns just as good as wood I have to buy."

Tuck was eccentric like that, in quaint charming ways. He was, to put it politely, thrifty. Mama, not so polite, told him he was tighter than ten pounds of potatoes in a five-pound sack. He never filled up his gas tank, choosing instead to buy a couple of gallons at a time. He might have pockets full of money, but he'd stop and get fifty cents' worth of gas. He had an old army trunk in the hallway of his house that was his version of a bank. He put in it what he called "a little piece of money," saving it for "a rainy day."

When it came to food, he would splurge a little. He and I would go to W. G. White's, a one-of-a-kind mercantile store on North Cherry Street in downtown Winston-Salem. Tuck and I could walk around town together without drawing the hateful stares that he and Mama attracted. It was acceptable for a white boy to be watched by a black man. Everyone just assumed Tuck was my rich white father's "boy."

W. G. White's was across from the Big Bear supermarket and the City Market, where we'd met him when we thought we needed to be supersecret. They specialized in meats, sausages, country hams, rock candy, fruits and nuts, beans in barrels, and all sorts of things you just didn't see anywhere else.

Tuck would buy expensive country ham or sausage, saying, "We deserve to have at least a D taste." *D*—that was his way of saying *damn*. He didn't cuss much unless he got worked up over something, and then *damn* was as bad as he could cuss.

He was also very proud of his personal appearance;. "If you run around in raggedy clothes, nobody's gonna take you serious." Sometimes, after going to W. G. White's, we walked a few blocks to the R. J. Reynolds building to get our shoes shined. He kept his hair short and well groomed and kept his mustache and "Soul patch"—as he called his goatee—well shaped. He even gave himself manicures. His house was always spotless and so was his car, which was always washed, waxed, and clean inside. He was everything my father was not.

35

Chocolate Milk

On June 16, 1962, my dream of becoming a brother came true. Mama, sensing the time was at hand, sent me to Aunt Goldie's on Friday to spend the weekend. Aunt Goldie knew only what the rest of the family had been told—that she was having a baby and the father was dead.

Tuck took Mama to City Hospital after her water broke on Saturday night. He couldn't go in. All he could do was help her to the emergency room door and watch while the woman he loved, who was about to give birth to his child, waddled into the hospital alone.

Mama gave her name as Sallie Spainhour, and listed the father, a fictional truck driver, as deceased. Sometime Saturday night, Randy Steven Spainhour was born to a woman named Sallie who had no insurance and no husband. Randy was light-skinned, the color of chocolate milk, but there was no mistaking his heritage. His light brown curly hair and his color gave him away. Aunt Goldie came into my cousin's room where I was sleeping, woke me up, and told me matter-of-factly that I had a baby brother. I lay awake the rest of the night, thrilled at the news.

Mama lay awake, too, but scared out of her wits in an all-white hospital under an assumed name and with a beautiful brown baby son. Aunt Goldie left the next morning for the hospital. Mama had begged her not to, but she was going anyway. Why was Sallie being so secretive about the baby? Why didn't she want anyone coming to the hospital? Those were questions that Aunt Goldie kept asking. Society, especially in the South, had no sympathy for Mama. It was a shameful thing that she was having a baby because it wasn't her husband's, never mind that she was separated from him.

The secrecy and the never-ending safety measures we practiced each time we visited Tuck were about to be exposed. Aunt Goldie parked her Mercury in the parking lot of City Hospital and walked to the front desk. She asked for the room number for Sallie Spainhour. Mama had explained the use of the fictitious name by saying she was ashamed for having a baby out of wedlock and didn't want to bring shame to her family. Aunt Goldie went to Mama's room and found her holding her baby son.

"Goldie, what are you doing here?"

"Well, I came to see you and make sure you were all right. You're in here alone. I couldn't just sit by and let that happen, not to my sister."

"But you shouldn't have come. I'm going to be sent home this afternoon. You could have come by the house."

Goldie, unaware that she was about to discover a secret, said, "Well, I'm here, so let me see the baby."

Mama protested, made excuses, and tried to discourage Goldie, but it was inevitable. Reluctantly, she handed her newborn son to Aunt Goldie. She cradled the infant and pulled back the blanket that had been covering his face. Goldie gasped in shock. Here in her arms lay a baby boy with kinky light brown hair as soft as rabbit's fur, little mahogany eyes that sparkled, and skin the color of chocolate milk. In a voice shaking with panic, Goldie blurted, "Sallie, this baby ain't white!"

"I know, Goldie, but he's still my son." There. The secret was out. There was nothing more to hide.

Recovering from her shock, Goldie asked, "My God, Sallie, what are you going to do?"

"Well, I'm going to raise my sons."

It was not in her nature to do otherwise. She was not going to turn her back on her children. She wouldn't run away. She would do the right thing because that's how she'd been raised.

Goldie handed Randy back to her sister, and with tears in her eyes and her head shaking in disbelief walked out of the hospital—and out of Mama's life forever. Goldie then picked me up at her house and drove me to the Gardens. When I arrived home, she said, "Now you stay inside. Your mama's going to be home in a little while." Then Aunt Goldie drove out of my life, too. It had begun.

Mama came home that afternoon in a Blue Bird cab with my baby brother.

"Honey, this is Randy Steven," she said, beaming. "Your little brother."

"Can I hold him?" I asked.

"Sure, honey."

Randy felt light and fragile in my arms. He was fast asleep, his precious little face so peaceful. I touched his soft skin. At my touch, his eyes fluttered open. He peered up at me with those beautiful innocent eyes and stole my heart. "Why is he twisting his mouth around, Mama?"

"He's hungry. Babies need to eat a lot."

"Should I make him some scrambled eggs and toast?" Mama and Grandma had both taught me how to cook because, as Mama once said, "You can't be expecting your wife to do all the cooking."

Mama smiled. "I know you make a good breakfast, honey. But babies can't eat scrambled eggs and toast. They need milk." She showed me how to make Randy's formula, and how to fill and warm the bottle. Later she was sitting on the couch, feeding Randy, when someone knocked on the door. I walked over and opened it, and in walked Uncle Bill.

I was happy to see him, but the minute I saw the look on his face I knew something was wrong. He'd just returned from the road, and it was evident he'd talked to Goldie. "I came to see for myself, Sallie," he said, without so much as a hello.

"See what, Bill?" Mama said, tears coming to her eyes as she sat on the couch feeding Randy.

"You know. I went by Goldie's and she told me you had a nigger baby."

The words hit me like a brick, and I stood glaring at Uncle Bill, my hero.

"He's my son, Bill. Gene's brother and your nephew."

"Ain't no nigger baby any kin of mine—and from today on, you're no longer my sister."

I was stunned. *There's no way Uncle Bill said that. I must be hearing things. He looks so upset. I've never seen his face like that. He's saying things that aren't in his heart; they can't be. I can't believe what I'm hearing. Never in a million years would I have ever expected this, not from Uncle Bill.* I started to cry.

"I'll always be your sister, Bill."

"No, you're not, not anymore you ain't."

"Why ain't Mama your sister, Uncle Bill?" I asked, tears running down my face and my heart breaking.

"You're too young to understand, honey," he said, now near tears himself.

"No, I'm not," I said. It tore at my heart to see Uncle Bill and Mama like this. I knew how much they loved each other. This wasn't right; nothing could justify this.

"Tell him, Bill. There's no reason to hide anything from him. He knows everything, I've never kept the truth from Gene."

"Your Mama is a nigger lover, honey," Uncle Bill said.

"That's not true," I cried. "Tuck loves Mama. He's a good man, and he's my friend."

My declaration stunned Uncle Bill. He took a long look at me. "I love you, honey," he said. "And I love your mama, too. But I don't want any niggers in my family."

He turned to Mama and said, "So it's your choice, Sallie. Which will it be? We can stay together as a family, just like we've always been, or you can choose that nigger over your family."

I looked at Mama. She was in agony and her heart was broken. I knew how much she loved Uncle Bill and how much Mama and Tuck loved each other. Why was this coming down to a choice? There was no choice to be made; we were all family, and families stick together. Uncle Bill could have been mad and cussed and raised hell, but to disown his sister was just not what Grandma had raised her children to do.

For a long time Mama said nothing. Tears fell from her eyes and soaked the blanket Randy was wrapped in. I saw tears in Uncle Bill's eyes. Seeing the two people I loved the most in the world crying because they were about to lose each other turned me inside out. I couldn't stand it.

I was wailing now like I had at Grandma's funeral. Why did Mama have to choose? Why couldn't we all be a family? Randy is my brother and Tuck is my friend. Why can't Uncle Bill accept that? Both men have such good hearts and love Mama and me. Why did the color of Tuck's skin matter so much?

Mama wiped her tears away. "This is the second worst day of my life, Bill," she said. "The worst was when Mama died. I love you and always will. But I also love Tuck and I love my sons—both of them. And if loving them means losing you, so be it."

Uncle Bill didn't say a word. He turned and walked out the door and out of our lives. After he left, we held each other tight and wept as if someone had died.

So the die was cast; we had been disowned. There we were—just Tuck, Mama, Randy, and me, seemingly against the world.

"I'm sorry things came to this, Gene," Tuck said to me after dinner at his house. "I never meant to cause your mama and you any pain."

"It's not your fault," I said. "If Uncle Bill and Aunt Goldie could get to know you, they'd feel different."

"It's a sad, sad thing, but too often people see what they want to see. To some people, the color of my skin is all they see and they never look beyond that. I was thinking maybe we should move north somewhere so your mama and I could get married," Tuck said. "We could live together as a family, and not have to look over our shoulder all the time. What would you think about that?"

"I wouldn't mind, I guess, but ain't there people who hate up north?"

"Of course. There are people who hate everywhere."

"Then what good would it do for us to move?"

"Your mama and me could get married without breaking any laws. You wouldn't mind if I married your mama, would you?"

"No," I said. "I think you two should get married."

He smiled. "Then we'll look into moving up north. We'll make plans and talk about it some more." I was convinced that Tuck would be a good husband to Mama because it was obvious he loved and respected her. And I knew he'd be a good dad to Randy and a good stepfather to me. I admired and respected him. He was a decent man with a wonderful sense of humor. He was a proud man who walked with dignity and held his head high. Despite living in a Jim Crow world, he bowed to no man. He was a Mason, a "Keeper of the Seal," a high honor, and wore his ring with pride. He volunteered and worked at his church, where he was a senior usher. He was a well-respected member of his community who could be counted on to lend a hand.

I had no doubt he'd make a wonderful stepfather. But I wondered, as I put a stack of clean dishes in the cabinet, if the white world of the South would ever allow him the opportunity to prove my judgment of him. It pained me that he was denied the same God-given rights that most Americans took for granted.

36

Leaving the Gardens

Late in the summer of 1962 Mama went back to work, but with no one to take care of Randy during the week, she could only work weekends. We'd go to Tuck's house on Friday afternoons and Mama would drive his car to work. She worked until the store closed on Fridays and all day on Saturdays. Since Randy's birth, I hadn't visited my dad; to do so would have been pure torture. He had never been willing to pay child support, and now he had a reason not to: Randy. Several times he had been brought before a judge, and each time Dad promised he would pay. But he didn't, even after he twice had been threatened with jail.

We needed the money Dad was obligated to pay in child support. In all, he was over four hundred dollars behind. So on a warm October day I took the bus across town. I got off at the corner of Waughtown and Old Thomasville Road and walked about a mile to Grandma's house. When I stepped into the house, I expected the worst—and I wasn't disappointed. The moment I sat down on the sofa, Dad and Grandma moved in like vultures and perched themselves on either side of me.

"You know your mama is a nigger lover, don't you?" Dad snarled.

"No sir."

"And do you know that she's living in sin?"

"No sir."

"She sure is," Grandma Cheek said. "She's sinned against God and nature by having that mongrel baby. She's going to burn in hell."

"But before she goes to hell," Dad declared, "she'll go to jail."

"What do you mean?" I asked.

"Someone told me it's against the law in North Carolina for her to have a mongrel baby. If I wanted to, I could go down to the police station right this minute and tell them to arrest her and that damn nigger."

"Maybe you should, son," Grandma said. "She's a disgrace."

I listened to this hate boil out of them while I seethed. It was no use to say anything. Hate and ignorance this deep couldn't be overcome with a few words from an eleven-year-old boy. I knew if I protested, I wouldn't get any money and I might end up making things worse. So I sat as if I were stone deaf and endured their bashing.

"So your nigger-loving mama wants me to pay child support, huh?"

"Yes sir."

"I bet she'll spend it on that mongrel baby," Grandma said.

"Tell her to go to hell," he said, glaring at me. "I ain't giving her a penny. Why don't that dirty nigger support you? In fact, tell your mama and that nigger to go to Mississippi. They know how to take care of niggers and nigger lovers down there."

He was talking about the recent riots and killings in Oxford, Mississippi. James Meredith had become the first black man to enroll in Ole Miss, and it wasn't sitting well with the Mississippians—at least not the white ones, and their opinions were the only ones that mattered there. The riots that followed had cost two blacks their lives, while seventy-five others had been injured and hundreds were arrested. Mama, Tuck, and I had watched CBS News with Walter Cronkite as he reported on the chaos in Mississippi. We watched President Kennedy plead for a peaceful solution. John Fitzgerald Kennedy was a hero in our house. "He's a great man who has a heart for the colored people in this country." That's what Tuck said about the president.

Mama worshiped the ground the man walked on, and said of him, "You can see it in his eyes when he talks. It comes from the heart."

I ignored Dad's reference to Mississippi. As I got up to leave, he said, "Tell your nigger-loving mama that she'll hear from me. I'll make her pay for what she's done. I swear I'll make her pay."

Seemed to me, I thought as I walked back toward the bus stop, he'd already made her pay more than enough.

Mama, Randy, and I made it through the rest of 1962 by the skin of our teeth, but by the spring of 1963 the housing authority was breathing down Mama's neck for $11.20 in back rent. We had to move—again. I was devastated. Piedmont Gardens had become more than a house. I was happy there, and had made friends with every kid in the sprawling project. We raced each other around the quiet streets on our bikes, played basketball, and romped in the common playground, never noticing the differences in the color of our skin.

"I'm sorry we have to keep moving," Mama said. "I know it's hard on you. But we have no choice."

We found a place in one of the poorest neighborhoods in town, and Tuck and James helped us move in. It was a small two-bedroom house near the corner of Moravian Street and Old Lexington Avenue in East Winston-Salem. The house was a smaller, inner-city version of the old farmhouse in Kernersville, but worse. It sat on cinder blocks. It had peeling, warped clapboard siding and double-hung windows with sheets of plastic covering up holes where the glass should have been.

A large oak tree was the only living thing in the hard-packed dirt front yard. For days I moped around. I hated the house and I hated the neighborhood. Old Lexington Avenue, with its never-ending roar of traffic, was less than fifty feet from our front door. We couldn't have been more poverty-stricken. There were a few things that made the old dilapidated house somewhat tolerable. One was Tuck's aunt, who lived just down the street. She kept an eye on us and helped care for Randy. Another was the recreation center. It had a nice baseball field and a basketball court. Then there was Mr. Clyde, the Pied Piper of the neighborhood. Whenever he drove up in his old produce-laden pickup, people young and old crowded around. Mr. Clyde was a white farmer who was liked and respected by everyone. He was conscious of just one color—green. He hawked his wares to anyone who could buy them. After doing business with folks for a while and getting to know them, he'd let them have stuff without paying, saying, "You can catch up with me next week."

With what little money we had, Mama relied on Mr. Clyde's fresh produce and liberal credit practices. Our kitchen table sported something from his farm daily: squash, okra, tomatoes, green beans and corn, homemade sweet-cream butter, fresh eggs, and the best country ham that ever graced a southern breakfast table.

The neighborhood was all black with the exception of us and two other families. The house to our right belonged to a white family, the Shells. They were rabid racists who wouldn't even talk to us after they'd seen little Randy. The one on the left belonged to a single white mother, Mrs. Poteat, and her daughter, Molly, who were both friendly country folks.

To white society we couldn't have sunk any lower. By moving into this seedy part of town, and by Mama having a mixed baby, it seemed as though we had lost our membership in the human race.

On Wednesday night, August 28, 1963, we were sitting in Tuck's living room watching the nightly news. The Reverend Martin Luther King Jr. had given a speech on the steps of the Lincoln Memorial, and they were showing excerpts. The grounds in front of him were carpeted with men, women, and children, mostly black but some white. I listened to his words: "I have a dream that my four children will one day live in a nation where they will be not be judged by the color of their skin but the content of their character. I have a dream . . ." I sat and took it all in. The crowd roared at Dr. King's words, and my own hopes soared.

Next to me, in an old worn-out rocking chair, was a man who looked nothing like me. I had known him now for eighteen months. In that time I had come to respect him, love him, and admire him. He treated me like I was his own son and more importantly he treated me as a friend. All that had been required of me was to give my "Secret Friend" a chance. Was that too much to ask? "If you want to know what kind of person a man is, give him a chance to show you," Tuck once told me. It seemed so simple, but in a world of bigots, it was out of the question. Was it possible for a man such as Dr. King to change all that?

One week later my strings to Dr. King's dream were cut. I was jerked from my sleep by loud noises coming from our front yard. It sounded like a Fourth of July celebration. I looked at the clock. It was a few minutes after two. Through the thin curtain, I saw a bright, flickering glow. *It can't be the streetlight*, I thought. *This is too bright, and streetlights don't flicker. This is more like flames from outside. What could be burning out there?* I sat up in bed, not certain what this commotion was. The noise hadn't stirred Mama and Randy. Their bedroom was in the rear of the house, and the door was closed.

I heard what sounded like firecrackers again, and then muffled voices just outside my window. I got out of bed, walked to the window, and pulled back the curtain a little. What I saw staggered me. A giant wooden cross was ablaze right in our front yard. Three men in white robes and hoods stood beside it. "Death to nigger lovers!" they shouted.

I froze, dumbfounded. One of the three Klansmen pointed a shotgun to the sky. I saw a flash as the orange flame raced out of the barrel. To my horror, I realized that what I had mistaken for firecrackers had been gunshots. "Death to nigger lovers!" the man shouted again. His hooded comrades picked up the cry.

The door to my room flew open. "Get away from there, Gene!" Mama screamed. As she said that, another shot was fired.

"Who are those men?"

"Get away from there, I said! It's the Klan!"

I backed away from the window and turned to look at Mama, who was clutching Randy to her chest. "What do they want?"

"They're here because of your brother."

My fear turned to rage, and it burned hot like the flames of the cross in our front yard. *Why are these bastards picking on a poor little baby? What has he done wrong? I wish I had a shotgun. I'd shoot the bastards where they stood and go back to bed, and let the neighborhood dogs feed off their dead bodies. How dare they hide behind sheets and hoods in order to scare a baby and his mama?*

"Shouldn't we call the police?" I asked.

"I wish we had a phone," Mama whispered.

We were trapped. The three Klansmen continued shooting their guns into the air and calling Mama every horrible name their perverse, ignorant minds could conjure up. We sat against the far wall, prisoners in our own living room.

"Mama," I said. "Can I go into the kitchen and get a knife?"

"What for?"

"To stab those bastards if they come inside."

Under normal circumstances such language from her son would have warranted a response, but these were not normal circumstances.

Though I was eleven, I was big for my age, and strong with the body of a teenager. And the loathing I felt for these three men outside made me feel ten feet tall and bulletproof. I remembered Grandma's last words, that I should protect Mama. I felt I was capable of protecting her and Randy even from the Klan.

"Okay, honey."

I went into the kitchen and picked up the longest, sharpest knife I could find. I returned to the living room and stood facing the door, waiting for the hooded cowards on the other side. Mama sat on the couch, rocking back and forth, trying to keep Randy quiet. This visit by the Klan was a warning. They were just trying to scare us. After a few more minutes, as the flames began to die down, one of them yelled out, "We'll be back, nigger lover, and next time we'll burn your fucking house down."

"I'll be waiting for you, you bastards," I whispered. I heard the roar of a car, and I rushed to the window just in time to see it turning right onto Lexington Avenue.

Fearing they might return, I sat at the door in a straight-backed caned chair, knife in hand, watching over Mama and Randy until the gray light of dawn crept through the curtains. When Mama woke up from her fitful sleep, she fished through her purse and gave me a nickel. "Go call Tuck and tell him what happened," she said, still shaking.

I unlatched the door, stepped down from the rotting porch, and stared at the charred remains of the cross. I kicked at the ashes and muttered, "Bastards."

I ran to the small store on the corner and called Tuck from the phone booth. I let the phone ring twice and hung up. I knew if Tuck was home he would call me right back. It was our system for saving a nickel. A nickel bought enough potatoes at Red's Market for supper.

Seconds later Tuck called back and I told him what had happened. There was a long pause. I could tell from the heavy breathing that he was furious. "Are you all okay?"

"Yeah, we're okay."

"Good. Now don't worry. I'll be right over. Tell your mama to be ready to leave."

I went back and told Mama that Tuck was on his way. I sat on the front porch watching for his car. Five minutes after making the call, I saw it turn the corner. I went back into the house to get Mama, who was holding Randy in one arm and Randy's baby bag in the other. We hurried out the back door and through a narrow alley leading to the street behind our house. A couple of yards away, Tuck sat in his car waiting, a determined look on his face.

"Are you all all right?" he asked as soon as we were inside.

"We're fine," Mama said.

Tuck kept checking the rearview mirror as he drove toward his place. He took a different route, making sure every few seconds we weren't being followed. When we pulled into the driveway, I saw Tuck's son-in-law James sitting in his Pontiac holding a shotgun. Two other cars filled with members of Tuck's Masonic Lodge were nearby. "Are you and the children okay?" was the first thing James asked Mama when he walked in the house.

"We're fine," she said.

"Now let those hooded cowards show their faces here," James said. Tuck decided it would be safer for us to stay with him for a few days. During that time, a car filled with armed black men guarded us. After we eventually moved back to our house, we remained under the protection of this armed guard for several weeks. Word was out that we had the kind of lethal protection that not even the Klan wanted to mess with.

37

"Dutdown"

Summer turned to fall and the nights grew colder. We'd buy coal as money allowed but we'd run out and there'd be nothing in the house to burn. I started taking the coal bucket and walking the mile or so to the Sunnyside Coal and Ice Company. I'd walk past the glue factory, where the smell of cooked broken-down horses turned my stomach. I'd walk past Devonshire Street, where my beloved grandma once lived, and tears would well up in my eyes. I'd wonder what she would have said about our lives now that we were living on the outer limits of society.

Once I reached the coal yard, I'd walk between the tracks where the coal cars unloaded. I'd fill my bucket up with stray pieces of coal no bigger than golf balls. They were free, and free was what we could afford. Being small, of course, they burned quickly in the stove. They never lasted until morning, but quick-burning coal put out more heat than no coal at all.

Mama was still working part time at Kress's. She worked three days a week, from two o'clock until the store closed around nine, and Saturdays.

Tuck was attentive to Randy, and on those Saturdays when he was not working he would take care of him. I'd spend the day down-town with Mama. She'd give me fifteen cents, and while she worked I sat next door in the Royal Theater, watching the Children's Matinee.

The matinee played all day. It started with cartoons and was fol-lowed by the Three Stooges, the Little Rascals, or Roy Rogers movies. Mama would come to the theater on her lunch break. As an employee at Kress's, she received a free lunch, so during her break she'd bring it over and we'd sit together in the lobby, or outside if the weather was nice, and share it.

During the week when Tuck was working and I was at school, his aunt down the street would take care of Randy until I got home from school. Mama had trained me well in the care of my little brother. I knew how to feed him, how to change his diaper, how to give him a bath, and how to rock him to sleep in my arms. On nights when he was cranky, I'd be the one who could get him to sleep.

Randy was toddling now, and he was easier to care for and more fun to play with. On those Saturdays when Tuck and Mama both worked, I'd pull the mattress off my bed and shape a pair of socks into a football. I'd kneel at one end of the mattress and Randy would stand at the other facing me with his little arms drawn up to his chest waiting to catch the ball, poised like a running back, giggling.

I'd hold my hands out like a quarterback under center, the socks in my right hand. I'd glance from side to side and yell out, "Blue 77, blue 77, hut-hut," and then throw the socks to Randy. He wouldn't catch them, but he'd pick them up and waddle toward me. I'd tackle him onto the mattress, and then provide the play by play.

"Randy Tucker for a gain of five yards; second down." At that point, Randy would run back to the far end of the mattress and we'd start all over again with the "hut-hut," which Randy pronounced "mutt-mutt."

Every few runs I'd yell "Touchdown!" and then raise my hands up to the ceiling to signify the score. Randy would yell, "Dutdown, Dutdown!" with his arms high over his head, dancing from side to side and giggling. Most days, when we started this game, it would consume us, and I'd lose all track of time. I wouldn't realize how late it was until I heard Mama open the door. "My goodness," she'd say, smiling. "Have you two been playing since I left?"

"Yes ma'am," I'd say. "Randy is training to play in the NFL."

"Dutdown! Dutdown!" Randy would shout, as I pulled the mattress back onto the box spring.

Randy and I were as close as two brothers can be. We were inseparable, and I took him everywhere I went. More often than not, I was reminded that he was a lightning rod for prejudice.

One day at the grocery store, Mama was holding Randy and I was pushing the cart down the aisles. We stopped in the cereal aisle, along with a few other shoppers. Randy was fussing and everyone turned in our direction. They glared at Randy, then at Mama, and then at me.

Randy was the odd one out. Several people began snickering. Others turned away in disgust. We continued shopping. A bearded man in bib overalls, who appeared to be mulling over the difference between cornflakes and Wheaties, looked up as we walked by. "Nigger lover," he muttered under his breath.

"What did you say?" I hissed, my body drawn up in a knot.

"Don't, honey," Mama, said, pulling me away.

The man towered over me, staring down at me with his walrus face, but I was ready to fight him right there.

"It's not worth it, honey," Mama said as she led me down another aisle.

"Why don't they just leave us alone?" I said. "Why can't they just mind their own business?" I glanced at Randy, who by now had quieted down and was smiling as he played with the house keys.

This harassment was a constant presence when we were out with Randy. Its unrelenting nature made me defensive and quick to buck up. I'd cuss someone out in a heartbeat, and would stand toe to toe with anyone I heard calling Mama and Randy names.

The sad part was, all of the harassment came from whites. No black person ever said an unkind word to us or gave us dirty looks. Our tormentors included the police, who now staked out Tuck's place like it was the headquarters of the underworld.

The harassment I feared the most came from my own family. Every time I visited Dad, he would spew such hatred about Mama that it frightened me. I despised visiting him, but I had to. It was my choice to do it; Mama never asked me to. Though he wouldn't pay child support, he'd give me a few dollars whenever I came over. I'd have to sit and listen to him and Grandma rant and rave while I bit my tongue. One Saturday I snapped; I'd heard all I could take. I hadn't been in the house a minute when he started in on me.

"You tell your nigger-loving mama to kiss my ass. I ain't giving her money to support that half-breed mongrel."

He was sitting in his chair with a can of Budweiser next to him. I stood up and faced him my anger overflowing. "You're a worthless excuse for a human being, you know that?" Grandma—who was sitting on the couch—let out a gasp like she'd been punched in the stomach. Dad's birthmark glowed. He started to get up and I took a step toward him.

"Go ahead. Get up. What are you going to do, hit me? I ain't scared of you no more, you drunk. I ain't going to run. Go ahead, get up." He settled back into the chair and his face turned ghost white. I continued my rant. "I tell you what. Keep your damn money, I don't want it. As far as I'm concerned you can both kiss my ass." I walked out and slammed the door.

38

Coming Apart at the Seams

In mid-October Mama went down to the Forsyth County courthouse to beg the judge for the child support Dad still hadn't paid. She had filed four other complaints with the court over Dad's failure to pay child support. After each filing, Dad was faced with the threat of prison. With the help of Uncle Bobby or Grandma, he'd pay a fine and walk out, promising to get caught up. But he never did. He had gone back to work at the Aluminum Awning Company in Winston and was making thirty-six dollars a week. He found spending his money on drinking more worthwhile than paying child support, and by this time he was $413 behind.

Because he refused to pay, we found ourselves once more in desperate financial straits. We were on the verge of losing even our run-down house on Moravian Street. Tuck was giving Mama money, but it just wasn't enough. We continued sinking lower and lower.

It was October 12, 1963. School was out that day, so I took care of Randy while Mama went to town. We played football on the mattress and ate lunch. When she came home, Randy and I were sitting on the couch reading a book. She was jubilant.

"I have great news, honey," she said.

"Did you get the money?"

"No, but the judge told your dad that if he didn't pay me by the end of this week, he was going to jail."

"That's a lot of money, Mama."

"It sure is, honey, and once we get it, I'll pay the landlord what I owe him, then I'll take you shopping for new clothes. I'll save the rest. And this year we'll have a special Christmas. What do you want Santa to bring you?"

"You know there's no Santa Claus. I'm twelve years old now."

"But you still want presents, don't you?"

"Sure."

"Then make a list."

That evening, when we were over at Tuck's house, Mama was telling him about the judge's ruling. "It's about time the court did something to make him fulfill his responsibility," Tuck said. "A man ain't a man if he don't provide for his children." Always cautious, Tuck added, "But what makes you so sure he'll pay this time? The court gave him a suspended sentence the last time and he didn't pay."

"This time he's going to jail, Tuck," Mama said. "And the judge meant it."

On October 21 a warrant was issued for my father's arrest. When he appeared in court, Judge Heffner gave him one last chance. He told him that he could avoid going to jail if he paid two hundred dollars immediately. Dad promised he would and walked out of court. October turned to November and we still hadn't seen a penny from him.

When I came home from school on Friday, November 15, Mama was smiling.

"Did the money come?" I asked.

"No. But we'll have it Monday."

"How do you know?"

"The sheriff came today. He gave me papers that say I should appear in court."

"What if he doesn't pay?"

"Then he's going to jail. And knowing your dad, he don't want to go to jail. I'm sure he'll have the money this time."

On Sunday we went over to Tuck's for supper. It was decided that Tuck would stay home from work on Monday and watch Randy because there was no way they were going to take him into a courtroom. Mama told me that I could miss school and go with her to court for the big payday.

"I'll give you a call after the hearing," she told Tuck. "Then you and Randy can come and pick us up. Once I have the money, I'm going to take Gene shopping for some decent clothes."

I woke up the next morning at the crack of dawn, my breath showing as I shivered under the pile of Grandma's old quilts. It was freezing cold in the house. The coal fire had burned out, and there was no more coal to burn. I knew if we didn't get the money from Dad, I'd have to make another trip to the railroad tracks.

Mama had the oven on to warm the kitchen, so I went in there to get dressed. I had gone through a growth spurt during the summer, and none of my old clothes fit me. My raggedy gray slacks were so short that I looked like I was expecting a flood. My long-sleeved shirts had become short-sleeved shirts, and the threadbare blue polyester coat had turned gray from old age. I put on a black clip-on tie and a pair of clodhoppers that Gomer Pyle wouldn't be caught dead wearing.

"I look ridiculous, Mama," I said.

"Don't worry, honey. After we get the money, we'll go to Sears and get you some new clothes."

"You need some new clothes, too," I said. She was wearing her only nice dress, one with green brocade. I had burned a hole in that dress one day in a fit of insanity. I'd been stoking the fire with the poker. Fascinated by the bright red glow, I held the poker and looked at the bedroom door. *Can a red-hot poker go through a door of solid wood?*

I stabbed the door with the poker and it went through the wood like it was butter. The hole it left was so small I doubted Mama would notice it. What I didn't realize was that behind the door hung the one pretty dress she owned. She did notice the hole in the door and her dress. I went outside and picked a nice sturdy switch for a butt whipping that day.

She put on her old coat to cover the hole, and we left for the bus stop. The bus pulled to the curb and stopped. Mama checked her watch. It was 8:15 A.M. "I don't want us to be late," she said. "Court starts at nine o'clock sharp."

She dropped a quarter into the container and we sat near the rear of the bus. As the bus began to move, I began seeing myself in new clothes. "I just can't believe it. Shopping for clothes!"

"We sure are, honey," Mama said, putting her arm around me. She leaned over and kissed me on the cheek. "You know I love you very much. A mother couldn't ask for a finer son. You've been my rock of ages these past few years, and Randy is lucky to have such a wonderful big brother." Her eyes glistened.

"Thanks, Mama," I said. "You're the greatest mama in the world, and Randy is the best brother. I love you both more than anything."

39

The Steps to Hell

We rode the bus toward downtown Winston-Salem in silence. I stared out the window at the houses passing by, wondering what kind of people lived in them and what their lives were like. Mama stared straight ahead. From time to time she fidgeted with her hands. She didn't like these confrontations with my father.

Half an hour later the bus stopped in front of the Mother and Daughter Department Store. The bright pink facade of the building glowed bright in the morning sun. We crossed the street, and she reached into her purse and pulled out her Pall Malls. "We have a few minutes, honey," she said. "Do you mind if we sit here on the bench while I smoke?"

"I don't mind," I said. While she smoked, I turned around and looked up at the ominous gray stone walls of the courthouse and the sculpted lion heads that guarded the entrance. Their eyes seemed to be staring at me. My eyes wandered to the police cars parked across the street. I didn't trust the police anymore. It made me mad to think about them busting into Tuck's house just to give us a hard time.

"It's almost nine," I said.

She crushed her cigarette with the heel of her black pumps. "Well, honey," she said, taking me by the hand, "let's go get this mess over with."

We climbed the wide marble steps leading into the courthouse, and the lions' eyes followed me as if warning me danger ahead. All of a sudden fear took hold of me and blocked my courage.

The double doors to the courthouse opened into a large hallway with a cavernous ceiling. Freshly polished black marble floors reflected the pale light from the brass light fixtures hanging from the ceiling. The hard floor echoed with each step we took, filling the enormous hallway with the sound of two solitary walkers.

"This place is big, Mama," I said.

"Yes, honey, it is." Still holding hands, we continued down the hall. My heart stopped when we reached the large wooden door at the far end. There, sitting on a dark brown wooden bench outside the door, was my father. He was leaning over, his elbows resting on his knees. He fidgeted with a pack of cigarettes, his face blank. He wasn't alone, and my courage collapsed. My heart raced and a voice inside my head screamed out, *Run! Hold on to Mama's hand and fly out of the building, and don't look back.*

I knew something was wrong when I saw Grandma and Uncle Bobby sitting next to him. In front of the bench stood a man whom I'd never seen before. He stared at us as we made our way to the door and then turned away. His silver-gray hair and fancy suit reminded me of a TV preacher.

Dad was dressed in the one suit he owned, a dark blue pinstripe, and a white shirt with a red tie. Uncle Bobby wore a brown suit with a camel-hair overcoat draped over one arm. Grandma was wearing a tan dress with brown and maroon flowers. She fiddled with the brown leather purse sitting on her lap.

Why are they here? I thought. *And why are they so nervous? Is it because Dad doesn't have the money and they're afraid he's going to jail?*

No one acknowledged us in any way. Sitting at the far end of the large hallway, as far away from the Cheeks as possible, was a startling surprise to me—Uncle Bill. He was nervous. His head was bowed and he stared at the floor. He glanced up from the floor, and our eyes met for a split second. I was about to say hi when an anguished look washed over his face and he turned his gaze back to the floor. He had that look that I'd seen on his face before, when he'd let a cuss word slip out in front of Grandma. He was ashamed.

Sitting across from Uncle Bill were our next-door neighbors, Mr. Shell and his mousy wife. The two unabashed racists never looked up. Their presence sent a thousand alarm bells ringing in my head. *Something is wrong, dead wrong. What are all these people doing here? They aren't here to watch the judge make Dad pay the four hundred and thirteen dollars he owes in child support. What's going on?*

Mama tightened her grip on my hand as we filed into the courtroom. A feeling of hopelessness washed over me. We were all alone. I wished Grandma Pearl were still alive. I knew she'd be walking with us no matter what. We made our way down the center aisle separating two rows of benches. Mama held on to my hand as if she was afraid a giant would reach down from the ceiling and snatch me up.

"What are Uncle Bill and the Shells doing here, Mama?"

"I don't know, honey," she whispered, "but don't worry about them. Everything's going to be all right."

I didn't feel as though everything was going to be all right. My stomach was in knots, and I could barely swallow. We reached the front row, and Mama sat down on the right side of the aisle. "You sit here, right behind me," she said. She patted the blond wood of the bench and I sat down in the seat behind her. In front of us loomed a massive, dark brown wooden desk. The polished surface reflected every ray of light in the ominous courtroom. It was the largest desk I'd ever seen and it rose up high out of the floor like a monument.

Seconds later, when I heard the sound of the huge doors in the rear of the courtroom opening, I turned around. I watched my father and his entourage walk down the aisle toward us and take seats on the left side of the aisle. Still, they didn't look at us. No greetings, nothing. Their silence and their inability to look at me spoke volumes, and sent drops of fear trickling down my spine. A sickening feeling in my gut told me that something horrible was about to happen. Impending doom crept over me and smothered my frail courage. My father didn't need all these people with him in order to pay child support. What was he after?

While these questions raced through my mind, the door behind the podium swung open. A policeman in a tan uniform walked in followed by a woman carrying what appeared to be a typewriter. She sat down at a small desk on my right, and the policeman said, "All rise. The Honorable Judge E. S. Heffner Jr. presiding!" Everyone shuffled to their feet as the white-haired judge, dressed in a long black robe, walked up to the bench and sat down.

40

Cast the First Stone

"Be seated," Judge Heffner said, and then got straight to the point. "In the matter of the custody of Jesse Eugene Cheek, are we ready to proceed?" Judge Heffner asked.

What? What did the judge just say? What did he mean by custody? My mind ran wild. Weren't Mama and I here to collect child support?

I turned and glared at my father. *Look at me, damn you.* He sat stiff, staring straight ahead. I looked to the back of the room. Two armed policemen stood guard, one on either side of the door, their hands clasped behind their backs.

For the final time the voice in my head screamed out, *Get up, grab Mama's hand, and run! Try to get out that door before the judge goes any farther.* But I couldn't move. Desperation had glued me to the seat, and my heart was trying to beat its way out of my chest.

Sensing my panic, Mama turned and put her hand on my knee and patted it. "Don't worry, honey," she whispered. "Everything will be okay. Nothing's going to happen. The Lord is our protector." She muttered a prayer under her breath, and I prayed, "Jesus, please help us. Don't let us be hurt. Please, Jesus." My prayer was cut short by Judge Heffner's booming voice. "Mr. Cheek," he said, "are you ready to proceed?"

The man with the silver-gray hair stood up and said, "Your Honor, Fred Crumpler. I'll be representing Mr. Cheek in this matter. And, yes sir, we are ready to proceed."

"Very well," Judge Heffner said. He turned and looked at Mama. "Mrs. Cheek, are you represented by counsel?"

"No sir," she replied in a shaky voice.

Judge Heffner said, "Are you ready to proceed?"

Say no, Mama! I screamed out in my mind. *Say no!*

"Yes" was all she could say. I'd never seen her so anxious. Her color was ghostlike and her breath came in short labored gasps. She knew something was about to happen, I could see that. As for me, I felt like I'd stepped into an episode of *The Twilight Zone*. I was expecting at any moment to hear Rod Serling's voice say, "Submitted for your approval, a boy and his mother await the hand of fate."

"Very well," Judge Heffner said. "Mr. Crumpler, call your first witness."

"Your Honor, we call John Shell." Mr. Shell stood up and walked to the stand. A small man with a large nose and snow-white hair, he looked like an aging weasel. He'd been our next-door neighbor for over a year and had never spoken to us. He had a daughter about my age, whom he'd forbidden to play with me or even to set foot in our yard. Several times when I'd been out playing in the yard, his daughter had tried to speak to me over the fence. Each time, Mr. Shell would come to his back door and yell, "Martha! Get away from that nigger lover's house." Martha would blush and whisper, "I'm sorry," then turn and run.

Mr. Shell cleared his throat and began to speak. He testified that Mama was a bad mother, that I should be taken away from her because she was carrying on with a Negro man, and that he'd seen her walking around with a baby with kinky hair who appeared to be half Negro. Mr. Shell went on to testify that almost every evening, between seven fifteen and eight, he'd seen a Negro man drive by our house in a blue Chevy and honk the horn. Soon after she would sneak out and not come back for hours.

Mr. Shell's testimony enraged me. I wanted to jump up and yell, *Liar! You dirty, rotten, hateful liar! Mama never left Randy and me alone at night—never.* As Mr. Shell continued to malign Mama's character, my hate for him grew. I didn't think a judge would believe such a brazen liar.

After Mr. Shell's testimony, I saw a flicker of a smile cross my father's face, and I wanted to cry. The judge asked Mama if she had any questions for Mr. Shell. Intimidated and unsure about what to do, she said, "No, Your Honor."

Next on the witness stand was Mrs. Shell. She parroted what her lying husband had said, and added her own twisted spin by saying Mama was unfit because she was guilty of race mixing. Sitting there I wondered, *What does race mixing have to do with a mother's love?* From the day I was born she had provided for me, protected me, and sacrificed her own well-being to ensure that I had as normal and happy a childhood as the circumstances allowed.

Mama had no questions for Mrs. Shell, either. A triumphant look on her face, Mrs. Shell left the stand and sat down next to her husband. The next witness called was my father.

As I watched him walk to the stand, I wished I had a gun so I could shoot him before he uttered the first word. *He's the cause of all this*, I said to myself, as he was being sworn in, promising that he'd tell the whole truth and nothing but the truth. *What truth? Whose truth?* I thought. *There is no truth here. This isn't about the truth. It's about revenge.*

For a moment he glanced my way and our eyes met, and he saw the hate I felt for him. He lowered his head as he began to speak. He recounted how he and his brother Bobby once found Mama at Tuck's house. He also said that he hadn't paid child support because I wasn't in a fit home. He told the judge that once I was placed in a proper home, he would begin paying it.

Then he said something that stunned me. He confessed that he was an alcoholic and an epileptic, and was unable to provide me with a proper home. He concluded by saying that he hoped the court would find me one where I'd be raised with good morals. Hearing him say this, I wanted to scream, *You drunken bastard! Why are you taking me away from Mama when you can't even provide me with a home?*

Any doubt of what kind of man he was was answered that day. My father was a cruel and hateful man. If he loved me, if he was concerned about my well-being, wouldn't he go out of his way to provide me with a decent home? Wouldn't he sacrifice something to raise me "with good morals," instead of saying he was a drunk?

I prayed that the judge, sitting high above us, God-like on his throne, would see through this charade. The judge must be wise, I thought, recalling the story from the Old Testament about King

Solomon. It was a story that Tuck loved to tell. Bible stories were a staple of our conversations. *Does this judge possess the wisdom of Solomon? He has to, he just has to.*

The next person to take the witness stand was Uncle Bobby. His exterior unfazed by the unfolding drama in the courtroom, he confirmed Dad's story about finding Mama at Tuck's house. He told the judge that he couldn't provide me with a home because he already had a child of his own. He said he hoped the court would rule that I be placed in a foster home, where I'd be raised properly.

He insisted that I'd be happier there than living with Mama. He said she was a bad mother because she was in a relationship with a "colored man." If Uncle Bobby cared at all about my happiness or me being raised properly, then why didn't he offer to give me the kind of proper home that he accused Mama of not providing? He'd never shown any concern for my happiness before.

After Uncle Bobby came Grandma. I cried when she took the stand against us. Mama and I had loved her. Grandma stunned me by testifying that she was a sick old lady who'd been advised by her doctor that it would be bad for her health to take care of a teenage boy. *Then why is she taking care of a grown-up boy like Dad?* She ended by telling the judge that she hoped the court would rule that I be placed in a foster home for my own protection because Mama was a bad mother who couldn't raise me in a proper Christian way.

As Grandma left the witness stand, I knew that the Cheek family hated Mama so much that they intended to punish her by taking me away. They didn't give a hoot in hell where I ended up, that was obvious. But by getting back at her, they were destroying me, and that never crossed their narrow, hate-filled minds. Mama had tarnished their golden reputation by leaving her husband for a black man. In their warped minds that was worse than stooping into the gutter to pick up trash.

The final witness in this charade was the last person I ever expected to see testify—and the final blow to my heart.

41

The Trip to Hell

Uncle Bill knew in his heart that Mama was the best mother a child could hope for. He'd witnessed evidence of that with his own eyes my entire life. When he took the stand, I knew that blind hatred and ignorance made him turn his back on what Grandma Pearl had taught him, that we should love others as we loved ourselves regardless of color. Thank God, she was not here to see him sit down on that witness stand. Deep down, I knew she was watching, and that her tears on this day could feed a thousand rivers.

When Uncle Bill took the stand against her, Mama and I started crying. It was just too much to bear. It ripped my guts out to hear him attack his own beloved sister.

Stifling sobs, he repeated the same old falsehood that Mama was not a fit mother because she was in a relationship with a "colored man." He also said that my father was "a good-for-nothing drunken bum" who couldn't raise me. Uncle Bill stunned me by joining the chorus of liars, saying I should be taken away from her and placed in foster care for my own good. As he got up to leave the stand, he looked at me. "I'm sorry, honey. I didn't mean to hurt you. I'm doing what I think is best for you. Honest." With that, he burst out crying and stepped down.

I wanted to scream. *The hell you didn't mean to hurt me. You, of all people, know how much I love Mama, and you know that it will destroy me if I can't stay with her. You know that she's the one person in this courtroom, in the whole world for that matter, who'd lay down her life for me—and for you, too.* But I didn't scream, I had no breath in my body. I didn't believe the nightmare that was unfolding right in front of me. I was in shock. My whole body was numb. I shook uncontrollably, cold to the bone.

Why would these people, all saying how much they loved me, want to hurt me so much by taking me away from the one person I loved most in this world? What crime had Mama and I committed? Did we deserve to be condemned like this? I tried to comfort myself with the hope that the judge could see through this charade. No judge in his right mind, if he had a heart, would permit such a terrible thing to happen to a boy and his mother.

I listened as Judge Heffner, my last hope, called Mama to the stand. By now, Mama was hysterical. Staggering, she managed to stumble to the stand. I wanted to stop this thing, to stop the pain that was now crushing her in front of my eyes, but I could do nothing but watch in disbelief.

Between sobs she spoke in a voice full of anguish and despair. The thought that her beloved son, the child she'd done everything in the world to raise right, was about to be taken away from her—not because she was a bad mother but because she had fallen in love with a black man—was more than she could bear.

"I'm not perfect, Your Honor, I've made some mistakes in my life. But I'm a good mother to Gene. I don't have much education. I've worked in a mill all my life. But since he was born, Gene has been the most important person in my life. I've always done what's best for him, Your Honor. Please don't take him away from me." She paused and gave my father a look that stabbed. "I've raised him without any help from his sorry father." Tears streaming down her face, she looked at me. "I love you with all my heart. I'd die for you." She turned her tear-streaked face to the judge. "Please, Your Honor, I beg you, please don't take my precious son away from me."

Mama's words flew across the courtroom, and my heart stopped beating. I was cold again, so cold. I watched my life melt away before my eyes. When she finished testifying, the silver-haired lawyer approached the stand. "Mrs. Cheek, you've sworn to tell the truth and nothing but the truth?"

"Yes."

"Well, then, can you tell this court who the father of your child is?"

"What child?"

"The child known as Randy."

Terror swept Mama's face. "I don't remember his name. He was a truck driver who was just passing through Winston. I heard he got killed in a car wreck."

"I see," he said. "Can you please tell the court what hospital Randy was born in?"

"I don't remember," she said, panicked by the thought that they could somehow trace the birth records.

"Are you willing to swear under oath, Mrs. Cheek, that one Cornelius Tucker, a Negro man, isn't Randy's father?"

There was horror on Mama's face. I was dead inside and my agony was complete. "Yes," she stammered, "I'm willing to swear that he is not the father of my child."

I glared at the faces of the judge, Uncle Bill, my father, and the other people in the courtroom. It was clear from their expressions and sidelong glances that no one believed Mama's desperate but understandable lies.

What choice did she have? Had she admitted the truth—that Tuck, a Negro, was the father of her son—she would be confessing to a felony according to North Carolina's anti-miscegenation laws. And if she was convicted of a felony, she and Tuck faced prison, and what would happen to Randy and me then? I studied King Solomon's face. Would he be merciful?

Mama left the stand weeping and saying over and over again, "I'm a good mother. I love my son. Please don't take him away from me."

The judge summoned me to the witness stand.

Every ounce of strength had been sapped from my body. I could feel my entire body and mind shutting down. I prayed for Grandma Pearl in heaven to reach down and once more reassure me. I wanted to hear her sweet voice whisper, *There, there now, it's okay, it was just a bad dream, it's over now and I'm here.* But it was not a bad dream, and there was nothing anyone on this earth could do for me now.

"Go on, honey, everything will be all right."

I took the witness stand, tears running down my face like twin waterfalls. I tried to calm myself so I could speak because I wanted to make the judge see the truth, to know what was in my heart. Right this minute I felt nothing but hatred. Hatred for the judge. Hatred for Dad. Hatred toward Grandma and Uncle Bobby for being the kind of cold heartless people they were. Hatred toward the Shells for their own vicious hate, and hatred toward Uncle Bill for abandoning Mama and me when we needed him most. It was this hatred that gave me the strength to speak in defense of Mama.

"Young man," the judge asked in a gentle voice, "do you attend school?"

"Yes sir," I said. "I'm in sixth grade."

"Do you want to continue living with your mother?"

"Yes sir, with all my heart. I don't want to live with anyone but my mama. She's the best mama in the world."

"Are you sure of that?"

"Yes sir. Don't listen to these other people here." I pointed with my finger at my father and his entourage. "They are all liars. They don't know my mama. She loves me more than anything. She's a good mother. Please, sir, don't take me away from her and my baby brother. They're all I have." With that, I busted out crying again, overcome with total despair. "If anyone tries to take me away from Mama, I'll run away. I'll kill myself."

I was hysterical as the judge told me to step down. Mama embraced me and we both cried. We were alone in our tears—except for Uncle Bill, who was crying like a baby and wringing his hands as if he was trying to wash away something dirty. My father couldn't look at me and continued staring straight ahead.

Weeping and clinging to each other, we just sat there and waited for the ax to fall. Our helplessness and tears failed to move the judge. He delivered his sentence for Mama's unpardonable crime—loving another human being whose skin color was different from her own.

"Mrs. Cheek," he said, "it is evident that you have had a child born out of wedlock, fathered by a Negro man in the presence of your son Gene. You therefore cannot be deemed a fit and proper person to maintain custody of Gene."

"Liar!" I screamed, rising to my feet. "How dare you say those things about my mama!"

The judge ignored my outburst. "This court is merciful and intends to give you one last chance to repent before passing judgment, Mrs. Cheek," he said.

Mama's face brightened. "Thank you, Your Honor."

"You can keep Gene," the judge said, "if you give up your illegitimate child with the Negro man. If you choose to keep the illegitimate child, then I have no choice but to recommend that Gene, for his own protection, be taken away from you and placed in foster care. The choice is yours."

I was stunned by the judge's words. Mama howled with grief. How could he present a mother with such a choice? He called that merciful? What kind of a monster was he? Something swept over me. A wisdom that I didn't know I possessed flowed into me. Whether it was Grandma Pearl, or God himself, I summoned the strength and wisdom that I needed.

I could not let my mama make this choice. It would destroy her as if the judge himself had plunged a knife into her heart. In an instant I knew what I had to do. I leaned over to her and whispered into her ear, "Mama, if they take Randy, we'll never see him again. He's just a baby. Let them take me away. I'm twelve years old. I know how to find my way home."

Before she could protest, I stood up and yelled at the judge, "Take me, not my brother!"

"No, no, you can't do this!" Mama screamed. "You can't do this to my son!" Mama's anguish went unheeded. Judge Heffner, the mighty Solomon, said, "It is the ruling of this court that Sallie Anderson Cheek is not a fit and proper person to have custody of her son Gene. The moral conditions in the home are unfit; she is training him to deny all authority, and is failing to provide for his discipline. It is now therefore ordered and adjudged that Jesse Eugene Cheek, for his own protection, be removed from the custody of his mother, Sallie Anderson Cheek, and be placed as a ward of the court in the care of the Forsyth County Department of Public Welfare, where he shall remain pending placement in a suitable foster home. Court dismissed."

The judge's words echoed through the exploding chambers of my heart, and I came apart. I threw my arms around Mama, and we clung to each other in desperation. *This isn't real. It's a nightmare. It has to be. Why is this happening to us? What did Mama do to deserve this? What did I do?*

Mama was wailing, her body racked by fits of anguish. She trembled as she held on to me. "No, you can't do this!" she screamed to the judge. "You can't do this! He's only twelve years old!"

My agony turned to rage. *I can't let this happen. If I hold on, they can never take me away from her.*

Two policemen, who had been waiting inside the entrance to the courtroom, strode down the aisle and grabbed my arms and hands. I fought them but my strength was no match for two grown men, and they tore me away from my mother.

"No! No! Leave him alone!" Mama shrieked, her arms reaching out in a frantic but futile effort to grab on to me. Between waves of sobs, she shouted, "He's done nothing! Leave him alone!"

"Let me go, let me go!" I howled as they dragged me toward the door. Insane now with fury and consumed by one thought—to get away from them and rush back to Mama's side—I twisted and fought with all my strength, but their iron fingers dug into my arms like shackles. The bailiff held on to Mama now as she struggled to break loose and rescue her beloved son.

As they hauled me up the aisle, I reached out with my feet and tried to jam them under one of the courtroom benches, anything to halt this madness. *If I can just stop them for a minute, if I could just talk to the judge, I can make him see he has made a terrible mistake.* But as we approached the courtroom doors, I knew there was no waking up from this real-life nightmare. My fate was sealed. I looked to my left and my eyes locked on to my father.

"I'll kill you for this!" I shouted. "Do you hear me, I will kill you for this!"

Down the wide hallway we went, my feet making a horrible screeching sound as I tried to dig them into the polished black marble floor. On through the courthouse they lugged me, and I continued to fight them with each step. They pulled me out the door and down the steps to a waiting patrol car, shoved me inside, and slammed the door.

"Where are you taking me?" I asked.

They didn't answer.

"Where's my mama?"

Again no answer.

"You can't do this!" I shouted. "I want to stay with Mama!"

Still, neither cop uttered a word. Trying to see through the tears, I studied the car door. Maybe I could open it and jump out. Damn, there were no handles. I was a prisoner. The car headed north up Cherry Street and, a few minutes later, pulled into the parking lot of a building I recognized—the Juvenile Detention Center. A jail for juvenile delinquents, JDs, bad boys—whatever people called troublemakers, runaways, thieves, and bullies. I was none of those. I was a victim—a victim of prejudice, hatred, and stupidity.

My despair turned to pure loathing and contempt for the cops as they half carried me into an office where a lady in a brown uniform walked down a narrow hallway and unlocked a thick metal door. The policemen shoved me through the door and slammed it shut with an ominous boom. I looked around. My world was now a gray cinderblock room with a small bed, a stainless-steel toilet, and a narrow barred window high off the floor.

There was no escape. I threw myself onto the bed and cried with a hopelessness I never thought possible. Every part of my body ached. My tears came in floods as desperation and misery settled over my body like a fever.

From somewhere, I heard a muffled voice that injected both hope and sorrow in my heart. *Is it her? Is it Mama? Yes! Yes it is!* She was outside the detention center, pleading for someone to let her in. "Please let me see my son! Please let me see him for just a minute! He's done nothing wrong! He doesn't deserve this. Please let me see him for just a minute!"

Mama's anguished cries ripped at my heart. I wondered how anyone could listen to the cries of such a tormented soul and not offer comfort. How could any human being stand by and witness such pain and not lift a finger to help?

But no one let her in. The mere thought that I might never see her again made me sick to my stomach and I fell to my knees. I clutched my head in my hands and rocked back and forth, moaning in agony as I listened to her hopeless sobs.

After what seemed like an eternity, all was quiet. They had forced Mama to leave, and I was now all alone. Consumed with an unbearable grief and convinced that all hope was lost, I cried myself to sleep. For three days I cried, slept, and cussed. I had no visitors, no contact with the outside world, just a metal tray of food slipped without comment under the door, and left uneaten.

My solitude ended when a woman came to the door, slid back the little metal window, and told me I should get my things together because my social worker was coming to take me to a foster home. *I have no things*, I wanted to shout. *I came in here with just the clothes on my back. Do you hear me? I have no things! No family, no home, no hope.*

"What day is it?" I asked, not moving from the cot.

"It's Thursday morning," she replied, closing the window.

I had lost track of time. The minutes, the hours, the days were all indistinguishable. I had lost my will and hope. I felt like a kite whose string had broken in the howling winds of March, broken loose from my lifeline and whipped around at the mercy of a merciless wind.

I didn't know what a social worker or a foster home was. All I knew was that whatever they were, I wasn't going to like them, and they weren't going to like me. The transformation was complete; the innocent, frightened twelve-year-old boy dragged from the courthouse and locked away for three days was gone. The pieces of his innocence were scattered about the room and ready to be swept into a dustpan and thrown away. His fear—poured out through his tears—had soaked into the pillowcase. I am what's left, and I am not afraid. Anger has washed over me like a tidal wave and filled my heart with hatred. Hatred for all those responsible for my transformation. I am determined—determined to survive so that one day I will see those responsible paid back for what they did.

42

An Altered Life

The woman guard opened the door. "Get your things. The social worker is here to take you to a foster home."

I wanted to go home, but I knew that wouldn't happen. I thought of the words Dad used to say to me, some of his perverted drunken wisdom. "Want in one hand and shit in the other; see which one gets full faster."

She unlocked the door and opened it, and the face of a strange woman peered in. She was young, in her midtwenties, with a pleasant but not beautiful face. She wore a dark blue skirt and white blouse. She smiled at me but I didn't return the smile. I could see other boys idling in their cells. Some were pretending to look at books or magazines, but I could tell from their glances toward my cell that they were checking out the social worker through the corners of their sad and longing eyes, perhaps wondering if someone would be coming to get them soon.

"Hello, Gene. I'm Miss Adams, your social worker," she said.

"What's a social worker?"

The smile widened. "Well, I work for the county. I help find suitable homes for children in your situation. That's what social workers do."

"I don't need a suitable home," I snapped. "I already have one. Just let me go back to my mama."

Miss Adams's smile faded. "Well, Gene, I'm sorry but that's not possible right now. The court has placed you in our custody because it feels you shouldn't be living with your mama. Your daddy wanted it that way. I'm here to take you to a foster home."

"What's a foster home?"

The smile returned. "Well, a foster home is just like a regular home. There's a mother and a father and they take good care of all the foster children who live with them, and raise them like their own. A foster home is a nice place."

"Please, Miss Adams," I begged, "don't take me to a foster home. I know I won't be happy there. I just want to go home. Please take me home. My mama is a good mother. She loves me. She needs me. Please take me to her."

My pleading seemed to have an effect on Miss Adams. Her eyes welled up as if she was about to cry. But then the professional in her reasserted herself. "That's not possible, Gene," she said. "The court has decided. Its ruling must be obeyed. You can't go on living with your mama. I promise you, you'll be happy in your new home."

"Where are my things?"

"They're in my car," she said. "I picked them up on the way here."

"Is my mama okay?"

"She's fine."

"And my little brother?"

"He's fine, too."

Knowing that Mama and Randy were okay gave me the strength to face whatever was next in this hideous nightmare that not even Poe could have invented. Wiping my eyes, I followed Miss Adams outside into the crisp November air. I squinted as my eyes adjusted to the bright sunlight. Cars honked in morning traffic; everything seemed normal. But I knew that nothing was normal. Everything had changed for me. Forever.

I was about to begin a new life in a strange place with a group of strangers. Riddled with fear and doubt. I nevertheless felt that somehow, some way I would find a way to go back home. We reached Miss Adams's cream-colored Pontiac Bonneville, which was parked alongside the street next to a police car. I climbed in the back and sat next to an old cardboard suitcase held shut by string. I realized that it was Mama's.

"All your clothes are in there," Miss Adams said, starting the engine.

As we drove toward the foster home, not a word was spoken between us. I fought back tears. For comfort, I held the tattered suitcase to my chest, knowing that it was covered with Mama's tears, and that it was something for me to remember her by. I stared out the window in silence. I was committed now to simple survival and a pledge to myself: *Whatever is next for me, I'll survive, and I'll find a way to get home.* As we passed Memorial Coliseum, Miss Adams slowed the car and pulled into the driveway of a big two-story white house on the corner of North Cherry Street and Deacon Boulevard. She pulled the car around back and turned off the engine.

To my left sat a small wooden building separated from the house by a hard-dirt yard. In front of me was a chain-link fence with the coliseum and fairgrounds beyond it.

"Well, here we are," Mrs. Adams said.

In silence, I stepped out of the car and glanced around. Staring down at me from a second-floor window was the face of a five-year-old boy. The eyes were sad, too sad for a child. They belonged on the face of a man old enough to have felt years of pain and sorrow. As I looked into his eyes, the boy held up his right hand, palm out. He wasn't waving, just holding it up. I nodded and extended my own hand. I could hear Grandma saying, *When you think you've got it bad, look around. You won't have to look far to find someone who has it worse than you do.*

I had learned my first lesson. I was not a small, frightened child who had lived some horrible life that left those sad eyes as evidence. I walked into the house through the back door and into the kitchen. Sitting at a table big enough for a platoon were a man and a woman. She was a large woman with short-cropped red hair. She was stout, big-boned, strong looking, and suited for the hard work of farm life. She looked up at me over thick glasses too small for her wide face, and said to me, "Hello, I'm Mrs. Hayes, and this is my husband, John."

Without speaking, I shook her hand and turned to the man. John Hayes was a tiny man with brown piercing eyes and a large nose. He looked like a hawk, all eyes and beak. There was no smile on his face as he shook my hand.

While Mrs. Hayes was talking to Miss Adams, I glanced out through the kitchen and into the living room and saw four small children, including the sad-eyed boy, sitting on the floor. I heard Miss Adams saying good-bye to Mr. and Mrs. Hayes. She turned to me nodded, smiled, turned, and went out the door, no words, no good-bye, and just like that she was gone.

Ms. Hayes led me through the living room and up the stairs to a bedroom with three single beds. She pointed to a bed on the far wall underneath a small window and said, "You take that one, Gene. You can go look around outside until supper is ready if you want to." Then she left the room.

I put Mama's suitcase under the bed, walked back down the stairs, and headed for the back door. Two small girls not much older than three sat in the living room floor playing with a notebook and colored pencils, laughing and chatting away in hushed tones. Sad Eyes and another boy around five were sitting on the couch watching TV. Sad Eyes looked up at me. I stopped in front of the couch.

"Hi, my name is Joey," he said. "How old are you?"

"I'm twelve. How old are you?"

Sad Eyes smiled, exposing the gap where his front teeth used to be. "I'm four." Then he asked, "Will you make Mark stop picking on us?"

"Who's Mark?"

"He's their real son"—pointing to the kitchen—"he's mean. I don't like him, but you're bigger than he is, so you can make him stop."

He was looking at me as though he was sure I was there to rescue him. I thought of my own baby brother and said, "Well, I don't know him yet, but I'll talk to him about picking on you. Okay?"

"Okay."

I walked through the kitchen and out the back door and into the backyard where a path cut its way through a patch of low brush and little dirt mounds. It ran along the chain-link fence, and I followed it until it came out of the brush just a few hundred yards below Ernie Shore Field, the baseball stadium where Mama and I had spent so many warm summer nights. I crossed the road to the stadium and walked along the fence that circled it. I thought about the times she had brought me here, and I started to cry and plopped on the ground. When Randy was born, one of the first things I thought about was how great it would be to have a little brother to bring to the games here.

That dream was now floating in the wind, not owned by me anymore.

When I was cried out, I headed back toward the house. Entering the yard, I saw a kid about my age, a little smaller, leaning against the wall next to the back door. I walked through the screen door and onto the porch where he stood.

"You must be the new one. I'm Mark and this is my house," he said, making a point.

"Well, good for you," I said, looking him square in the eyes.

"You getting smart with me?" he asked, taking a step forward. Then he made a mistake. "You the one with the nigger-loving mama?"

Something in me snapped. This punk kid represented all those people I had spent days hating. Without warning and moving with the speed of light, I lunged forward and pinned him to the wall with my left forearm. With my right hand made into a fist, I pounded his face. He tried to fight back, but in seconds it was over. He slumped to the floor bleeding from his nose and mouth. He was crying now, and I leaned over him. I grabbed a handful of his hair and jerked his head back so that our eyes met.

"Never say anything about my mama. Do you understand me?"

He nodded.

"And don't let me hear that you picked on any of these other kids. If you do, I will stomp a mud hole in your ass and walk it dry. Do we understand each other?"

He nodded again, and I let go of his hair just as his mother came through the back door. "Here now," she said. "What's this all about?"

Without answering, I walked into the house and through the kitchen, not caring about the food sitting on the table. I was too tired to eat, so very tired. Drained, I headed for the bedroom. Sad Eyes looked up at me from the table and smiled. I winked at him and went to bed.

43

My Finer Nature

The next day was Friday, November 22, 1963, and since I wasn't starting school until Monday, I sat in front of the TV watching a game show.
No one said anything about the confrontation between Mark and me,
and he kept his distance, his face bruised and swollen.

"We interrupt this program to bring you this news bulletin from
Dallas, Texas. The president of the United States, John Fitzgerald
Kennedy, was shot and fatally wounded . . ." The reporter continued
but there was little point in hearing any more.

I was in shock. Tuck had said Mr. Kennedy was a champion of the
common man. "He will do great things for blacks and poor people in this
country." Mama agreed, and in our house Mr. Kennedy ranked right up
there with Martin Luther King and Santa Claus. I felt like I was caught
in another nightmare. First my family's destruction, and now the murder
of a man who in our house had brought the hope of hope. His death and
my own destruction were forever joined together in my memory.

That afternoon I found several empty Coke bottles at a con-
struction site and cashed them in. I used the money to call Mama at
Tuck's house. After several minutes of crying and talking about
President Kennedy, she told me she was moving in with Tuck. They
had talked about it, and there was no other choice now. The world was
no longer safe. My removal from my home and the president's death
were proof enough.

I was glad Mama and Randy moved because I had been worried
about them alone in that house next to that lying racist Mr. Shell. I

could imagine the smirk on his face every time he saw Mama. The pain of the courtroom would come crashing down on her every time she looked at his hard-hearted face. By moving in with Tuck, she and Randy would be safer.

Maybe now that I was gone, the Cheeks, at least, would leave them alone. So the day after JFK's assassination, Tuck and James loaded up our few possessions and hauled them to Vargrave Street.

On Monday I enrolled in the sixth grade at Lowrance Middle School about ten blocks from the house on Cherry Street. Each morning Mark and I walked together to school. Since that first-day encounter on his back porch, we had reached an understanding. I was physically superior and angry enough to unload that superiority on him, and he understood that.

November turned to December and I survived somehow, but I had changed. The change in me had not been slow and measured. To the contrary, it had been quick and uncontrollable. Mr. and Mrs. Hayes saw the change and left me alone. My social worker had noticed as well. I read a report she'd written and left on her desk: "Gene is dependent on his mother, and I have serious concerns about his ability to conform and accept being placed in a foster home." Mama, Tuck, and even my little brother noticed the change, and Mama cried all the harder because of it. What had changed in me is what the writer Robert Penn Warren called my "finer nature."

A part of me that had been dormant had surfaced. A hardness had been shaped by watching Dad drink himself into abusing Mama and me. My softer, finer nature had been forged into hardened steel. That day in the courtroom had ground and polished that steel into a razor's edge.

I stumbled on, each day putting one foot in front of the other, and survived. I went home for Christmas Day. It was just my third visit since I'd been taken away. It was a sad, subdued day void of any Christmas magic. Mama cried as the clock ticked away the passing hours. On the ride back to Cherry Street, she looked at me and said with tears in her eyes, "I'm so sorry, honey. I'm so sorry. This is all my fault."

"No, it's not, Mama. You didn't do anything to deserve this. It's the world's fault."

Just after the New Year, Mrs. Hayes asked me to fetch her husband from his shop. Mr. Hayes was a cabinet builder, and his small shop sat behind the house. I could see him through the dirt-streaked window as I approached the shop. I opened the door in time to see him pulling on a bottle of Jack Daniels. As soon as the door squeaked on its hinges, he lowered the bottle to his side, and his surprise turned to anger.

"Jesus Christ, don't you know how to knock?" His face was flushed from being caught in the act and, no doubt, the Jack Daniels. His speech was slurred and his face shined beet red. I was the son of an alcoholic and schooled in the art of recognition. I had spent years watching and learning the signs. It was important for my survival to avoid a drunk. To avoid one, you need to know one. That I had missed it up to now was in itself an accomplishment for Mr. Hayes. He had gone to great lengths to keep his secret safe. Now here we stood.

I didn't reply to his question, but smiled and said, "Mrs. Hayes sent me to get you. There's a phone call for you." With that, I turned and walked out the door of the shop and headed toward the ballpark. It had become my sanctuary. I could hear Mama's laughter ringing across the diamond and see her cheering in the wooden bleachers down the first-base line, her long golden hair moving in a summer breeze. When I missed her too much, I came here.

I also came here to think. I had something new to consider now with my discovery of Mr. Hayes and his love for the bottle. His drinking would, or could, have dire consequences for their happy little foster home. One of the first things Miss Adams had told me was that Social Services did not allow drinking by the foster parents.

I walked along the edge of the outfield fence to my favorite spot beyond the center-field fence where a scaffold was attached to two light poles. By climbing onto the scaffold, I could sit and look out over the field. Although it was January, the grass on the ball field was emerald green. I mulled over my newfound information. It was obvious that most of the Hayes's income revolved around these foster kids who came and went like the clouds. Jack Daniels could change all that. I decided to tell Mrs. Hayes about my discovery. I'd then suggest to her that my silence concerning her husband's drinking was a fair exchange for allowing me to come and go as I pleased.

I took the little transistor radio that Mama had given me for Christmas out of my coat pocket and tuned it to WTOB. Ruby and the Romantics were singing, "Our day will come." Listening to the song, I hoped it was an omen for good things to come. Everything to me came down to one word—*home*. That afternoon I told Mrs. Hayes.

"When you sent me to get Mr. Hayes, I caught him drinking," I said.

The blood left her face, and her eyes narrowed into a harsh glare. She'd been expecting this. I smiled at the thought of Mr. Hayes standing in front of his domineering wife and dutifully delivering the bad news of my discovery. "What do you want for your silence?" she asked cutting to the heart of the matter.

"I want to see Mama whenever I want. I'll let you know where I'm going and when I'll be back. I think it's a fair trade."

She didn't say a word; she just nodded as the blood rushed back into her face. I could feel the heat of anger radiating from it. With that, the deal was done.

44

Leaving

9:00 A.M., Friday, September 18, 1964

The sky is clear and bright on this late summer morning. The city skyline standing out against the Carolina blue sky looks like a postcard, and the R. J. Reynolds building stands in the middle reflecting the morning sun like a diamond. The warm morning air hangs heavy with the sweet, earthy smell of cured tobacco. Taking all this in one last time doesn't seem worth the trouble. I don't care about such things this morning, though that isn't the whole truth. That makes it sound as though it's just this morning that I don't care. The truth is all the caring in me is gone, taken out down to the roots and replaced with something else—some overpowering feeling of despair, sadness, and anger beyond measure. I am consumed by these emotions, and at this moment I'm not sure I will ever care again; not sure I can, not sure I want to.

Six months earlier I had my thirteenth birthday in the company of strangers, and now I was leaving for good. But I wasn't going home. I was leaving my hometown, my mama, my brother, Tuck, and everyone I knew. I was leaving not by choice but by force.

Miss Adams was driving me to the Boys Home of Lake Waccamaw in North Carolina. Mama's old dilapidated cardboard suitcase—holding the remnants of my life—was in the backseat. I was scared, mad as hell, confused, and pissed off at the whole world. The life I lived for twelve years was no longer recognizable. A life spent surrounded by the love, strength, and wisdom of the people I loved was no more.

There was no conversation between Miss Adams and me as she pointed the car east out of Winston-Salem. I had no desire to speak to her; she was by my reckoning responsible for the ongoing ruination of my life. She had arranged for my placement in Boys Home because, as she said in her report, "Gene is very dependent on his mother, and I have serious concerns about his ability to conform and accept being placed in a foster home."

Outwardly, I was a normal thirteen-year-old boy. I might have been a little big for my age at five foot six, 140 pounds. I had short, light brown hair and green eyes streaked with gold. I also had an extraordinary connection with and love for Mama, and I thrived on that love. Miss Adams's assessment of me was right on the money. I didn't want to conform, nor accept being in a foster home.

After I discovered that Mr. Hayes was an alcoholic, I forged a truce and came and went as I pleased. I informed them of where I was going and when I'd be back, but I never conformed to the rules they applied to everyone else. When I felt the need to see Mama, Randy, and Tuck, I went by city bus, bicycle, or sometimes walked across town. This didn't sit well with Miss Adams. She would come by the foster home to check on my progress, and I wouldn't be there. When asked about my whereabouts, Mrs. Hayes would give the one true response she could give, "I don't know." When Miss Adams asked me about these absences, I lied and said that I was working at the ballpark or caddying at the country club. I did both of those things so the statements were true—just not accurate.

This battle of wills, mine versus everyone else's, went on for months. Miss Adams knew I was going home, but couldn't catch me at it. I saw Mama once a month under Social Services supervision. On occasion Mama was allowed to pick me up, and we would spend the day unsupervised. It was on these rare occasions that I saw my little brother and Tuck.

My clandestine trips home led Miss Adams to broach the subject of Boys Home. She brought it up one day at her office. My immediate, emphatic response had been, "No, no way."

"It's more like a summer camp," she reported. "You'll get to see your mama and brother more often. They send all the boys home when school is out, including Christmas."

Her words had fallen on suspicious ears. Being across town from Mama and knowing I could see her brought some comfort. Being at the other end of the state would bring no such comfort. I had to admit that Miss Adams's tale of spending Christmas and summer at home sounded good, but my distrust of the system was rock hard.

Mama didn't buy her spin, either; she was against the move from the start, and her reply had been swift and direct. "I would never agree to have Gene sent that far away. We'd never see each other."

Mama had no say in the outcome, and neither did I. It was the Department of Social Services, Miss Adams, and Dad's signature that gave birth to this journey. The insolence and rebellion growing in me seemed like a normal response to me. Miss Adams was befuddled by it and sought explanations. To her, my response to having been yanked away from my mother and brother was abnormal. How should I respond? How would she respond? What if one day she came home from work and found that she no longer lived in her house, and in place of her family, there were strangers? Would she find my sedition so objectionable and hard to understand then?

We rode on two-lane blacktop highways, passing through countryside dotted with tobacco fields, dairy cows, and small towns with names like Snow Hill and Aberdeen. My heart grew heavier with each mile that passed. I spoke when Miss Adams asked a question, and then in brief detached sentences. My thoughts were on Mama, Randy, and Tuck, and when, or if, I'd ever see them again.

What if this Boys Home is more like a prison camp than a summer camp? What then? Afraid, full of doubt and dismay, I wondered, *How will I make it now without Mama?* One fact remained. She was my mother and I was her son, and that bond would not break. Foster home hadn't broken it, and neither would Boys Home.

We were traveling now alongside swamps, savannas of long-leaf pines growing in carpets of wiregrass, swollen cypress trees, pitcher plants, and cattails segregated from the highway by a blackwater canal.

Spanish moss hung in immense steel-gray shocks from every tree that rose out of the black water. The road, Highway 70 East, ran straight like a yardstick, cutting its way through this strange diluted land.

I was a city boy from the Piedmont of North Carolina, a land of rolling red dirt hills, thick hardwood forests, tobacco fields, cornfields, city streets, and sidewalks. Now we were speeding by the great Green Swamp of eastern North Carolina.

About 1:30 P.M. we reached Lake Waccamaw, a berg with two gas stations, a small grocery store, and a one-room post office. We crossed over train tracks, and I caught my first glimpse of the home—two long, ranch-style brick buildings, their backs facing the road. No fence, no walls—I had expected one or the other. What I saw could have been a church retreat or, though I was unwilling to believe it, a summer camp.

The campus was dotted with more such buildings. The driveway into Boys Home lay beside a two-story white antebellum house that had been in a previous life the home of wealthy southern royalty. Sitting on a hill overlooking Lake Waccamaw, it now served as the administration building and home to the director.

The grounds were well tended and tailored with flowers, blooming shrubs, and fresh-mowed grass. In the middle of the campus stood row after row of majestic pecan trees. All over fifty feet high, they seemed strong and regal, laden with pecans and adorned with long flowing draperies of Spanish moss. The moss hung in the trees as though a giant child had thrown it on a handful at a time.

The long brick buildings, called cottages, were the homes to sixteen boys and a housemother. The money to construct each cottage was donated by a civic-minded organization that believed it could make some difference in the world. The Civitan Cottage on a little hill had been the first one built. Considering where it sat in relation to the others, it had at the time been considered the last one the home would ever need.

The Lions Cottage, built in 1960 to meet the increasing need, stood across the driveway from the big white house. At the far end of the Lions Cottage sat the Jaycee Cottage, the latter in the row of two I had seen from the road. The campus and the sidewalk turned left at the end of the Jaycee Cottage, traveled a few feet, and passed in front of the Kiwanis Cottage.

Miss Adams parked her car on the coal-black asphalt parking lot. She got out of her car and said to me, "Pretty place, huh?"

Yeah, it's real pretty. You stay here and I'll go back to Winston. That's what I wanted to say. Instead I said nothing and stared at my new home.

45

The Welcoming Committee

Run! Run! I told myself. But where would I run to? How far could I get? I wanted to cry, but crying would be a sign of weakness, and this place looked like it would eat the weak. I pulled my suitcase from the backseat and followed Miss Adams as she walked toward the big white house.

She was opening the side door as I caught up and we walked inside.

"Hi, may I help you?" the woman asked, looking up from the desk.

"Yes, I'm Miss Adams from Forsyth County Social Services, and this is Gene Cheek."

"Very nice to meet you. I'm Miss Gentry." Turning to me, she smiled and said, "How are you, Gene?" The kindness was evident and real in her eyes.

"I'm fine, ma'am, thank you," I replied, forcing myself to return her smile.

"Why don't you both have a seat. I'll get Mr. Burgess. He's in the office this afternoon." She walked off and came back with a small man by her side. He walked to where Miss Adams and I sat.

"Hello, I'm Jack Burgess, one of the counselors here."

Miss Adams stood and so did I. "Mr. Burgess, I'm Miss Adams and this is Gene Cheek."

"Hello, Gene. How was your trip?" he asked, ignoring Miss Adams. He was about five foot six, small in structure, brown hair cropped in a crew cut. On his big nose rested a pair of thick glasses. He stuck out his hand.

I shook it. "Hello, Mr. Burgess. The trip was fine, considering, I mean, I guess." The last bit sneaking out of my mouth before my brain had a chance to look it over.

"I know how you feel—coming to a strange place and all—leaving your family and friends," he told me. "But believe me, you'll do just fine here. It's not so bad. You'll be okay."

I was grateful for the words of encouragement, but I had my doubts.

"I need to talk to Miss Adams for a few minutes and fill out some paperwork. Everyone's still at school, so why don't you take a walk and have a look around. The lake is down at the bottom of the hill behind the big house. You can walk down, have a look, and come back in about thirty minutes. Then I'll show you around."

"All right," I said and headed for the door.

Miss Adams turned to me and said, "Gene, I'll be gone when you get back. I wish you the best."

"Okay" was all I managed to say. I strolled outside and spotted the lake, but what beauty it held was lost to me. My stomach churned. Fear and doubt consumed me, almost knocking me to my knees. I had spent days trying to prepare myself for this inevitability. My months in the foster home had changed me and I had taken on a hard edge, but that edge deserted me now. I'd thought I was prepared. What a joke. How does a kid get prepared for sitting front row at his own destruction?

Here I was seemingly a million miles away from my home, fighting back the fear. I was not the same terrified child I had been one short year ago. Oh, I was just as scared, but I had learned to conceal my trepidation behind a mask of roughness. Now my self-defense took on the persona of being too hard to be afraid. The kids I would be meeting in a while had no doubt made similar adjustments. They would be just as hard. Would I be strong enough? If not, could I become invisible like the wind, there but not seen?

I walked down the hill as all these thoughts ran through my head. I thought about Mama's tear-streaked face when we'd said good-bye yesterday and I began to cry. *Shut up, you big baby!* I screamed at myself. *Your mama ain't here now, you can't show any weakness—not here, not in this place.*

I walked to the gazebo at the end of the pier and gazed out over the dead-calm lake. I reached down into my sock and pulled out my cigarettes. It wasn't a habit yet, just a part of the disguise as the rough streetwise kid. The exterior showed a determined *I-don't-take-no-shit* resolve, but the interior shook with the fright of a new puppy about to piss all over itself.

I flipped the cigarette into the lake and started back up the hill with all the bravado I could muster. I wondered what kinds of kids were here. I figured they were tough ones, JDs and kids from the streets who tangled with the local police, then Social Services, and ended up being sent away. The answer would be evident soon enough. I turned the corner at the big house and found Mr. Burgess standing in the driveway.

"Perfect timing," he said. "Your social worker just left. Grab your stuff and I'll show you to your room."

Mama's ragged cardboard suitcase sat outside the door. I picked it up and fell in beside Mr. Burgess.

"We try to keep the guys together according to age," Mr. Burgess said as we walked down the sidewalk toward the back door of the cottage. "All the guys in the Lions Cottage are about your age, so we'll put you there for the time being." He opened the back door. We walked into a long hallway with linoleum tiles polished to a high gloss, and painted cinder-block walls. On opposite sides of the hall were doorways, each leading to a bedroom. I stood looking into the door on the right. Four single beds equally spaced sat against the wall on the right. At the head of each bed was a small cork bulletin board. At the foot were a desk and chair. Across from the desk were four identical closets built into the wall with three drawers below. Beige draperies drawn into the corners helped frame a row of windows along the outside.

A door led to the bathroom, which had green tile that covered the floor and marched up the walls. Two stainless-steel sinks sandwiched between two shower stalls were on the right, and two toilet stalls stood on the left. At the far end of the bathroom another door led to another bedroom, identical to the one I had just been in. The place was industrial, clean, and functional.

Mr. Burgess pointed at the last bed in the first bedroom and said, "You can take that bunk. Put your stuff in the closet for now, and I'll show you the rest of the house and introduce you to Mrs. Maultsby."

I put the old suitcase into the closet and walked with him to the end of the hall. To the left was the living-dining room; to the right, a room with built-in lockers, bookcases, and a few chairs. "Mrs. Maultsby will give you a locker and a combination lock so you can keep your personal stuff secure in here," he said.

Beyond the living room was the housemother's apartment. Mr. Burgess walked to the door and knocked. A woman who looked like everyone's grandmother with cotton-white hair and glasses opened the door. "Hello, Mr. Burgess," she said, not looking at me.

"Mrs. Maultsby, this is Gene Cheek. He's going to be in your cottage. If you'll take over for me, I need to get back to the office." Then he left.

"It'll be a little while before the school bus comes," she told me. "Why don't you just have a seat, read, or just relax till the rest of the boys get here." Not waiting for a reply, she went back into her apartment.

I walked into the room where all the lockers were and picked up a *Boy's Life* magazine. In a few minutes a boy about my age walked in. He was a little shorter than me but stocky and tough looking even though he was wearing Coke-bottle glasses. I looked up at him.

"What you looking at?" he snapped.

"Nothing." I said, and went back to the magazine.

"Good," he said not moving, "because I don't like people staring at me."

"I wasn't staring at you," I replied.

"You calling me a liar?" he said, his lip drawing up into a sneer.

"No," I replied, seeing where this was heading.

"Well, hell, I think you're calling me a liar. You think I'm stupid? Where you from?"

"Winston-Salem," I answered, looking down at the magazine.

"Nothing but queers from Winston-Salem," he said staring at me with dark eyes three times their normal size behind those glasses.

"Hey, look, I just got here. I don't want no trouble." I stood up for the first time and faced the mean-looking punk, who was obviously trying to get my goat.

With that, the kid took a step toward me. "Well, you're in the wrong place if you ain't looking for trouble. You think you're tough?"

Quick as a cat, he flashed out and punched me in the mouth. I reeled in pain, dumbfounded. I touched my fingers to my lip to check for blood, but there wasn't any even though he'd popped me pretty good. A chickenshit grin crept over his face. If I didn't fight back right now everyone would know about it, and I'd be marked as easy prey. I'd be everybody's punching bag. In a split second I made my decision, right or wrong. My fist flew out, landing squarely on the guy's nose. His thick glasses flew across the room and broke in half when they hit the wall.

"Hey, man, you broke my glasses. What the hell you do that for?"

"You hit me, I hit you."

Just then the front door opened and fourteen noisy boys filed into the house. I turned from the kid who was picking up his glasses and walked toward the living room, not knowing what to do.

"This ain't over," the kid said, glaring at me.

"Anytime," I replied in my toughest-sounding voice. But my knees were shaking, my gut hurt from the grapefruit-sized knot inside, and I was seconds from breaking down. I turned and walked out of the room. I guessed this guy must be the head of the welcoming committee. Some welcome. I mustered up the courage and went to meet the others. I became the center of attention. They all stopped what they were doing and looked me over as if they were inspecting a hog, trying to decide the best way to slaughter it. Which one will be the next one to pop me in the mouth?

46

Christmas, 1964

I circled the creosote-caked telephone pole searching for the dry side. A cold, soaking December rain pelted me from all directions. I leaned out from behind the pole and looked east down the straight-line black-top that disappeared into the mist just a few hundred yards away. Where was the bus? The guys who were eastbound—Willie, Sammy, Mike, Buddy, and the rest—had nodded and flipped us off—the Boys Home version of a friendly good-bye—as they boarded their bus fifteen minutes earlier.

The rest of us were westbound. Henry and Johnny were going to Charlotte, Wayne to Salisbury, and Ray all the way to Forest City. We all stood waiting in front of the Lake Waccamaw Esso station, already soaked to the skin and cutting each other. "You didn't get hit by the ugly stick, the tree fell on you." That's a cut. It was called cutting because, like a scalpel in the hands of a surgeon, words can be sharp. At Boys Home, it was an Olympic sport.

Learning the art of cutting was crucial to survival. But more important to survival was learning how to take it like a man. If you didn't, cutting would become relentless and it would wear you down until you broke. You couldn't break here. To do so was a sign of weakness, and the sharks feed on the weak. There weren't that many sharks in Boys Home, but there were enough, and they had a nose for blood.

I was going home for the first time since I'd arrived in September. It had been only three months ago, but it seemed longer. My adjustment to the home was under way. I had learned who to avoid, what to avoid, and how to avoid it. I had made a few friends, and not too many enemies. I had been in a few fights because in this testosterone-driven place avoiding confrontation was difficult. I was one of a hundred boys who had scores to settle, and since the people we felt truly culpable weren't at hand, we took it out on each other. But I had to change that face now. I had to put on my happy face, the one I wanted Mama and Tuck to see. They had enough worries on their plates without having to worry about me any more than they already did.

At last the Greyhound pulled in front of the gas station and we climbed aboard. People of every shape, size, and color were riding the dog home for Christmas, wherever home was. Army men in their pressed dress green uniforms and spit-shined shoes would be getting off in Fort Bragg while many more would be getting on. I wondered how many of these young men would be going to that country called Vietnam. How many would not come back to ride the bus for another Christmas? A former Boys Home resident, Bryant Powell—a legend on campus—had been killed in Vietnam in October.

As the bus roared on, I leaned my head on the seat back and watched as the gray world outside the window sped by. Christmas had once been a magical time to me—in some previous life it seemed. I peered through the rain-streaked window as we passed the altars of those who still believed in Christmas magic. Small towns were decked with lights and wreaths strung from pole to pole. The picture windows of fine brick houses and the warped wooden windows of tiny clapboard shanties all displayed the ornaments of this festive time. Dark green Christmas trees, large and small, twinkled and sparkled from a place of prominence and honor in every home. I thought about last Christmas, my first away from my family. I'd been in the foster home living with strangers. At the time, I didn't think it could get any worse. Now here I was riding a Greyhound that would take me home to Mama, Randy, and Tuck, and on the tenth day a Greyhound would take me back to Lake Waccamaw and Boys Home.

I called home collect every Saturday at 1 P.M. to let Mama know that I was adjusting, and that it wasn't such a bad place after all. I knew in her mind that it was something else, something out of a Dickens novel. Her firstborn was two hundred miles away, out of reach and out of touch. She would think the worst and worry and cry, as she lay sleepless, imagining what sort of place her son was in. Once I got home and she was able to look at me and hug me, and hear me tell her about the place, she would feel better. It wasn't so bad once you learned how the machine worked.

Boys Home ran like a well-oiled military machine. The routine was as steady and constant as the humidity. During the week, reveille sounded at 6 A.M., breakfast was at 6:30, and the bus left for Hallsboro School at 7:15 A.M. It returned to campus at 3:15 P.M., and we had fifteen minutes to change clothes, grab a snack, and report for work. Work consisted of swinging a sling blade, a hoe, a pick, a shovel, or an ax. We cleared and reclaimed land from the swamps that surrounded the campus one foot at a time. And we worked mile-long rows of corn and pole beans.

Work ended at 5 P.M., and we had thirty minutes to shower, change clothes, and get ready for supper at 5:30. Between 6 and 7 P.M., we were free to do what we wanted so long as we didn't leave campus. Mandatory study started at 7 P.M., when we all had to be at our desks in our room. We studied, read, or pretended to do those things for two hours. Afterward we had thirty minutes to get our clothes ready for the next day, smoke a cigarette, or watch TV. Lights went out at 9:30 P.M. This iron schedule had no deviations until the weekend came.

On Friday nights we had free time until 10 P.M. We could go to the skating rink, a mile or so from campus up the Lake Front road, or attend the football game at the high school. We worked a half day on Saturdays and had the rest of the day to socialize, coming back to campus for supper and then free again until 11 P.M. If you were old enough and lucky enough to have a girlfriend it was a good night for sitting in the girl's parlor listening to records. Maybe, if you were real lucky, you'd get a kiss before walking back to the campus. On Sunday morning everyone attended church. We'd all dress up in our lone coats and ties and walk to the Baptist, Presbyterian, or Methodist church. After services it was back to campus for Sunday dinner; we'd eat fried chicken, mashed potatoes, fresh green beans, and homemade sheet cake for dessert. Our free time ended at five o'clock Sunday afternoon when the military machine regained control of our lives.

Running this machine was Rube McCray, a big guy with hands the size of whole hams, a full head of silver-white hair, and a ready smile. He was six foot four and over two hundred pounds. A former football player, he had coached tiny William and Mary College to national prominence from 1944 to 1950. He came to Boys Home at the request of A. D. Peacock, who'd founded the home in 1950 and was its director until 1958. That year he'd lured Mr. McCray away from taking the head coaching job at Georgia Tech, offering him the director's job. Mr. McCray sent his regrets to the university and came to Boys Home.

He had a great sense of humor, a fine sense of fairness, and was as tough as pine knots. His staff consisted of three counselors, a housemother in each cottage, and his wife, who directed the Boys Home choir. There were two ways to beat the machine's monotony— playing sports and joining the choir. I did both.

I forgot Boys Home when the bus stopped in front of Red's Feed and Seed in Kernersville. I thought about the three times that Mama and I had walked through this town. Once we trekked from the dilap-idated farmhouse to catch the bus to Winston to shop. The second time we returned from town, me with a new bow and arrow in my hands, and Mama crying because her legs and feet were sore and swollen. Then once more—the night we left Dad.

The bus was now heading west up Waughtown Street, and famil-iar sights of my old neighborhood passed by the window. Hill Middle School, our old apartment, and, just a few blocks south, Grandma's old house. The bus turned north onto Stadium Drive, taking me past the Red Shield boys club, where I'd learned to swim. Then past Bowman Grey Stadium where I had gone many Friday nights to watch the stock car races with Uncle Bill, and once or twice with my dad. We passed by Vargrave Street, and I could see Tuck's house from the window. I could have gotten off and walked there, but the car was gone and I knew they'd all be waiting for me at the downtown bus station.

When I got off the bus, Mama was standing under the awning out of the rain. Her face lit up like she was seeing me for the first time. Tuck was sitting in the car, Randy crawling over him like he was a set of jungle bars. Tuck waved to me. Mama rushed toward me, crying. I dropped my suitcase and threw my arms around her, and we both sobbed. "See?" I said, stepping back and holding my arms out wide. "I'm all in one piece." She laughed, but kept crying.

We walked over and I threw my suitcase in the back and climbed in. Tuck turned, tears glistening in his eyes. "Welcome home, Gene. It's so good to see you." He stuck his hand back and I shook it. "Hey, Tuck, it's great to be home."

"Ene, Ene," Randy said as he came flying over the seat and landed in my lap. He put his little arms around my neck, "Ene, Ene, where u bin?"

"I've been thinking about you, little brother. Did you miss me?"

"Es, I mit u. I wuv u."

"I love you, too."

We had a good Christmas, and a good visit, but we were just pretending. Pretending that everything was okay, pretending that the ten days would never end, and pretending that what had happened to our lives hadn't changed us. But it had. I was angry, and my hatred toward Dad and all those who'd taken the stand that day in court burned in me like a cancer. I was consumed with it. My reason for existing was to get even. I didn't give a hoot in hell about anything else. Mama's face had a sadness on it that had become as permanent as her golden-green eyes. She tried to hide it but it was unmistakable.

On my next to last day at home, Tuck took me to W. G. White's as our last fun day together. On the way back he stopped at Dewy's Bakery to buy some sugar bread. When we came back to the car, he didn't start it. Instead, he turned to me and said, "Okay, it's just you and me now. How are you doing, really?"

I started crying, and the hate and anger I had been trying to hide for two years came out as I unloaded my soul to my Secret Friend. He sat and listened—tears streaming down his cheeks—as I told him how I just didn't care anymore. How my hatred for Dad and Uncle Bill and Bobby and all those others so totally consumed me that I truly just didn't care about getting good grades or making friends.

When I was finished, he put his hand on my shoulder and said, "You can't go on hating all these people, Gene. It'll eat you up inside. You're a fine boy, a good boy, and I know it's easy to hate those who did this terrible thing to you and your mama. But, son, you have to let it go. You're a better man than they are. Their hate will do its dirty deed to them. You must let it go and turn your focus on doing your best at everything—grades, friends, sports. Promise me you'll do that."

I nodded. "It won't be easy, but I'll try."

"Your mama is trying, too."

"What do you mean?"

"She still has a lot of hate toward those same people, though she'd never say anything to you about it. We talk about her feelings all the time. She's learning to let go, but she's still filled with guilt over what she's done to you."

"Mama did nothing wrong but to love me and to love you."

Tuck smiled. "Yes, but your mama is plenty worried about you. She and I and Randy are here together and you're so far away and all alone. If she knew you were okay, she'd be okay."

The next day as we were saying good-bye at the bus station, both of us trying to control our tears, I whispered in her ear, "Don't worry about me, Mama. I'm going to be okay. I promise."

As the bus pulled away from the station, I saw her crying and shaking like a willow tree in a windstorm, and I died a little more.

47

No Happy Ending

Hours to days, days to weeks, weeks to months, months to years—that's how time passed at Boys Home. By 1969, my senior year, I had been at the home for several lifetimes—or so it seemed. I adjusted as the time moved on. I made it. Hell, I liked it. Boys Home had become my home, and the guys there were like my brothers. Mr. McCray was a father figure and Mrs. Gore, my housemother for the last several years, was my second mother. I was popular on campus and at school. I was captain of the football team and dated all the popular girls. From the outside, looking in, I was a normal, happy, well-adjusted young man. From the inside looking out, I was a confused, angry, lonely young man who didn't know who or what he was. My guilt at being happy in my altered life, my continued hatred toward my father, and my desire to pay the world back was the underlying wind that kept me afloat.

It was also during my senior year that another rock was laid on the pile already smothering my heart. I fell hard in love for the first time. Her name was Joyce. She was a tall, sinewy, raven-haired beauty whose large dark brown eyes melted me every time I looked at her. She was a junior, a cheerleader, and homecoming queen.

Her parents were good, hardworking middle-class folks who had always treated me fine. Her little sisters were crazy about me, and I think that helped her parents feel okay about me.

At Christmastime she and I exchanged gifts. I bought her a cameo necklace and she gave me a green cashmere sweater. We sat in her living room listening to Peaches and Herb singing "Love Is Strange" and talked. That's when I told her about Tuck and Mama and Randy. I saw no signs that it changed her one bit. Nothing passed between us, no cosmic signs, no look on her face, nothing. She was unfazed.

Our romance continued—until she told her parents about my family secret. This new information was more than they could tolerate. A few days later Joyce and I had a date. I borrowed one of the Boys Home's old station wagons and went to pick her up. Her mother came to the door and said, "Joyce is not here. She's out with Billy." Billy was her former boyfriend. Before I could say a word, her mother slammed the door in my face.

That was that. I never went out with Joyce again. For the rest of the year she avoided me at school; she wouldn't even look at me. Her friends told me she didn't want it that way, but her parents insisted that she have nothing to do with a boy whose mama was "shacked up with a nigger." I tried to call her, but her mother wouldn't let me talk to her. I tried to talk to her mother, but that was fruitless, too. I shut my eyes after that and stumbled through the rest of the school year blind.

As graduation approached, Mama announced on the phone that she was taking the bus down to see me graduate. I was thrilled with that news. Mama had never been to Boys Home, she'd never seen any of my games, and she'd never met my friends. When an article appeared in the local sports pages about me, I'd clip it out and send it to her. When the choir sang on TV during Christmas, she watched and called all her friends to tell them to watch as well.

My life at Boys Home wasn't a subject of conversation when I was at home. I could see the pain on her face every time I started to tell her about my friends or the girls I dated. Just sitting around looking at my high school annual was enough to make her cry.

You can't turn back the hands of time, so they say, but Mama tried to do just that. In her mind and heart I was the child she had loved and nurtured before that day in 1963. She saw me in no other light. Her and Tuck's life revolved around loving Randy and mourning me. Their social life was the church, Hanes CME church. Mama was the one white face except on a few occasions when I went with them.

Mama was a member now and on the junior usher board, and she was wholeheartedly accepted.

After my removal from her custody, the beast of hatred seemed satisfied. Dad continued to pave his road to hell and left everyone else alone. I hadn't seen him in five years and hadn't heard one word from him. The same held true for the rest of the family, with the exception of Uncle Bill. He sent me money from time to time, and if his truck driving took him near Lake Waccamaw, he'd stop and visit for a while. When I was home during Christmas he'd come by the house and take me shopping. The pain he must have felt from playing a part in my removal was evident on his face. His heart was broken, and inside he was dying.

Besides Joyce, I told one other person during my five years at Boys Home about my altered life. I wasn't ashamed; I was scared of losing acceptance, scared of losing my friends, and scared I'd have to fight my way through each day. I told Wanda, a girl I'd dated off and on since the eighth grade. She had one of those hearts you never had to question. She was as sweet as apple blossom honey, and a good friend. She was Beth all over again. I kept it all in and hidden behind a mask of laughter and competition. The anger and unadulterated hatred I felt was the fuel to my engine, and it ran wide open. My teachers liked me, but I was a terrible student and they all knew I just didn't care. I couldn't tell them why I didn't care, I just didn't. My life was treading water, never moving forward or back, content to stay in place.

June 6, 1969, Mama rode the Greyhound bus into Whiteville, fifteen miles west of Lake Waccamaw. I picked her up in Boys Home's 1968 white Ford station wagon.

We rode down the old blacktop heading toward the lake. Mama hadn't been out of Winston-Salem in fifteen years, maybe longer. But this was not a vacation. The scenery of the swampland and the beauty of the lake might as well have been the Badlands. There was no beauty in this land for her. She was here to see her beloved son—all grown up without her—take his final steps into manhood. We were strangers. Oh sure, we loved each other, but we were strangers nonetheless. In Mama's mind it would always be November 17, 1963, and tomorrow she was not going to the courtroom. She would take her two sons and, with the help of the man she loved, they would run away and live happily ever after.

"You want me to show you around campus?" I asked as we turned down Old Lake Road and passed the home.

"No, honey, I can't do that."

"It's okay, Mama, it's okay."

She started to cry and I put my hand on hers. She cupped my hand in both of hers, held it to her eyes, and wept. I took my hand from her and turned into the motel parking lot. Then I took her hands in mine and together we cried.

"I'm sorry, honey, I'm so sorry." Her words came in between the sobs, forced out one at a time with short gasping breaths.

"Sorry for what, Mama? For loving me? For loving Randy? For loving Tuck? You've never done anything to be sorry for. This wasn't your fault. I've spent the last five years around boys whose parents don't give a hoot in hell about them. I feel sorry for them; they've never known what the love of a mother feels like. Every night I've closed my eyes knowing that I had a mother who loved me more than life itself. I thank God every day that you're my mama. I thank him every night for Grandma and her wisdom. She taught you to love and not to hate, and to have compassion in a world where the compassionate get thrown away. You're the reason I am who I am. Without you and Grandma in my life, what would I be? Nothing. It's your blood and hers that run through my veins. I know more than anyone what you have sacrificed for your sons. I know the power of the love in a mother's heart. I love you with all my heart, and I know you love me. You never have to tell me you're sorry."

48

The Beginning and the End

April 1995

We rode silent through the countryside, my wife Kathy and me. The warm April sunshine joined the sound of Eric Clapton's "Tears in Heaven" and filled up the car, but I barely noticed either. I was far away with my mind on Mama. I had tried to call her five times since Friday afternoon and got nothing but her answering machine. Now it was Sunday morning and there was a stone in the pit of my stomach. It wasn't like her not to return my call. I'd gotten up early and over coffee tried to call her one more time, figuring I'd catch her before she left for church. But there was no answer.

I woke up my wife. "Will you come with me to Mama's?"

She looked at me through sleepy, questioning eyes. "Why?"

Good question really. Why? We hardly spoke these days; I'd been living in the basement for a year, and if we passed each other in the hallway, it was an accident. "I have a bad feeling. She hasn't answered her phone since I talked to her Friday."

During that conversation, she'd said a strange bruise had just appeared on her face overnight. "Does it hurt?" I asked her. "Are you sure it's not a spider bite?"

"It's not a spider bite, and it doesn't hurt. It's just there."

Mama was taking enough blood thinners and blood pressure medicine to treat the whole over-sixty crowd of Winston-Salem. If a feather fell on her, she bruised.

"Well, if it's not cleared up by tomorrow, I'll take you to the doctor."

"Okay, honey," Mama said, and we hung up. I'd been impatient with her; it wasn't in the words I'd said as much as the tone. I didn't have the time to talk to her. Saturday came and I was still wrapped in my own funk, mad at the world. I was miserable, my wife was miserable, and our life together was miserable. Our kids were out of the house now, so why did we continue the charade? I called again Saturday midmorning and left a message on her machine. "Mama, I think I'll come up tomorrow instead. Call me later." But she didn't call, and later that night I tried again. Still no answer. *She must be at work*, I thought. She worked five days a week as a certified nurse's assistant, and she loved her job. She was sicker than most of her elderly patients, but she never let on. Her patients loved her. Sometimes she worked the weekend. It wasn't so much for the money; she just liked taking care of people.

"Okay," my wife said from the bed, bringing me back to the here and now, "I'll get up and go with you."

An hour later we were making our silent way to Winston-Salem, sixty miles east of our home in Hickory. We'd lived there since coming back to North Carolina in 1985 from the West. Once a week, usually on a Saturday, I'd drive up to see Mama. We'd ride around town looking at the old places where we'd lived, or we'd take flowers to the graves of Grandma, Grandpa and Uncle Bill, and Tuck. That's what she liked to do, ride around looking at all the old places.

"I remember when Goldie and I were teenagers," she'd said one day. "We used to walk out here just to see this house."

We were two miles from town passing by the old Bridges estate with its wrought-iron gates and lion statues on either side. "You guys walked all the way out here just to look at this place?" I asked her, a tone of wonder in my voice.

"Yea, we loved it. We'd walk out here on Saturday morning and stop at Milner's drugstore and get an ice cream on the way home."

I loved those rides. We'd laugh and talk about the good old days, but we never talked about "the day." It had passed between us like a breath for thirty-five years. We couldn't or wouldn't talk about it; we just couldn't find the right time or the right words.

The stone in my stomach turned to a boulder as we turned the corner and I saw her car sitting in the driveway. I was hoping it wasn't there. I'd called from the cell phone thirty minutes earlier but she hadn't answered. Kathy looked at me as she turned off the car. "It'll be okay. Maybe the phone is turned off." The look on her face said she knew better. Mama wouldn't turn her phone off because she was afraid one of her sons might need her to work a miracle in our unmiraculous lives.

"Yea, maybe so," I said with no conviction in my voice.

We opened the gate and walked up the sidewalk toward the front door. The daisies that she loved so much were in bloom and lined the tiny sidewalk like it was the entrance to a fine big mansion instead of a two-bedroom row house in East Winston-Salem. Kathy reached the door first and tried to open it, but it was locked. I knocked. "Mama, hey Mama, it's me, your favorite son. Open up." No answer. Kathy reached into her purse and pulled out her key. She turned it in the door and pushed it open. As I stepped into the house the boulder was crushing me. "Mama, are you going to sleep all day?" I said as I walked in.

And then I saw her. She was slumped over on the couch, sitting in her housecoat. Her legs pushed straight out as if she'd recoiled at some great and sudden pain, the coffee table pushed out of place. She was dead. "Mama! Oh, God, no! Mama!"

Kathy rushed to her side, but it was no use. Anyone could see she was gone. Kathy picked up the phone and called 911 and I walked to the back porch and started to cry. All the old hates came roaring up inside me. *Well, you finally won, you sons of bitches. She's dead. You finally wore her down and killed her.* But there was nobody left for me to hate. They were all dead, too.

I was crying into my hands when Mama's voice came to me: *Don't cry, angel. Don't cry. I'm at peace now. I'm with your grandma and my daddy. Tuck is here and so is Uncle Bill. Don't cry. I'm at rest. Don't cry. Be strong for your brothers.*

Oh, my God. My brothers. I had to call them. Kathy sat beside me on the porch, her hand on my knee, as we watched the paramedics take Mama away. "I'm sorry, Gene. I loved your mama. She was a fine woman."

"I know" was all I could say. A little while later I called my brothers and laid my boulder on their hearts. They both said they would rush to Winston-Salem. Greg lived in Florida so it would take a while before he could show up, but Randy, who lived in Havelock, North Carolina, arrived about 5 P.M.

We cried and held each other. Strangely, there was a peace over us. It was as if Mama had convinced us that she was in a better place; it was what she believed. Her mama—my beloved grandma—and her daddy, and Tuck would all be waiting on her in heaven and they'd greet her with open arms. That's the way she'd expected to find it, and somehow we all believed it.

Randy and I called Mama's friends, the people she went to church with, and those who had been so important to her life for forty years. We called the nursing service where she worked. Everyone cried. Finally around 8 P.M. we were done. We were sitting in the living room, silently staring at the walls and ceilings, when the phone rang.

"Hello," I said.

"Hello, is Sallie there please?"

My heart sank. Here's someone I had yet to tell the news to. "No ma'am, I'm sorry but my mama died this morning."

"Oh, God, I'm so sorry. This is Mrs. Robertson. Your mama took care of my sister."

"Yes ma'am, I've heard her speak of you and your sister." Mama cried every time she talked about this new patient, Mrs. Sealy. Mama had told me, "She's mean to her, I can tell. As soon as I'm out of that house, she's mean to her. I feel it. I hate leaving her alone with her own sister."

Mrs. Robertson spoke again. "I wanted to tell your mama that my sister passed away this morning, but I had no idea—"

I interrupted her. "I'm real sorry about your sister, Mrs. Robertson. Mama thought a great deal of her."

"Your mama was a saint. My sister loved her."

"Yes ma'am, thank you." I hung up the phone.

I thought a moment and started to laugh. Randy and Kathy looked at me like I'd lost my mind.

I explained the conversation I'd just had. "Well, don't you get it?"

They both had confused looks across their faces.

"I had this picture in my mind: Mama got to the gates of heaven and told Saint Peter she had to go back for a minute. Saint Peter asked her why and she said, 'Well. I can't leave poor old Mrs. Sealy with her mean sister. She's got to come with me.' So she came back and took Mrs. Sealy with her. Now, ain't that just like Mama? She dies but still she can't quit worrying about someone else."

We laughed and cried. It was just like Mama.

Her concern about people and worry about things that she had no control over had killed her, one slow, agonizing day at a time. Her fight to keep hope alive in her children and family, and the belief that love conquers all, had worn her down like a steady drop of water wears down solid rock.

The death certificate wouldn't list "worry" and "struggle" as contributing factors in her death. The official cause was an aneurysm, swift and deadly. But worry and struggle had done it to her as sure as the world is a poorer place without her.

A few days later we said good-bye to Mama. Per her instructions, it was a simple graveside service. "I don't want no drawn-out funeral, just quick and to the point," she had said. Being the oldest, I followed those instructions to the letter.

As the long procession of cars rode down Maryland Avenue on our way to the cemetery, the inspiration of her life was like a bright shining light guiding us all. The funeral procession approached Martin Luther King Boulevard and I fought back the tears at what I saw. A young African American man had been strolling down the sidewalk. He was dressed in black baggy jeans, a dark blue FUBU sweatshirt, and a baseball cap turned sideways on his head. He stopped as the hearse carrying Mama passed. He removed his cap, held it over his heart, and turned to face the street. He was paying his last respects to a woman he scarcely knew. But he knew of her and he knew what had been lost in his neighborhood—another kind soul had moved on, and her passing left a hole in its fabric.

Mama had lived in that neighborhood in the center of a large African American community—one of the oldest in Winston-Salem—for thirty-five years. She had raised her sons there and buried Tuck. Her final resting place would be in Evergreen Cemetery next to him.

The faces of the people at her graveside were the last chapter in her life. Rich white faces streaked with tears, people who had become part of her extended family because she had cared for their loved ones and they in turn had fallen in love with her. Brown and black faces, young and old, rich and poor, members of her church or people from the neighborhood who were losing a part of their own family.

Mama's death had a profound effect on me. A mother's death has that effect on every son, but there was more to it for me. I'd been living a lie and she knew it. I was unable or unwilling to deal with the issues in my life, choosing instead to pretend everything was just fine. Things were not fine and Mama knew that. She loved me so much that she never came right out and said it; instead, she worried over me in silence.

I had let her down. I had been unable to remove from our lives the stain from that day so long ago, and now I never would. As I rode home alone after her funeral, I cried. I pleaded with God, "Just let me talk to her one more time," but I was only talking to myself.

Three months later I left my wife and moved out on my own for the first time in twenty-seven years. In fact, it was the first time I'd ever been alone. I'd been lonely for a long time, but not alone. I moved to an isolated cabin on Lake Norman, and the isolation smothered me for a while; then a strange thing began to happen.

I started looking at my life. I stripped it down to the bones and laid it all out in front of me, and there wasn't much to see. Bitterness and despair mostly, and lots of self-pity. Mama gave me a poem written by a man named Berton Braley for Christmas the year before she died. It was for this exact occasion. She knew I was going to dig up these bones and she knew she wouldn't be there for me, so she left me the poem. It was hanging over the fireplace as I started to read it; I saw it truly for the first time that night.

OPPORTUNITY
With doubt and dismay, you are smitten
You think there's no chance for you son!
Why the best books haven't been written
The best race hasn't been run.
The best score hasn't been made yet,
The best song hasn't been sung,
The best tune hasn't been played yet,
Cheer up for the world is young!
No chance? Why the world is just eager
For the things you ought to create.
Its store of true wealth is still meager,
Its needs are incessant and great.
It yearns for more power and beauty,
More laughter, love and romance, more loyalty, labor and duty.
No chance, why there's nothing but chance.
Don't worry and fret faint hearted,
The chances have just begun.

As I read those words, Mama's voice came to me as clear as if she were sitting beside me: *Your life ain't over, honey. It's just beginning. You're a good man. It's time you believed that of yourself. You can do whatever you want to do. There's nothing here to stop you, but you.*

And as quickly as her voice had come, it was gone. I cried that night but I made some decisions that would change my life. Mama was right, as she had always been. Nothing stood in my way but me. I took responsibility that night for my failed marriage, my failures as a father, and my own self-perceived failures as a man. I gathered up all those things from my past, and for the first time forgave myself for them. I thought of Mama and Tuck, my father, my grandma and uncle Bill, and I forgave them all for that day so long ago. I forgave Grandma for not being there when I needed her most. I forgave Mama and Tuck for falling in love and for risking everything for that love. I forgave Dad and Uncle Bill for their shortcomings as human beings. I forgave them all, but the most important person I forgave that night was myself.

I also made a conscious decision that night that somehow I would tell the story of that time long ago. I had always wanted to, and that night the process began. This book is the culmination of that night. I know now why Mama and Tuck fell in love and risked it all. They couldn't help it. Grandma wasn't there in the flesh that day in the courtroom, but the things that her love and understanding instilled in me gave me the strength to make it. I know why Dad and Uncle Bill did what they did that day, and it wasn't to hurt me. They did it because like so many people in the world today they feared what they could not understand. We all do it. The world has changed a lot since those days back in 1963, but it has not changed enough.

Epilogue

They say you can do anything when properly motivated. The existence of this book proves that statement. I'd like to say my motivation was pure, but that would be a lie. This book started as an act of vengeance. I wanted revenge on those—long since gone—who brought pain to my family and me. It changed from revenge to understanding and then finally to forgiveness. I can't pinpoint the exact time because it moved over me like the changing of a season, slow and deliberate. It wasn't until this process was near the end that I even noticed, but I'm grateful for it.

This book is equal parts desperation and inspiration. The desperation came because this story burned in me and my only chance for relief was to tell it. The inspiration came from all those who are remembered in these pages. Somehow, they channeled through me and brought this story to life. On my own, I wasn't capable of writing the first word.

My families, the Cheeks, the Andersons, and the Tuckers, took this journey with me in absentia. Mama, Dad, Tuck, my brothers, grandparents, uncles, aunts, nieces, nephews, cousins, and friends all stood shoulder to shoulder with me as I dug up these bones. If there's a lesson to learn here, it is *Love conquers all*. Now let me catch you up on some of the people whose lives these events affected.

They say you can't go home again. My life proves that; Lord knows I tried. My relationship with my mom was never the same after our years of separation. Though we fought it, the wheel of time moved on and our altered lives swallowed us up. In Mama's eyes I would remain the twelve-year-old boy she loved but somehow let down. She carried needless guilt with her every day of her life, and I carried my own guilt. I felt guilty that I adjusted to my changed life and couldn't remain the twelve-year-old boy I thought she wanted me to be. We never talked about that day in 1963 or the aftermath—it was just too painful for her, and I didn't have the courage. We ignored it like the old stoically ignore aches and pains. If you don't acknowledge them, they don't exist. My mom used to ask my ex-wife—in moments of private conversation—if I blamed her for what happened all those many years ago. Her guilt over that event was like a millstone around her neck, and I could never release her from it. I never admitted to myself or to her—and never consciously accepted, until I started writing this book—that indeed that twelve-year-old boy blamed his mama. By then she was gone and it was too late for us to deal with it.

I regret that now. Mama is gone and that conversation will have to wait for another place and another time. Lots of things remained unsaid, and doubts from our past clouded our future. This book is my attempt to set the record straight, and to tell Mama and Tuck once and for all that I don't blame them. My mother was the mother every child should have—kind, loving, and considerate. She was my friend, and I trusted her. I valued her opinion, and I saw, as I got older, that the things she had endured in her life did not break her; they made her stronger and more compassionate.

After my discharge from the navy in 1972, I married a girl from San Diego, California. We raised three children, Roxanne, Jennifer, and David. They are the best thing that ever happened in my life. Once they grew up, my wife and I found ourselves in the company of strangers—each other.

As a young man I pictured myself as a perfect husband and father. Now I know I was neither. I let the ghosts from my childhood haunt the kind of man I became. The past has a way of interfering with the future whether we want it to or not. So it was with me. It pains me now to admit those things to myself and to you, but there it is. When my marriage came apart and I found myself alone for the first time in thirty years, I had no one to blame for my failures but the man in the mirror.

My dad. In September 1985, having spent twenty-two years running from my own demons and having come to an understanding of
what it means to be a father, I sought to rebuild my relationship with
Dad. He was still living with Grandma in the house across the dirt road
from Aunt Lucille's home. The years of alcohol and living with his
demons had ravaged him. He'd lost an eye to cancer, his body was
emaciated, and he looked like someone out of a concentration camp.
But he hadn't changed one bit; a can of Budweiser was never far from
reach. I wanted to give him the chance to know his grandkids.

The things I wanted from him, he was incapable of giving. So
after a year of bringing his grandkids around to see him, I stopped. I
was not going to put my kids in a position where he could hurt them.
In the fall of 1987 he went into the hospital dying of cancer. I took off
from work for several days to visit him. If there was a chance that we
could make things right between us, I wanted that opportunity.

On October 9, 1987, I went to confront the man I had hated for
so long. In a daze, I made my way down the shiny floors of Baptist
Hospital to his semiprivate room. I found him asleep on the stark
stainless-steel hospital bed nearest the door, surrounded by all the
marvels of modern medicine. I was relieved to see that the bed next to
his was unoccupied. It would give us the privacy we'd need to expose
the explosive emotions buried deep in each of our tormented souls.

He seemed peaceful in his sleep, like a newborn baby. I had a
hard time remembering him as the mean and vindictive man I had
feared and hated as a child. Was this the seldom-sober alcoholic whose
mere voice had made me quake? Was this the heartless monster who,
on November 18, 1963, had strangled all my pity and love for him? For
years after that day, I prayed to God that he not go unpunished.

Now he was dying a horrible death. Had the Almighty afflicted
him with the deadly cancer that ravaged his body and left bones sticking out of his sagging, pasty white skin? Was this "Ye shall reap what
you sow"? Watching him struggle for each shallow breath, an IV drip
pumping both morphine and nourishment into his skeletal right arm,
brought tears to my eyes. I realized that I couldn't hate him anymore.

For a long time I sat on a stool at the foot of the bed, watching
him sleep. Tears continued to flow as memories of our tortured rela-

tionship flooded back. How much I'd wanted to love him, I thought. And how much my mother had wanted to love him, too. But alcoholism wouldn't let us near his heart. It guarded it like Cerberus, the watchdog at the gates of hell. It devoured his capacity for kindness, love, and empathy. It made prejudice and hatred the ruling passions of his soul.

The faint glow of the October sunlight filtered through the half-drawn blinds. There was a distinct smell of death in the chilled hospital air, and I knew my father didn't have much longer to live. His arduous journey was at an end. He was sixty years old, but alcoholism and cancer had withered him beyond his years. Why had I come to confront a ghost? I asked myself. My father's eyes fluttered open. He seemed startled to see me.

"Good morning, Dad," I said, as his one good eye focused on my face.

"Hello, son," he said in a weary, croaking voice.

Good, he recognizes me. He's not delirious. A silent minute passed.

"Dad, we need to talk," I said, almost choking on the words.

He turned his head toward the wall and said, "Sure, son, what is it?"

"The doctor told me he talked to you yesterday."

Without looking at me, he said, "Yes, we talked." His voice sounded faint and distant, as if his soul was already on that mysterious journey of no return.

"You know you're dying, right?" I said. "The doctor told you that, didn't he?"

"Yeah, he told me," he said matter-of-factly.

"Well, are you ready for that?"

No answer.

"Are you ready, Dad?" I repeated.

No answer.

He's silent because he knows what I mean, I thought. *But does he, or has the morphine quieted the pain and dulled his mind as well?* Courage overtook me, and I said, "Is there anything you have to say to me? Is there anything you want to tell me about what happened in 1963?"

For a long time he said nothing. Then he spoke, "No, son, there's nothing I want to say. Everything's fine. I'm okay. I'm ready to go."

I was stunned. Here he was on his deathbed, knowing what words I wanted to hear, words that I needed to hear and he needed to say. Yet still he couldn't bring himself to say them. Was it pride, stubbornness, or another act of vindictive cruelty?

"Are you sure there's nothing you want to say?" I asked.

My father didn't reply.

Oh, how much I wanted him to look me in the face and say those magic words, *I'm sorry for what I did to you that day, son. I never meant to hurt you. Please forgive me. No matter how angry I was at your mama, it was wrong for me to hurt you.*

But he didn't say these healing words. I don't even know if he was aware of how necessary they were. There would be no healing for my heart or his, this day. Twenty-four years after the fact, he was unrepentant, still consumed with hatred.

At that moment my own hatred and rage toward him returned. I wanted to tell him that I was mighty glad that alcoholism and cancer had shriveled him like a ghost, and that he was dying in agony. But I couldn't. My rage and hate passed like spent thunderclouds, replaced with pity. I felt sorry for him, sorry for his decision to cling to hatred even when he was about to go meet his maker.

For a long time I sat gazing at him, tears clouding my eyes. His face turned to the wall, as if fastened to it by unseen chains.

"Well," I said with a sigh of resignation, "I guess I'll head back then. For whatever it's worth, I want you to know that I forgive you. I don't hate you for what you did. I just wish you could have said you were sorry." I never saw him alive again. Although his words went unspoken, I had forgiven him, that was all I could do and what I needed all along.

My brother Randy. Randy lives with his wife, Susan, in Oklahoma. They have four beautiful children, Brittany, Jonathon, Walter, and their youngest, who bears Mama's middle name, Addy, and is her mirror image, both within and without. Randy is a living tribute to his parents; he is everything they could have hoped for in a son. We are as close today as we were when we played football on my mattress.

My brother Greg. Mama and Tuck had a second son together, Gregory. He was born on May 13, 1970, and is as dear to me as Randy. He and his wife, Tonya, live in Florida, and they have two children, Tamyra and Gerard. Although Greg was born at a different time in this country, he was not untouched by this experience. He is also a shining tribute to his parents, and I'm proud to call him brother.

Mama and Tuck were married on September 13, 1979, six years after the repeal of the anti-miscegenation law in North Carolina—to them it was but a formality. They were devoted to each other, and their lives, both together and individually, are examples to us all.

Tuck doted on Mama until the end. He died on May 29, 1981, after a year's battle with colon cancer, during which time he never lost his love of life, pride in his heritage as a black man, faith in Christ, and devotion to his family. He was sixty. He left a legacy that still lives in Winston-Salem. His grandkids are all proud of their grandfather, and he would be very proud of them. I am proud to have known him; he was my friend, and a man other men should strive to emulate.

Larry and Beth. I never saw my two best friends again. I hear Larry is a preacher now. I hope he is well, and I want him to know I still love him. I don't know what happened to Beth, but my hope is that life has given her the happiness that she gave me one summer a long time ago. I love her, too. Both their names were changed during the writing of this book, to protect their innocence.

Uncle Bill died in 1980. He told Mama just before his death that he was sorry for the role he played in my being taken away from her. He admitted that racial hatred blinded him when he went along with the Cheek family request to testify against her. He asked for her forgiveness, and Mama gave it to him. Uncle Bill called me before his death from brain cancer, and asked me to forgive him. I did. I loved him then and I love him still.

Aunt Goldie. After not speaking to Mama or seeing her for almost twenty years, Aunt Goldie also asked Mama for forgiveness. Goldie blamed her husband, her own weakness, and her fear of what her friends and neighbors might think for their estrangement. Mama forgave Aunt Goldie, too, and they rekindled their sisterhood and friendship. Sadly, we lost Aunt Goldie a few years ago. I forgave her and loved her then and now. Both Aunt Goldie and Uncle Bill came to respect Mama's decision to marry Tuck, and came to understand what a fine and decent human being he was.

My intentions in writing this book were to be honest with it all, to tell the story from the eyes of the little boy who saw it, felt it, lived it. I have done that and I am the better for having done so. In an effort to be clear and honest, there are a couple more things you need to know. Mama knew that day in 1963 that we were going to a custody hearing. She wanted to spare me the angst and fear of that, so she didn't tell me. I think her decision was the right one. She did hire an attorney for the trial, but he didn't show up. She was so certain they wouldn't take me that she went ahead with the trial. By the time it was evident what was happening, she and I were both in shock. She also appealed the decision, and she and Tuck hired an attorney. But their money and hope ran out. I believe with all my heart that they both did all they could to get me back. The wheels of southern justice (or injustice) ground them into submission.

I am often asked by those who know me if I can now lay this down and move on with my life. It would be nice if I could answer yes, but once again that would be a lie. The truth lies somewhere else. While writing this book, I did gain understanding, and with it came forgiveness, but I have not forgotten. The facts are this will remain a part of my life, as long as there is life. I'm not sure complete healing is attainable. I don't think I will ever forget, and I'm not sure that I should.

About the Author

Gene Cheek is a blue-collar son of the South born on March 2, 1951, in Winston-Salem, North Carolina. He has lived an unremarkable life with the exception of his children, grandchildren, and his own peculiar childhood. He lives in the Blue Ridge Mountains of North Carolina. This is his first book.